THE IMPACT INVESTOR

THE IMPACT INVESTOR

Lessons in Leadership and Strategy for Collaborative Capitalism

CATHY CLARK, JED EMERSON, AND BEN THORNLEY

A Wiley Brand

Cover design by Michael J. Freeland
Cover image: © Wavebreak Media/Jupiter Images
Copyright © 2015 by John Wiley & Sons, Inc. All rights reserved.

Published by Jossey-Bass
A Wiley Brand
One Montgomery Street, Suite 1200, San Francisco, CA 94104-4594—www.josseybass.com

Jossey-Bass books and products are available through most bookstores. To contact Jossey-
Bass directly call our Customer Care Department within the U.S. at 800-956-7739, outside
the U.S. at 317-572-3986, or fax 317-572-4002.

Wiley publishes in a variety of print and electronic formats and by print-on-demand. Some
material included with standard print versions of this book may not be included in e-books
or in print-on-demand. If this book refers to media such as a CD or DVD that is not
included in the version you purchased, you may download this material at http://
booksupport.wiley.com. For more information about Wiley products, visit www.wiley.com.

Library of Congress Cataloging-in-Publication Data has been applied for and is on file with
the Library of Congress.
ISBN 978-1-118-86081-6 (cloth); ISBN 978-1-118-86071-7 (ebk.);
ISBN 978-1-118-86075-5 (ebk.)

Printed in the United States of America

FIRST EDITION

HB Printing 10 9 8 7 6 5 4 3 2 1

Contents

■ ■ ■

Tables and Figures

Tables

Figures

Foreword

When I reflect on impact investing and its prospects of growth to a size somewhere between the $100 billion of microfinance and the $3 trillion invested in private equity and venture capital worldwide, I often think back to the origins of venture capital—the starting point of my professional life.

Venture capital was a response to the needs of tech entrepreneurs, just as impact investing is a response to the needs of a new generation of social entrepreneurs who seek to make a meaningful difference in improving people's lives.

No one had thought of creating ten-year, illiquid funds, investing in small companies with very limited track records of performance, led by young people with no business experience. The response came because people sat around a table and said, "We see the future, and we have to provide the tools for it." When I set up what became Apax Partners in 1972, few in Europe knew what an entrepreneur was, and fewer still believed that entrepreneurs would achieve much of consequence for our daily lives. Forty years later, they have completely transformed our world.

The microchip, the PC, the mobile phone, and the Internet, with its search engines and instant access to information and people, have revolutionized the way we live. They have brought a transformation as momentous as that which followed the creation of the alphabet and the invention of printing. Entrepreneur-led companies have overtaken those that led their fields for nearly a century. IBM was overshadowed in the space of a couple of decades by a start-up named Apple, which is now the largest company in the world by market cap; Microsoft, Amazon, Google, and Oracle made it from start-up to being among the world's top thirty companies in just three decades.

The tech entrepreneurial revolution was driven by innovation and risk taking. It transformed the mind-set of governments about how economic growth should be achieved. In the United States, in the space of twenty-five years, it has been estimated that fifty million jobs were lost by smokestack industries, while sixty million jobs were created by new companies.

Our prospect now is to provide social entrepreneurs with the financing they require, and in this important book, Cathy Clark, Jed Emerson, and Ben Thornley provide the first detailed insight into how that financing has—and widely ought to be—provided.

However, even as the outstanding funds profiled in *The Impact Investor* work tirelessly to pioneer a new "Collaborative Capitalism," there is much work to do building market and public policy infrastructure to help a new generation of entrepreneurs replicate their success.

The Social Impact Investment Taskforce and the Role of Government

Understanding this need for infrastructure and the paths to its creation has been the charge of the Social Impact Investment Taskforce, announced by UK prime minister David Cameron in June 2013 and established by the G8. By the time this book is published, this group, which I have been privileged to chair, will have just concluded its deliberations and published its report.

The Taskforce included a private and a public sector member from seven G8 countries and the European Union (EU), and observers from Australia and development finance institutions; it held hearings in different countries and created four working groups and seven National Advisory Boards to advise on the enabling infrastructure for impact investing in various local contexts. In total, the Taskforce has engaged more than two hundred of the world's foremost experts on impact investing in responding as vigorously as possible to the social challenges we face.

The Taskforce has played a particularly valuable role, clarifying the role of government in impact investing and informing the approaches of its different member countries by sharing examples and lessons from efforts in each jurisdiction.

For the United Kingdom's part, Bridges Ventures, which is featured in this book, provides one of the earliest examples. Bridges Ventures was created as an outcome of the UK Social Investment Task Force fourteen years ago, which I was also privileged to lead, and, after securing half of the funding for its first fund from HM Treasury, has gone on to become one of the largest impact investors in the world, with more than £400 million under management in both the United Kingdom and soon in the United States—an exemplar of what this book calls "Policy Symbiosis."

Another piece of enabling infrastructure in the United Kingdom that is particularly powerful is Big Society Capital, an investment "wholesaler" with £600 million of equity capital to invest in social investment intermediaries, comprising £400 million that has sat unclaimed for fifteen years in bank and building society accounts, and an additional £200 million from the United Kingdom's four largest commercial banks.

Big Society Capital has already put the United Kingdom in the lead in terms of its market structure and number of social impact investment participants. Two dozen social impact investment intermediaries of significant size exist: Big Issue Invest, Bridges Ventures, Charity Bank, ClearlySo, Impetus-PEF, LGT-Berenberg, NESTA, Social Finance, Social Investment Business, and Unlimited, to name but a few. Virtually all of these have been backed by Big Society Capital, which is building capital flows to these and other social organizations through equity, social impact bonds (SIBs), and unsecured and secured debt. At the start of 2013, £25 million was in impact investment managers' hands in the United Kingdom; at the start of 2014, the sum was over £150 million.

From the United States we have much to learn from the experience with the Community Reinvestment Act and the New Markets Tax Credit, which together bring more than $20 billion of investment a year to poorer areas of the United States. The US federal government has also provided outcomes funding for SIBs and is actively engaged in promoting impact investment through the White House Office of Social Innovation and Civic Participation.

In France, capital flows into social organizations have benefited from allowing pension contributions to go to funds that invest 7 to 10 percent of their assets in tackling social or environmental issues.

And across the EU, the European Investment Fund is leading the effort to develop impact investment management firms running sizable funds.

Optimizing existing ecosystems to support social entrepreneurship and investment is one important role for government. A second is to be a constructive commissioner of impact investment, focusing not on the layers of cost that impact investment necessarily involves but on the cost per successful outcome. And a third focuses on international development, where $150 billion is expended every year in aid, and governments are looking for more innovative and effective approaches to tackling the challenges of economic development and the social issues that constrain it, such as literacy, child malnutrition, and illness.

Addressing Constraints on Economic Development

Social entrepreneur after social entrepreneur, investor after investor, governmental minister after minister, and countless business leaders and financiers all came before the Taskforce and argued that a revolution was needed in the way we tackle social issues. Government resources available for this fall far short of increasing social needs. This is why I think that impact investment's time has come.

But to make progress, we must clearly understand the challenges at hand, and focus considerable energy on removing remaining barriers so that the breakthrough in thinking that has enabled impact investing—namely, the measurement of social outcomes and their linking to financial returns—really does provide social entrepreneurs with the keys to the capital market.

Cathy, Jed, and Ben define and describe a practice of Collaborative Capitalism that is broad—with the power to influence all business and finance—yet driven by impact investment that is initially concentrated in private markets, just as tech venture capital was.

Impact investing is indeed both an "approach," across asset categories, and also a part of the alternative assets class, where it offers a unique form of private investment that is largely uncorrelated to public markets.

Similarly, international economic development is a core objective for many impact investors—we are all for the incidental impacts of regular commercial activities in low-income communities, such as job creation—yet economic development is insufficient in and of itself. We must also address the *constraints* on economic development internationally, through the provision of services to tackle such problems as literacy and school dropout rates, the eradication of disease, training of the unemployed, and so forth. Driving capital through development impact bonds (DIBs) toward tackling these social constraints on economic development is one example of what the impact investing movement is all about.

Again, *the lynchpin is the realization that social outcomes can be measured,* for interventions on everything from recidivism, homelessness, foster care, and educational dropout rates, to malaria, early detection of diabetes, and sleeping sickness eradication.

I believe that within five years, we will know the costs of an intervention for most social issues, the savings government can yield from an intervention, the price a philanthropic donor or a government is paying in the market for the particular outcome, and the greater value to society—the secondary and tertiary effects—of someone being rehabilitated, for example.

The Taskforce is providing guidelines for metrics and benchmarks in dealing with key issues. Conventions will be set over time just as we have accounting conventions for, say, recognition of revenues in a software company. There will be professional firms carrying out independent verification, and organizations to gather information and make useful comparisons.

In the United Kingdom, we see, in private asset classes, financial products that strike directly at important social issues. SIBs are among them, representing a particularly innovative proposition by connecting financial performance directly to social outcomes. If average returns delivered are on the order of 7 percent, as expected, and these returns are "uncorrelated," because recidivism rates, adoption rates, and other social measures do not fluctuate with the stock market, this low correlation will offer valuable diversification benefits. If these returns hold up over time, this should lead to allocations to impact investing of several percent of total assets in most portfolios.

The Contours, Challenges, and Transformative Potential of Impact Investing

The authors of this book trace the history of impact investing back to socially responsible investing and the impulse to integrate environmental, social, and governance factors in public markets. I too am enthusiastic about an increasingly impactful approach to investing in public companies and look forward to seeing investors reward strategies designed with a measureable social outcome in mind. Among the actors emerging in impact investing are larger corporations focused on specific impact projects. Group Danone, for example, has created Grameen Danone Foods, a yogurt factory in Bangladesh whose mission is to help reduce childhood malnutrition, increase children's growth, and improve their concentration in school.

I also see a role in impact investing for corporations as outcome funders and mentors for charitable service providers addressing issues relevant to a corporation's business. For example, a company selling health products might want to be one of the outcome funders alongside government and health maintenance organizations for social impact bonds that seek to reduce the number of prediabetics contracting Type 2 diabetes.

For what are becoming known as "profit-with-purpose companies," sometimes known as "for-profit social enterprises," an important challenge will be "locking in" mission through special-purpose corporate forms, such as the B Corporation in the United States. Socially driven investors want assurance that these businesses will not abandon their mission. Corporate structures that enable entrepreneurs and investors to know that the mission of the business will be locked in beyond a sale of the business are an increasing feature alongside the presence of measureable social objectives.

Impact investing may reach scale sooner by capitalizing for-profit businesses, but it is likely to be most transformative for nonprofit, charitable organizations. In the United Kingdom alone, there are 160,000 charitable organizations, including many service providers to the less well off. Most are small and have no money. In 2000, the UK Social Investment Task Force estimated that three-quarters had insufficient capital to look ahead more than three months; more recent annual surveys of the US nonprofit market by the Nonprofit Finance Fund paint the same picture.

Figures from the United States also illustrate the problem of inadequate resources. Despite three-quarters of a trillion dollars in US charitable foundations, and nine million people employed in nonprofits, very few US service providers have managed to raise the funding necessary to achieve scale. Over a period of twenty-five years, fifty thousand US businesses have successfully crossed the line of $50 million in sales. How many nonprofits have done so in the same period? Just 144.

The primary reason nonprofit organizations face this predicament is that traditional philanthropy has focused on the act of charitable giving rather than on achieving social outcomes. It has given charitable organizations money for two or three years and then, as a well-intentioned sanity check, directed them to raise money elsewhere after that—oh, and not to waste any of it on their overheads.

Yet if business entrepreneurs had come to me at Apax with business plans that involved investing nothing on overheads, I would have shown them the door. The combination of unpredictable funding and lack of investment capital has prevented almost all charitable organizations from realizing their potential effectiveness and scale.

Philanthropic foundations have a special role to play in driving innovation in nonprofit organizations, and are gradually rising to the challenge. Some foundations now seek to measure outcomes from their grant activities, by way of qualitative if not quantitative criteria. Some are beginning to see impact investment as a very focused complement to philanthropic grants. Some are using their endowments to attract investors, as the Rockefeller, Bloomberg, and Pritzker Foundations have done by taking first-loss positions ahead of third parties. Some charitable foundations are beginning to see themselves as the natural drivers of impact investment, especially the kind that carries the greatest financial risk and the potential for the highest social return. They think it natural to achieve their social objectives through some direct investment from their endowments.

■ ■ ■

All investors will find this an informative and valuable book, a must-read for anyone serious about impact investing and sustainable business more broadly. For investors interested in improving people's lives, the book lays out a refreshingly detailed overview of the area. And Cathy, Jed, and Ben's predictions in their final chapter include many powerful ideas, including a number that chime with the work of the Taskforce: integrated reporting, the globalization of financial innovation, new concepts of fiduciary duty, and the importance of corporate and stakeholder alignment.

Impact investing, more than anything, needs leadership. And this leadership does need to be cross sector, or, in the authors' terms, multilingual. We need it from investors in a position to pilot entrepreneurial ideas; from larger, commercial institutions whose participation is helpful to scaling the sector; from philanthropists and foundations, who can take risks to catalyze impacts; and from policymakers, who can help create a multisector playing field more conducive to improving lives.

In truth, there are no more excuses for *any* of us not to act. Social outcomes can be measured. Governments are open to the best ideas on how to move forward. Investors are participating as the right products become available. The rise of impact investing requires only that we coordinate our efforts and, with careful urgency, bring the "invisible heart" of markets to help those whom the "invisible hand" has left behind.

Sir Ronald Cohen
Chair
Social Impact Investment Taskforce
Established by the G8

Preface

Picture . . .

. . . making an investment recommended by the local broker managing your retirement savings and then pulling up an app on your phone that shows the affordable housing development in your community that the investment is helping finance.

. . . seeing a news article on the need for more employment opportunities offering sustainable wages, benefits, and professional training for the people of your region and then reviewing the investment report from a local fund quantifying the precise number of jobs it had supported with your capital.

. . . collaborating with your start-up team to launch the business you've been planning for the past few years—and knowing there are investors on the other side of the term sheet as interested in the social relevance and intentional impact of your venture as they are in its financial health.

Over recent years, the world has been witness to an accelerated process of economic evolution coming simultaneously from the fringe and the mainstream. It is a fusion of previously disparate areas of expertise and a vision emerging out of traditional finance, community and economic development, environmental finance, and social entrepreneurship. Following two years of in-depth research, case-studying the experience and track records of twelve of the leading impact investment funds operating in markets around the world, *The Impact Investor* offers a window through which to view this larger transformation.

The work of the twelve funds has been significant. Among other things, they

- Created and sustained more than 1.3 million jobs in underserved markets
- Provided more than seventeen million people with access to finance previously beyond their reach
- Managed portfolios of impact investment with more than 40 percent of their investments going into women-led firms and 60 percent of their funds invested in businesses operated by individuals from racial and ethnic groups historically excluded from mainstream financial markets
- Have raised and invested in excess of $1.3 billion in impact capital

The funds represent but a snapshot of larger trends under way around the world—trends we believe have the potential to transform business and finance as we know them today. Although in some ways the managers of these funds are simply taking traditional business practices and applying them to new markets, they bring a profound new investment perspective that integrates economic opportunity within a social and environmental context. This investment perspective is a new analytic mind from which all financial professionals may learn. As you will see explored in the pages to come, these investors operate with what we call a "multilingual" skillset—with the capacity to speak profit and purpose, financial return and social impact.

If you take nothing else away from *The Impact Investor,* consider this:

There is a new way of investing that is in the process of deep evolution and no longer sits on the edge of mainstream economics and capital markets.

These managers do not think in terms of "do well and then do good" or "financial-social trade-offs." Rather, they think in an integrated way that intuitively seeks to capture the full nature of value through their investment strategies, seeking financial return *with* impact. They do not see impact as the unique domain of traditional channels of the public and nonprofit sectors. These actors and the funds they bring to market extend the work of previous investment pioneers and represent a potentially powerful force integrating numerous worlds into a single, sustainable whole.

These new approaches to investing are not being forced on markets, but are drawn into them at the same time as they are emerging out of them. The world is changing as we confront the shortcomings of an "either-or" understanding of capital—either you make money or you give it away—in favor of an integrated investment practice that rejects the short-term approach to managing long-term goals, with no consideration of off-balance-sheet factors such as worker health or the availability of water or the environmental sustainability of a company's supply chain. Some of the change under way in our world is about simple self-preservation (if you're a beverage company operating in emerging markets and are not taking water issues into account, perhaps you will be in a different line of work five years from now!); other parts come from those intentionally seeking to use investment capital to drive positive social and environmental impacts.

This book is just the latest stepping-stone in a growing body of research across the fields of social entrepreneurship, blended value, community development finance, microfinance, workforce development, impact assessment, sustainability, corporate responsibility, and socially responsible investing. In the past five years, more has been written about the purpose, scope, and activity of these fields than ever before, with increasing speed and regularity, from more diverse and global voices.[1]

What we add to the nearly daily drumbeat of new blogs and reports is a deeper empirical look at what is being done and accomplished by funds that have established a tangible track record, in order to understand this emerging field with fresh eyes and to more confidently predict what will come next.

What this track record of research points toward is the reality that impact investing is moving from anecdote to analysis, from the whipsaw opinion of hopeful pundits to perspectives informed by sharp experience and insights grounded in practice. Our research is drawn from the concrete experiences of twelve funds precisely because that level of in-depth analysis is what is now required to move our collaborative efforts from the initial questions of "Impact Investing 1.0" to the next level of informed execution.

It is no accident that Morgan Stanley, Goldman Sachs, UBS, Deutsche Bank, RBC, Bank of America, National Australia Bank, all of the High Street banks in the United Kingdom, and dozens of other major financial institutions throughout the globe are making strong plays in the impact investing arena. Other investors should take heed:

The train has left the station.
The tremors are being felt.

Mainstream investors are reframing assumptions governing traditional investing just as traditional philanthropists and socially responsible investors are reconnecting with their initial motivations to effectively manage assets and make use of capital to create a changed world—at the levels of individual, community, company, and market.

The rise of impact investing takes place against a larger backdrop of innovation within mainstream capital markets and newly emerging visions of the future of business. And much of this is now being driven by shifts in "consumer" demand, whether at the neighborhood level of individuals seeking to better the possibilities before them; the customer level of those seeking to align the power of their dollars with the world they seek to create; or the consumers of investment strategies and vehicles who are demanding greater transparency, less financial leverage, and expanded understandings of potential value creation generated by their capital.

The funds profiled in this book show us, concretely, what this collaborative new world looks like—in the emerging era of Impact Investing 2.0. The work of the twelve funds stands as a testament to the fact that capital can be structured to change the economic conditions of those who remain largely outside the economic mainstream.

While a great deal has been achieved, a great deal more must be done. We do not pretend to offer "the answer" to the many debates and discussions currently taking place in regard to the ability of capital and companies to advance positive change in the world; nor do we provide a template or defined road map. What we offer in the following pages is a set of organizational data points, experiences, and analysis to inform our next steps as we move forward together. We owe a great deal to these funds willing to open their balance sheets and reflections to outside researchers. And we are pleased to bring their lessons to all those committed to investing with impact to help advance the world to which we aspire.

August 2014   Cathy Clark
Durham, North Carolina

Jed Emerson
Granby, Colorado

Ben Thornley
Oakland, California

This book is dedicated to J. Gregory Dees

1950–2013

Mentor, Colleague, Friend

For using the power of words to plant a vision that has inspired a generation to think about how we each can use our talents to make the world better.

For defining social entrepreneurship as a discipline and not a personal hobby, drawing out in nearly every person he met the desire to engage with others collaboratively toward shared goals.

And, most of all, for quietly, sneakily nurturing the societal institutions, in education, finance, consulting, government, journalism, philanthropy, nonprofits, and business, making that vision come true.

THE IMPACT INVESTOR

Introduction

You don't need a weatherman to know which way the wind blows.
— Bob Dylan, "Subterranean Homesick Blues"

THERE WAS PROBABLY NO POINT IN HISTORY when life was truly simple and uncomplicated. Every age, every time, every life has its challenges, its complexities, its moments of uncertainty and change. Yet, in the midst of each age's challenges comes a moment of clarity: the need to engage in the Civil War, the ultimate validity of battling the Axis powers, the compelling righteousness of the civil rights movement.

Our moment is no different than others that have come before, save that the clarion call is for a new generation—figuratively and literally, as the Millennials step into new leadership roles—to advance new thinking with regard to the nature of capital and the practices of investing. We now live in a world where injustice and poverty, down the street or across the world, may be felt in an instant. One where environmental degradation threatens not just some future generations we'll never know, but the quality of life of our children. And what's being demanded, more clearly than ever, across generations, is the opportunity to align every facet of our lives with making a positive difference, with a broader vision of a life well lived.

In this respect, in a world that technology renders increasingly open and interconnected, capital markets remain one of the last bastions of imperviousness. Even though capital flows around the globe are one of the most powerful forces shaping our societies and economies, most of us still invest under the pretense that the impact of capital is divorced from its uses.

1

Yet even as our moment in history demands nothing less than a full accounting of the positive and negative outcomes of capital, a thorough understanding of our role in bending environmental and social systems toward justice, there will be those who continue their efforts to play the role of pundits on the sidelines as our modern Rome devolves into seeming chaos. Even as trillions of dollars continue to be invested with the sole consideration of financial return, and even as companies continue to be managed with an eye to a single, supposedly unencumbered bottom line of financial performance, the majority will see that larger forces are being unleashed in the form of a new capitalism—capitalism focused on the generation of financial returns, yes, but a larger, more holistic economic system operated with reference to previously "off-balance-sheet" factors, such as stakeholder interests and carbon footprint—and a host of additional factors increasingly understood to have influence on long-term value generation and financial return to investors, as well as to our well-being on the planet.

Capitalism will continue its evolution of past decades but increasingly turn outward, recognizing that economics and finance may no longer be viewed in isolation from those elements on which the capitalist engine itself draws. The *new* capitalism will continue to be revealed as the unifying backdrop against which innovations and refinements will emerge. The *new* capitalism will not pit asset owner against wage earner, or shareholder against stakeholder, or capitalist against community. Rather, the *new* capitalism clearly emerging through the mist of history is one of complements—not contradictions. It is a capitalism of integrated interests. It is a capitalism of shared futures and global markets played out in community contexts connected across the planet via the new wireless world and ultimate reality that value is a blend of environmental, social, and economic components—value is itself fundamentally whole and more than the sum of these parts. The legacy of the future will not be one of blind wealth creation but rather sustained value creation across generations. It is a capitalism of corporate and community commerce, of individual and societal change, and, ultimately, our undeniably common interests.

It is, at its core, a *Collaborative Capitalism*: the realization of a community's highest economic and social aspirations through the enterprising deployment of ideas, capital, and shared resources in pursuit of common impact.

It is within this broad flow of global collaborative capitalism that impact investing takes place.

As we will explore in the following chapters, impact investing is a banner under which a host of practices now gather:

- Mainstream, private equity investors seek to integrate environmental, social, and governance factors into their pursuit of financial returns.
- Pension fund fiduciaries invest with an eye to the health of the communities in which beneficiaries live, as well as their financial interests.
- Foundations seek not simply to make charitable grants but rather to draw on the full tool kit of capital under their control—grants, to be sure, but also program-related investments and public and private securities—all with an eye toward sustained portfolio performance and maximizing total impact.
- Individual investors gather on crowdfunding platforms, aggregating their hundreds into hundreds of thousands of dollars directed at various types of impact and multiple types of return.

In some ways, this is all new—yet in others, the song remains the same. Over a decade ago, following a presentation at the World Economic Forum in Davos that included a description of the vision and practices of what may now be defined as impact investing, an audience member rose to express how powerful he felt this new vision to be—and to point out that in many ways it was simply a return to the fundamental principles of the traditional, privately held family business managed not only for the benefit of the founding family but also for the community (if not the region) as a whole; the family's prosperity could not be separated from the place they called home.

Impact investing is old-school, fundamental investing and economic development with a twenty-first century sustainability wrap. It is what good business practice was, is, and will ever be. It is earth economics and family values and profit with purpose. In short, it is the visible tip of the iceberg within the larger global system of Collaborative Capitalism.

In the research on which our partnership is based, the three of us (re)discovered a set of truths that communities and societies have forgotten:

- The most effective strategies operate with awareness not simply of the corporate or capital context but with linkage to the "great around" represented by the public sector and the enabling environment it creates.
- The strongest form of capital is a "stack" of *all* capital coming from a variety of private *and* public investors—each tranche of which buys down risk, and positions enterprise for optimal performance, thus enabling opportunity to be captured for the benefit of shareholder and stakeholder alike.
- The best teams are diverse, with leaders who build from past experience a complex future that transcends silos and singular disciplines or doctrines.
- The organizations—whether for-profit or nonprofit or hybrid—that are built to best stand the test of time are those that do not seek to artificially separate corporate mission from financial discipline, but rather maintain mission as the touchstone on which financial sustainability is grounded.

As harbingers of a new way of doing business generally—or, more accurately, a revitalized understanding of back-to-basics truths—these axioms offer significant challenges to those who continue to maintain the illusion that the interests of capital and impact are antithetical. Business models geared only to financial performance, with no consideration of impact, will be decreasingly effective in generating consistent profits. This trend, in concert with the preferences of Millennials, who more than any generation seek to blend meaning with their work and money, mean that these models will quickly become bad business in shrinking markets.

Our Two-Year Study

We have reached the insights and conclusions in the following pages as the result of a two-year process of observing best business practices in Collaborative Capitalism through our examination of twelve outstanding impact investing funds that met or exceeded the expectations of their investors.

With a commitment to concurrently delivering attractive financial returns and intentional social outcomes, impact investors are at the cutting edge of Collaborative Capitalism, operating in markets often smaller, younger, and more idiosyncratic than mainstream investors have the stomach or capacity to tackle, and that demand cross-sector skills that many mainstream investors simply do not possess.

As a result, successful impact investing fund managers are extraordinarily creative, nimble, and resilient—all qualities we wanted to explore and learn from when we first culled an initial universe of 350 funds to 30 that were recommended by their investors.

We then decided on the final twelve funds, which were representative of the breadth of activity in impact investing, with track records of financial and social performance that were suitably robust and sharable. The twelve funds are listed here; their impact target areas are illustrated in Figure I.1. With the objective of understanding the key factors that had undergirded their success, we interviewed not only fund managers but also the investors in those funds, the recipients of investor capital, and the actors within their immediate peer group.

Twelve Top-Performing Impact Investing Funds

Aavishkaar
ACCIÓN Texas Inc.
Bridges Ventures
Business Partners
   Limited

Calvert Foundation
Deutsche Bank
Elevar Equity
Huntington Capital
MicroVest

RSF Social Finance
Small Enterprise
   Assistance Funds
   (SEAF)
W.K. Kellogg
   Foundation

Chapter 2 provides additional insight into the research process, which, in 2013, led to the largest-ever public release of performance data in impact investing, despite the fact that most impact investing funds operate in private markets and, with only accredited investors, are under no obligation to share information publicly. Our top priority was building trust with the funds, and holding fast to a detailed process of engagement that would ensure that

Figure I.1 Impact Targets of the Twelve Funds

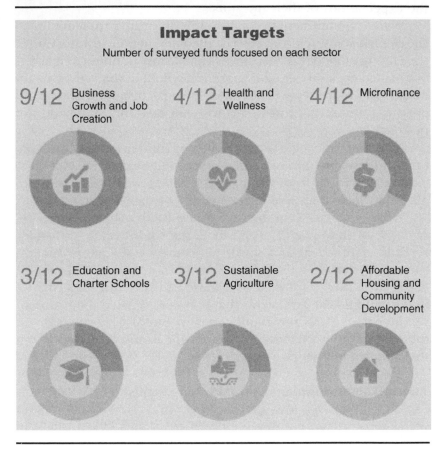

financial performance was contextualized alongside the complete, detailed story of their creation, governance, strategy, deployment, and relationship with investors and investees over the entire life of the fund. The aggregate financial and social performance of the funds is presented in Figures I.2 and I.3.

What we discovered was a sophisticated marketplace that is much less haphazard than many have thought, and a pathway of practice and expertise we invite you to explore in the following chapters.

Figure I.2   Fund Investors and Financial Performance of the Twelve Funds

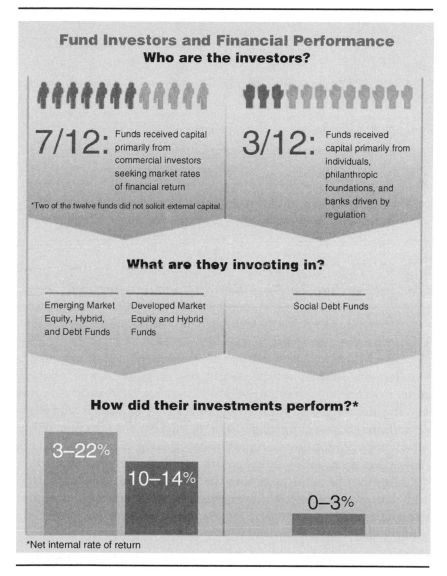

Figure I.3   Aggregate Impact of the Twelve Funds

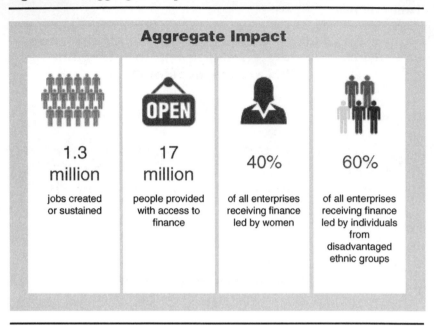

Audience

Our focus is impact investing—and practitioners in the field are certainly a core audience that will benefit particularly from new insights into the structural and strategic characteristics associated with high-performing impact investing funds. However, this book also has broader application, just as impact investing sits at the apex of Collaborative Capitalism. (We will discuss this in more detail in chapter 1.)

Although there are ongoing discussions regarding the nature and practice of impact investing, the concept really is quite straightforward:

Impact investing is capital management in pursuit of appropriate levels of financial return with the simultaneous and intentional creation of measurable social and environmental impacts.

What's important to understand is that the lessons of impact investing are also the lessons of Collaborative Capitalism, a larger field of practice that encompasses everything from corporate social responsibility (CSR) to operational and supply chain sustainability, public private partnership, and socially responsible investment (all in an effort to mitigate risk).

Increasingly, financial institutions *and* corporations around the world are using Collaborative Capitalism as a tool to proactively generate clear, positive social outcomes in addition to profits and wealth. This is a profound and transformational shift in what economic activity and capital make possible (adding an entirely new measure of extrafinancial performance). From the capital markets perspective, impact investing has the potential to forever change the way we consume financial services.

Consider this one data point from the World Economic Forum: *Although just 6 percent of US pension funds reported in 2013 that they had made an impact investment, fully 64 percent expected to in the future.*[1]

Even if it takes these pension funds decades to follow through and just half pursue the opportunity, the ramifications are clear: impact investing is going mainstream, pushing those already engaged in "risk-mitigating" capitalism to think more clearly about outcomes, and those unfamiliar with Collaborative Capitalism to quickly get up to speed.

The Impact Investor speaks directly to numerous audiences touched by Collaborative Capitalism and provides some of the following important insights and easy-to-apply tools:

- **For mainstream investors**, including commercial institutions, fiduciaries, and individuals, *The Impact Investor* provides actionable insights into the characteristics and performance of a range of proven impact investing strategies. It also paints a picture of the unique skills of impact investors, and the right questions to ask when weighing a fund's likelihood of delivering the financial and social value it promises. *The Impact Investor* also recommends concrete steps investors can take directly, in their own portfolios, to deliver positive social or environmental outcomes in addition to attractive rates of financial return.
- **For corporate executives**, *The Impact Investor* provides evidence a new era of Collaborative Capitalism is emerging—the next essential paradigm in business, building on CSR and other evolutions in thinking regarding the place of business in advancing social or environmental performance. By showcasing the

work of impact investing funds at the forefront of this trend, this book portends a set of practices that, in less than a decade, will become commonplace in all business settings. By studying the work of impact investors, business executives will gain material insight into a range of strategies for ensuring that their companies remain profitable and sustainable. Executives will also gain skills needed to be more successful operators in a world that is more sector agnostic than ever and populated by a new generation of Millennial customers.

- **Entrepreneurs** will learn what makes impact investors tick and the type of business approaches they typically invest in. This book will provide entrepreneurs with insights into partnering and working with investors, and the other multilingual skills and new approaches they should master (alongside impact investors) in order to be as effective as possible. Each of the impact investing funds we feature is also entrepreneurial in its own right. The lessons from the experience of these funds will be invaluable for any innovative business leader.

- **Community and social change agents** will gain insights into how capital can be used to drive social and environmental justice. The tools of finance are increasingly being appropriated to support community vehicles—nonprofits, businesses, cooperatives, social enterprises, and any number of other structures—delivering job creation and opportunities for expanding employment and development to those presently excluded from local and regional economies.

- **For teachers and students of business**, the book offers a range of new analytical frameworks for assessing the structure and rapid development of impact investing, created with the benefit of extensive primary data. These frameworks have broad business applications, and our research methods and approach to documenting performance can be applied in most markets. The book also presents clear paths for continuing research and opportunities for further academic and thought leadership. All students will benefit from understanding the operational approaches being applied by funds using cutting-edge financial instruments in pioneering markets.

- **For philanthropists**, the book presents a comprehensive overview of what it means to be "catalytic" by delivering a magnitude of social value never before seen as an intentional outcome of private investment. The book highlights the involvement of a number of philanthropic leaders in the funds we researched, two of which are private foundations. The book will help philanthropists understand what it means to engage in impact investing, how to get started, and the kinds of approaches that will increase the probability of success.

- **Public officials** will recognize a range of private investment strategies in *The Impact Investor* that have *already* been utilized by policymakers to drive the delivery of social and environmental impacts at scale. The book describes an ideal form of public-private partnership and the steps needed, primarily on the part of impact investors, to actualize this heightened form of collaboration. Public officials will see a powerful, evolving role for government in the development of impact investing, and the opportunity to stretch limited resources in innovative new ways. As essential partners in impact investing, public officials will benefit from the book's broader insights into the future of finance and business and its relationship to diverse constituencies, a perspective already at the heart of government.

No book can be all things to all people. Readers should know that much of our data and real-life examples of Collaborative Capitalism are drawn directly from impact investing funds. The rest is drawn from the broader literature and our personal experiences in the fields of impact, philanthropy, policy, and investment. Two of us have been private impact investing fund managers, and two of us have been foundation executives making grants and program-related investments, a key form of impact investment. One of us has been a business and finance reporter; two of us have written guidebooks for practitioners that include models and frameworks that, more than a decade after they were published, continue to be widely used across the social enterprise and impact investing sectors. We have experience in successfully changing the way people think about and understand complex topics. Two of us have been publishing and teaching on these topics for more than fifteen years each. One of us coauthored the first book ever published on the topic of impact investing; one of us was a public official focused on economic development before advising the largest pension fund in the United States on its impact assessment practice; and one of us helped create an emerging standard rating system for impact investing funds worldwide.

A Focus on Intermediaries

Through these experiences, we initiated our major collaborative research effort in 2011 with the strong belief that there is no better unit of analysis than impact investing *funds* for understanding the way capitalism is changing.

Why? Because funds interact directly with hundreds of enterprises and have ultimate responsibility for delivering the blended performance of financial as well as social and environmental returns on which the case for impact investing rests. They are the proverbial canaries in the coal mine of the larger sphere of Collaborative Capitalism. They are test beds and financial R&D labs, where in order to succeed, relationships and communication must be rock solid even while the work remains innovative.

Indeed, when impact investing funds succeed, many important results follow that may positively impact the development of Collaborative Capitalism: investors increase their investment, replicable financial structures emerge for new pools of fund capital, entrepreneurs have clear guideposts of what to expect of investment, and secondary markets more naturally emerge.

Finally, funds are also a crucible of accountability. As Bob Webster has written about the Grassroots Business Fund, where he is chief operating officer, the formal fund structure provides a "clear and transparent picture of fund financial flows," including management fees, legal costs, portfolio investments, investment interest, dividend, and principal reflows; "clear expectations for financial and social returns and any tradeoffs thereof"; and an "active seat at the governance table." They also "can incentivize the fund manager through some type of carried interest in the fund's performance."[2]

What's Ahead?

The Impact Investor is presented in three parts that examine how we got here, the current state of the market and its emerging best practices, and future implications.

In part 1, "Key Practices and Drivers Underlying Impact Investing," we describe the development and current state of Collaborative Capitalism and impact investing.

Chapter 1, "Inside Collaborative Capitalism," explores some of the big-picture trends driving the shift from incidental to intentional impact, including the use of business approaches in solving social challenges, a growing awareness of environmental and economic sustainability, and demand from a new generation of more responsible consumers and investors.

Chapter 2, "Raising the Curtain on Impact Investing," provides a comprehensive overview of this fast-growing market, introducing our twelve funds in detail, their performance, and the market of which they are a part. We also provide a new estimate of the total size of the global impact investing market, drawing on key subsectors, and propose a new method for categorizing impact investing funds.

In part 2, "Four Key Elements of Successful Impact Investing," we analyze current practice and delineate the four key elements of successful impact investing—and by extension Collaborative Capitalism—and provide a range of tools for implementing these practices:

Chapter 3, "Impact DNA," highlights successful funds' core approach to impact investing: a process of establishing a clearly embedded strategy and structure for achieving mission prior to investment, enabling a predominantly financial focus throughout the life of the investment. We call this approach "Mission First and Last." Knowing early and explicitly that impact is contained in a fund's DNA allows all parties (investors, investees, and the fund itself) to move forward with the investment discipline akin to any other financial transaction, confident that any possibility of mission drift can be effectively managed.

Chapter 4, "Symbiosis as Strategy," explores the ubiquitous role of government in impact investing, and the multidirectional relationships of trust and support that undergird effective public-private partnership. By nature, impact investors represent a marriage of public and private interests. They seamlessly integrate a commitment to improving public welfare with the power and efficiency of capital markets. Policymakers—who have a vested interest in maximizing the social and environmental well-being of their constituencies and hold massive power to influence the market through laws and regulations—are natural partners for impact investors.

Chapter 5, "The New Deal," focuses on the rigorous and creative strategies impact investors use to meet the diverse return objectives of a range of capital providers. By bringing different types of stakeholders to the table, cultivating "catalytic" investors, and doing the hard work of financial structuring, impact investors are able to support markets that would not otherwise be "investable," providing access to capital in some of the most underserved places and sectors.

Chapter 6, "Multilingual Leadership," discusses the inherently cross-sector nature of impact investing and the diversity of skillsets and strategic approaches needed if one is to succeed. Impact investors are expert at simultaneously seeing the world through the eyes of philanthropy (the "theories of change"), government (market failure and subsidy), and finance (the best use of capital; return on investment), which is a difficult but essential approach to master in the era of Collaborative Capitalism.

In part 3, "Looking Ahead: Trends and Challenges," we take all that we have learned and pose a simple question about the future. We claim that Collaborative Capitalism is on the march. What then are the signs we should look for to indicate that Collaborative Capitalism is storming the castle? What might still hold it back?

Chapter 7, "The Writing on the Wall" outlines ten trends to watch that will signal the arrival of a broader practice of Collaborative Capitalism on a range of investment and business activities, both mainstream and niche.

Chapter 8, "Concluding Reflections," brings together the themes and explores seven challenges the field must face to successfully bring forth this new vision.

Finally, we end with an "Impact Investor Resource Guide" that brings together all of the strategies and tools from chapters 3 through 6. This is an easy reference for those eager to move quickly to action.

Impact investing has been called a dark wood in which various new and exciting creatures bustle about and explore a new world of investing and impact. *The Impact Investor* points to the paths through the wood and confirms impact investors, social entrepreneurs, pension fund fiduciaries, and a host of other actors actually know a lot more about how to "do" impact investing than many have to this point believed. We do not have to wonder how impact investing may have the greatest impact—the fund managers and strategies in this book document how leading funds execute their strategies for high performance. We do not have to ask, "How does impact investing differ from traditional, mainstream investing?" The investors profiled in the following pages show how impact investing is not altogether "new" or different, but rather an extension of the fundamentals of sound investing practices. We do not need to ask, "What will it take for impact investing to go mainstream?" The practices and diverse pool of investors described in this book show that in fact impact investing has gone mainstream and that it is only a matter of time before we are truly able to see the depth and breadth of the adoption of impact investing practices within those mainstream markets.

Every era is an era of change. We need only to lift our heads or climb a nearby hill to gain a different perspective, to see the possibility of the changes taking place within our community, region, or market. This book provides an overview of promising investment themes and practices that portend a global economic transformation. The exponential growth of impact investing is well under way as we continue to see new ideas, strategies, and opportunities brought from the fringe to the center of capital markets the world over.

PART ONE

KEY PRACTICES AND DRIVERS UNDERLYING IMPACT INVESTING

1

Inside Collaborative Capitalism

*Collaborative Capitalism is the realization of a community's
highest economic and social aspirations through the enterprising
deployment of ideas, capital, and shared resources in pursuit
of common impact.*

COLLABORATIVE CAPITALISM IS MANIFEST AT MANY LEVELS and in many
ways, within and between companies, investors, and the markets
and communities in which they operate. It has evolved out of the
creative adaptation of business norms, practices, and relationships
to address the ultimate effect of capitalist activities on broader
social and environmental purposes. At the organization or company level, it is driven by what we often refer to as "mission"; at the
fund or investor level, it is usually in the details of the transaction,
in the price premium, in the metrics of accountability, or in the
ways that risks are mitigated to allow more stakeholders to achieve
their goals.

But let's get down to brass tacks. Collaborative capitalism is not
a theoretical construct. It is made real in myriad markets through a
wide range of business approaches and financial innovations.

Consider Fair Trade, a prototypical impulse of Collaborative
Capitalism applied to global value chains. A key concept of Fair
Trade is to recognize the supplier as a constituent of the business,
who is affected by lowered commodity pricing, such as for coffee or

This chapter draws on the e-book *Collaborative Capitalism and the Rise of Impact
Investing,* which was published as a prelude to this book by the three authors in
April 2014, available at www.bit.ly/collabcapital.

bananas. Fair Trade advocates have applied diverse sets of strategies to align the tools of capitalism with working to ensure a fair wage is offered to the supplier in local communities.

In essence, Fair Trade labels aim to make transparent the effect that a fair, living wage has on this constituent, and ask the customer to agree to pay for those benefits up front. Advocates of Fair Trade then use a host of accountability practices to ensure this price premium is protected all the way down the value chain.

The outcome at the end of this process—the targeted impact Fair Trade seeks—is a supplier farm, cooperative, or worker with a higher quality of life due to a higher income. This seemingly small innovation in the supplier-to-consumer relationship has become a practice hundreds of companies may now build on and extend to other areas of corporate practice. Collaborative Capitalism–based movements and industries are born of effective innovations like this.

Peer-group-based microfinance is another example of Collaborative Capitalism at work. In this case, the transparency of peer pressure within a borrower group replaces the need for hard collateral assets, transforming local peers into stakeholders who are highly motivated to ensure regular payments, and obviating the need for layers of risk protection by the lender.

In our introduction, we presented this idea of Collaborative Capitalism as a larger field of practice encompassing everything from corporate social responsibility (CSR) to operational and supply chain sustainability, public private partnerships, and socially responsible investment. Indeed, it is a broad term we use to describe many different impulses with various terms and names. In this chapter, we explore the roots of Collaborative Capitalism, define its subfields more concretely through the Collaborative Capitalism pyramid, and parse three essential elements of Collaborative Capitalism: transparency, attention to constituency, and an outcomes orientation.

The Roots of Collaborative Capitalism

There are three major trends that, taken together, have fused into the widespread practice of Collaborative Capitalism. They include the acceptance of a social role and responsibility for business as a core aspect *of* business, the development of a new feeling of "agency" among the Millennial generation and entrepreneurs, and the realization that risk mitigation by investors can be aligned with achieving better outcomes—both financial and extrafinancial.[1]

The Social Role and Responsibility of Business

Since the time of Andrew Carnegie and John Rockefeller, charitable organizations—alongside or as a complement to government programs, and fueled by the profits of business success—have been counted on to fill gaps in the fabric of society left by the failures of markets to meet human needs and potentials.

Some would say the historic vision of the role of charity as the sole agent advancing a private sector social agenda is very much in the past. Today, business itself is viewed as one of many stakeholders in a system that perpetuates inequity.

"I truly believe that capitalism was created to help people live better lives, but sadly over the years it has lost its way a bit," said Virgin's Richard Branson in 2011. "The short-term focus on profit has driven most businesses to forget about the important long-term role they have in taking care of people and the planet."[2]

Writing in *Atlantic* in November 2013, Chrystia Freeland described the concerns of a number of other high-profile critics:

> "Capitalism, even 150 years ago, was more inclusive; there was more of a sense of social responsibility," Dominic Barton, [the global managing director at McKinsey] told me. Today, trust in business is declining. "The system doesn't seem to be as fair or as inclusive. It doesn't seem to be helping broader society."
>
> Barton's concern is shared by David Blood, former head of Goldman Sachs Asset Management, who cofounded Generation Investment Management with former vice president Al Gore a decade ago. "Some people say income inequality doesn't matter. I disagree," Blood said. "We are creating a situation in which only the elite of the elite can be successful—and that is not sustainable." Both men worry that if capitalism doesn't deliver for the middle class, then the middle class will eventually opt for something else. Barton says that business needs what he calls "a license to operate," and without a new approach, he fears, it risks losing that license.[3]

Attempts to understand the business community as a morally legitimate and important actor in the resolution of these problems have followed naturally, because of what are perceived to be at least four key assets.

First, businesses have important sets of **relationships**, such as with suppliers and value chains, entities they may nudge, negotiate with, or block. They also have influence over their workforces and often the communities in which they work, and they can set hiring policies, implement broad training programs, or encourage healthy and positive environmental behavior among employees and their families through internal rewards and programs. Large companies may choose with whom they do business in every community, from the local bank to the food vendor. They wield an influence rivaling that of local governments.

Second, businesses have **operational capacity**, which means they can have direct impact on all sorts of outcomes and ideas. Large manufacturers can, for example, experiment with efforts to reduce harmful environmental effluents coming from their factories and, when they discover what works, serve as conduits for that knowledge. Companies of all sizes in all industries, from Stonyfield Farm (organic yogurt) to Interface (sustainable carpets), have spent a great deal of time and energy experimenting with new ways to be environmentally sustainable and in the process spreading the word with more credibility and authority than a nonprofit in the same field might have. Small private companies have the power to be R&D labs for new ways of doing business (as Ben & Jerry's was from its inception) and, when they get large, to efficiently operationalize global implementation of those innovations (as Ben & Jerry's can do now, as a subsidiary of Unilever). As philanthropy and government working in lockstep may have done fifty years ago, so business today represents the potential of a whole value chain in the production of social and environmental outcomes and influence at the same time that business generates financial returns for shareholders.

Third, businesses have the **power to create markets** that allow others to emulate and follow their formulas for success. Very few industries are made up of a single business—successful value chains, customer bases, and innovations tend to create clusters, and many businesses flourish in them, sometimes for decades, before a new disruptive innovation comes forth and a new industry takes over.

Fourth, businesses have **access to capital** at levels that dwarf philanthropic resources—and sometimes governmental will and capacity—to scale solutions. The kind of investment capital that Coca-Cola can access to ensure the availability of clean water for its own global supply chains almost certainly supersedes what the most dedicated philanthropically supported nonprofits or separate government agencies can do to develop clean water systems and try to maintain them. And a start-up company may access more capital for social good than nonprofits that are many decades old, if it has a scalable business model. For a social change maker, this ability to scale what works and sustain it over time is the impact equivalent of pixie dust—magical stuff that dreams are made of. Although there are plenty of problems that cannot be addressed by business and for which government and nonprofit attention is essential, smart change makers look for the most effective solution agents, and increasingly they are turning to business as a key partner in their efforts.

With power comes heightened responsibility. Many believe it is in businesses' interest to wield their influence to provide social good alongside financial return. As Rockefeller Foundation president Judith Rodin argues, "This new way of doing business extends beyond just the mainstreaming of 'impact investing.' The needs of business blend the lines even further, as businesses look to philanthropic models to keep their value chains sustainable and their customers and employees healthy and secure. As companies expand globally—especially into the developing world—it will no longer be profitable to exist without taking the community and the work force in which they work into consideration."[4]

The profound role for business in society may seem obvious and has been a fact well understood for decades by titans of industry, such as Henry Ford. But we must remember efforts to include business in discussions about explicitly improving society and the world have been relatively recent. For example, the United Nations Global Compact, an initiative to encourage businesses worldwide to adopt sustainability policies and to report on their implementation, was not created until 2000. Financing for Development, a UN conference held in Monterrey, Mexico, in 2002, was the first meeting of its kind to include the private sector as a formal "interlocutor," alongside the public sector (UN member states) and nongovernmental organizations.[5]

The New Fiduciaries: Millennials and Entrepreneurs in the Lead

Large companies are increasingly being held to account for the risks of *not* behaving sustainably, including in public markets through investment strategies that make use of negative and positive screening for environmental, social, and governance (ESG) factors. However, the strongest impulse to execute business strategies with impact and attract capital aligned with that purpose has been in the realm of smaller, private business creation and in educational programs grooming new leaders, where the recent growth and appeal of social entrepreneurship are undeniable. As Katie Smith Milway and Christine Driscoll Goulay report in a recent article, "MBA programs today are minting not just captains of industry, but also crusaders for social good. Any program teaching business skills needs to train their graduates to serve both companies and society. This means equipping would-be entrepreneurs with an understanding of multiple bottom lines and equipping would-be corporate professionals with intrapreneurial vision to connect business interests to social value. Steeped in both social and business principles, this new breed of MBAs will be able to navigate complexity and create opportunities to sustain the world we live and work in."[6]

For example, Net Impact, a membership organization of students interested in the intersection of impact and business, has grown from seventeen members in six chapters in one country in 1993, to more than forty thousand members in 315 chapters in over ninety countries in 2013.

This trend in education at the graduate level is based not on hope but on a major demographic and capital transition that is under way. The baby boom generation, recognized for its interest in how its actions affected society, is passing the torch to its children, who now express interest in affecting society even more than their parents did.

Although generalities have their limits, on the whole the culture of the so-called Greatest Generation, coming from the era of the Depression and World War II, was one where folks believed in hard work during the week and volunteering and recreation on weekends; their idea was that you spent a life gathering assets to retire on and, if you were lucky, to give to your children and community as you got older. The baby boomers' generation was about social change and revolution as a path to enlightenment and personal fulfillment. Granted, only a minority of boomers dropped out of society for good—indeed, their greatest impact lay in changing society's mores and values from within—but on the whole, the legacy of this generation was a rejection of traditional thinking and beliefs, moving us from a 1950s/Cold War mind-set to a 1960s/1970s counterculture mind-set. The Millennials—today's current crop of future leaders in their twenties and thirties—are pursuing a path between, a middle road of "profit with purpose." To many Millennials, the idea that you would spend a life working for a single company and then retire to do what you always wanted to do is as much anathema as the prospect of living in a commune and making a living selling handcrafts.

In addition to a sense of purpose, there is also a new sense of agency, empowering these young people to bring their talents and energy to bear, not simply as activists, but as agents of change. They are willing to work not just to knock down established systems as their parents' generation sought to do but to use their creativity and insight to build new solutions. The Ashoka U slogan "Everyone a changemaker" has swept over college campuses, blending with the hot trends of design thinking and rapid, lean, start-up prototyping. The energy of Silicon Valley has met the purpose impulse, and the result is a new fascination with social innovation.[7]

Many have studied this new generation, puzzled at the seeming contradiction: coming out of the recent Great Recession, young people are willing to earn less to ensure that their work addresses social and environmental issues. A 2011 report commissioned by the Career Advisory Board and conducted by Harris Interactive found that the number-one factor young adults ages twenty-one to thirty-one wanted in a successful career was a sense of meaning.[8] Deloitte's 2011 Millennial survey showed the same results; over 50 percent of Millennials believe the purpose of business is primarily innovation and societal development (see Figure 1.1).

Figure 1.1   Primary Purpose of Business According to the Millennial Generation

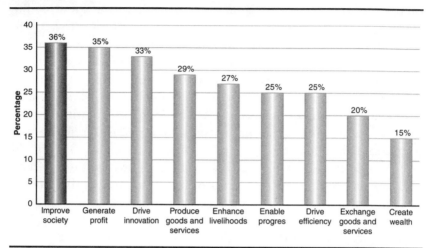

Note: All figures are the percentage of 4,982 survey respondents in eighteen countries, all of whom had college degrees, were employed full-time, and were born after January 1982, answering the question, "Which of the following words and phrases match your own belief as to what business is for?"

Source: Deloitte Global Services Limited. (2013, January). *Millennial Innovation Survey.* http://www2.deloitte.com/content/dam/Deloitte/global/Documents/About-Deloitte/dttl-crs-millennial-innovation-survey-2013.pdf.

Almost 50 percent of Millennial respondents believe business leaders today think too much about the short term and are entirely focused on profit. And around a third of Millennials believe today's business leaders lack awareness of the wider society.[9] Similar results have been found as Deloitte has repeated this survey over the last three years; in 2014 Deloitte noted, "Millennials believe the success of a business should be measured in terms of more than just its financial performance, with a focus on improving society among the most important things it should seek to achieve."[10]

The younger generation is not alone. The field of philanthropy as a whole was bitten—hard—by the business bug in the late 1990s, as Seattle and Silicon Valley entrepreneurs started to cash out and contemplate what to do with their newfound time and money.

In fact, the growth of "social entrepreneurship" as a field of study in graduate business programs in the early 2000s coincided with the emergence of these new philanthropists, attempting to blend what they knew of successful business practices, such as venture capital investing, with philanthropic objectives.

The "venture philanthropy" and "philanthrocapitalism" movements were born, and it is no accident that investors such as George Roberts of KKR and John Doerr of Kleiner Perkins, together with social entrepreneurs they funded, jumped into the emerging space and began to define it in the early 1990s.

In fact, the two largest philanthropies in the United States dedicated to the pursuit of social objectives through entrepreneurial activity and investment were later created by the two founders of eBay, Jeff Skoll and Pierre Omidyar. Now, more than fifteen years after they emerged from their company as paper billionaires, each of them has put hundreds of millions of dollars to work supporting mission-driven entrepreneurs and the systems that support them.

The two are heralding and celebrating the type of ingenuity that gave them their wealth, and are working hard to apply those skills to address the globe's most pressing problems. Skoll, Omidyar, and other successful entrepreneurs, such as Steve and Jean Case, who have been pioneers in bringing entrepreneurial practices to philanthropy, are also working to contribute to the discussion among the Giving Pledge billionaires—ultra-high-net-worth individuals who have pledged at least 50 percent of their assets to charity.

This group, consisting of some of the world's wealthiest individuals and families, is following the example of Bill and Melinda Gates's and Warren Buffett's bold attempts to understand and share the lessons and rewards of their philanthropic pursuits. These discussions are not about philanthropy alone, but also include explorations of impact investing practices. As these efforts continue to create successful track records, in twenty years we may have, not a handful of significant entrepreneur philanthropists using investment as a tool to achieve social outcomes, but hundreds if not thousands.

Although the exact definition of *social entrepreneurship* has been elusive to some, for business leaders the term resonates powerfully.

In the early 1990s, a small set of pioneering entrepreneurs—such as Anita Roddick of the Body Shop, Gary Hirshberg of Stonyfield Farm, and Will Rosenzweig of the Republic of Tea—started spreading their ideas and meeting regularly to explore the potentials and limitations of managing business for social good. Together, through organizations they and others founded—such as Social Venture Network, Business for Social Responsibility, and Net Impact—they created clubs of like-minded businesspeople, all striving to create what have been called "social ventures" or "mission-driven companies": businesses with social objectives. These entrepreneurs came together to support each other's work and share best practices.

Investing in Impact Enterprises

Mainstream capital markets have only recently started to catch up with social entrepreneurs. Back in 1992, a few of those CEOs realized that you cannot be a successful impact entrepreneur without the alignment of your key stakeholders, especially funders and investors. Without alignment over the mission-driven activities of the business, many entrepreneurs found that their best plans were waylaid in the pursuit of profits by those investors. The group Investors' Circle was created to identify investors who had interests in the mission side of the business; it would invest in their growth, patiently and creatively nurturing both the teams and the field to help develop successful social capitalists. The group, now more than twenty years old, has invested $175 million in more than 275 companies and funds, and it has invested in some of the brands and companies that are now household names. Zipcar (sustainable car sharing), Honest Tea (iced tea with an ethical supply chain), and many others received capital from investors who recognized an enterprise model blending social impact and financial return.

The CEOs of many other ventures who did not seek out mission-aligned capital found out the hard way what can happen: investors may turn your business away from its commitments to paying employees a living wage, from fair trade suppliers, or from customer segments that are not imminently profitable, such as low-income people in developing countries. Today mission-focused and other investors are collaborating intensively to help successful ventures scale, but recent research shows that many entrepreneurs still report looking for mission-aligned capital in the early stages of their company's development.[a]

[a]Clark, C., Allen, M., Moellenbrock, B., and Onyeagoro, C. (2013, May). *Accelerating Impact Enterprises: How to Lock, Stock, and Anchor Impact Enterprises for Maximum Impact.* https://dl.dropboxusercontent.com/u/7845889/AcceleratingImpactEnterprises.pdf.

Fast-forward a decade, and we see the notion emerging of a new form of capitalism to recognize and protect the for-profit mission-driven impetus, realized in the idea of the B Corporation (which was developed by members of Investors' Circle, described in "Investing in Impact Enterprises").

The B Corporation certification was designed to affirm and clearly signal a business's commitment to "solving social and environmental problems." Going beyond the many *product* certifications, such as LEED for buildings or ISO standards for labor, which audit the footprint of a specific product, the founders of B Lab, the nonprofit that manages the B Corporation certifications, wanted to provide a *company* certification as a transparent and comparable holistic record of an entire company's social and environmental impact. The goal was to create a trustworthy signal to employees and investors that a company was not just green-washing its intentions. B Lab also insisted on the need for legal protections for these companies dedicated to stakeholder interests, to protect them from the strict interpretations of fiduciary duty that have become the norm for the last few decades.

Soon thereafter, new corporate forms arrived, such as "benefit corporations" and "flexible purpose corporations," building on the legacy of more narrowly designed special-purpose vehicles, such as low-profit limited liability companies (L3Cs) in the United States and community interest companies (CICs) in the United Kingdom. Some of these new corporate forms require companies to declare their mission intentions from the outset and to regularly report back on them in annual reports, ensuring transparency and accountability.

The fact that the number of new, emerging socially oriented businesses remains relatively small—certified B Corporations, benefit corps, flexible purpose corps, and L3Cs together constitute probably less than 1 percent of the businesses created in the United States today—is beside the point. They are a community of practice and a beacon, with hundreds of examples, of what is possible; interest and attention in emulating the model are surging. In the United States, for example, according to B Lab, as of December 2013, more than twenty states had passed legislation allowing companies to incorporate as benefit corporations within their state, including New York, California, and, significantly, Delaware, which holds the largest share of all new business incorporations. Also in December 2013, there were more than 894 certified B Corporations in over twenty-nine countries. Governments around the globe are exploring similar programs with the goal of stimulating businesses that are good social citizens.

As the norms and practices for socially oriented businesses develop, it has also become easier to identify companies whose impacts match their objectives. And within the many organizations emerging to support investment in businesses with social objectives—including the expanding SOCAP conferences; the Global Impact Investing Network; and even mainstream groups like the World Economic Forum—we see activities focused on how to blend the pursuit of outcomes with new forms of metrics, transparency, accountability, and attention to stakeholders.

The agency of business as a force for social good is quickly becoming established.

Aligning Risk Mitigation and the Delivery of Better Outcomes

The development of new notions of business practice has been paralleled by an evolving understanding of what constitutes a sound investment strategy.

That the definition of "sound" investment strategy evolves should be no surprise to anyone familiar with the history of capital market development. For example, there was a time in the State of New York when fiduciaries were not allowed to invest in anything other than bonds issued by the State of New York.[11] Most today would see this as severely limiting; clearly, the definition of what constitutes responsible action on the part of fiduciaries has shifted significantly since those days. It continues to mature as fiduciaries explore various strategies for fulfilling what they understand to be their obligations as overseers of capital. Others have addressed this question of the emerging definition of fiduciary duty and responsible investing; as it continues to evolve, many have documented movement in a direction that allows—indeed, increasingly requires—fiduciaries to consider more than simple financial performance alone in the allocation of capital.

It would be a mistake to think sustainable or impact investing is a completely new way to invest or in some way detracts from how fiduciaries previously approached good investment practice, though this is an easy trap to fall into. In this worldview, negative screens remove investments from consideration, limiting the potential investment universe and possibly decreasing potential future returns; in other discussions, impact investing is thought to require investors accept a lower rate of financial return in exchange for potential future social or environmental returns.

In truth, sustainable and impact investing are not about limiting investor options or returns. Rather, effective impact and sustainable investing *augment* traditional investment discipline with enhanced perspectives and additional information, for the purpose of allowing asset owners or fiduciaries to make better decisions regarding their investment strategies and risk-and-return expectations. After events including the Enron scandal, the BP oil spill, and self-dealing among various actors on Wall Street, which contributed to the 2008 financial crisis, prudent investors increasingly recognize the importance of this kind of thinking.

One of the most significant investors to tackle these issues has been CalPERS, America's largest public pension fund, in the state of California, with over $278 billion in assets as of December 2013. CalPERS is charged with management of retirement assets for current and former employees of California public schools, local agencies, and state employers. As can be imagined, it is not in the business of either taking unreasonable risks or losing money on behalf of its pensioners. That said, it is for precisely this reason that the fund is moving to integrate more aspects of sustainability into its investment approach.

Janine Guillot, former chief operating investment officer at CalPERS, led the adoption by the CalPERS Board of Administration of a set of investment beliefs that have set a new standard for institutional investors.[12] They include statements such as these:

- **A longtime investment horizon is a responsibility and an advantage.** This requires CalPERS to encourage investee companies and external managers to consider the long-term impacts of their actions and favor investment strategies that create long-term, sustainable value.
- **CalPERS investment decisions may reflect wider stakeholder views,** provided they are consistent with its fiduciary duty to members and beneficiaries. CalPERS names its primary stakeholders as members/beneficiaries, employers, and California taxpayers.
- **Long-term value creation requires effective management of three forms of capital: financial, physical, and human.** Governance is identified as the primary tool for aligning the interests of CalPERS and the managers of its capital.
- **Risk to CalPERS is multifaceted and not fully captured through measures such as volatility and tracking error.** This belief states that, as a long-term investor, CalPERS must consider risk factors that emerge slowly over long time periods but that could have a material impact on company or portfolio returns, such as climate change and natural resource availability.

Each of these notions draws on ideas fundamental to sustainable investment practices and in keeping with the goals of many impact investors. CalPERS invests for secondary social benefits in addition to financial returns in a relatively narrow and targeted fashion. However, in establishing heightened principles of transparency and accountability in capital markets, CalPERS plays a broader catalytic role in driving Collaborative Capitalism.[13]

In effect, by making it plain that many core concepts of sustainable investing are simply a function of good investment practice, CalPERS is effectively saying all long-term asset owners should take these factors into account. As Guillot explains: "As a general rule, sustainable investing should just be about good investment practice. That's thinking about your time horizon and what risks and returns are relevant to a particular investment over your time horizon. If you're a long-term investor, thinking about some of the risks that get labeled as 'sustainability-related risks' is essential—environmental risks, human capital risks, governance risks, including whether a potential investment (whether it's a public company or private vehicle) is governed in a way that will enable it to succeed over the long term. Thinking about those kinds of issues is just good practice."

This is the same notion that led David Blood, together with Al Gore, to create Generation Investment Management. Blood argues that the integration of sustainability (or ESG issues) into traditional financial analyses is not a screening process but a research process: "As long-term investors, we fundamentally believe that sustainability issues can materially impact a company's ability to sustain both earnings and a long-term competitive advantage. ESG analysis gives us a more complete picture of business performance."

Other investors are following suit. In its excellent report *Climate Change Scenarios: Implications for Strategic Asset Allocation* and its follow-up report, *Through the Looking Glass: How Investors Are Applying the Results of the Climate Change Scenarios Study,* Mercer, a global consulting firm, documented the experiences and practices of a leading group of institutional investors augmenting traditional financial analysis with consideration of ESG factors. In *Through the Looking Glass,* the authors note how "within the group of project partners, a large proportion of funds had well-established, active engagement policies and practices in place prior to this study. It was in this area we found the most commitment from investors to take action: a large majority of partners reported the findings of the study strengthened their conviction for the need to engage with companies and policymakers to tackle climate risk management."[14]

Jane Ambachtsheer, a partner at Mercer and adjunct professor at the University of Toronto, makes the observation that there are a host of risk factors sustainable investors can explore with greater confidence: "What is your governance framework around the time horizon over which you're investing? Think about quarterly capitalism; are you part of that problem? Are you part of the solution? Do you believe it's a solution? Is it hitting your bottom line? If the answer is yes, what are you going to do about it? . . . [and] on the ESG risk management side, are your fund managers playing with a full deck of cards? Are they using ESG analysis to help them in their corporate valuation, in their risk assessment, how they engage with companies?"

All of this matters, however, only if we can show the practices of sustainable and impact investing actually deliver the returns of financial and social value creation that investors seek. On that front, the jury is in. Deutsche Bank Group's 2012 benchmark metastudy titled *Sustainable Investing: Establishing Long-Term Value and Performance* is unequivocal on the point of materiality:[15]

- 100 percent of the academic studies agree that companies with high ratings for CSR and ESG factors have a lower cost of capital in terms of debt (loans and bonds) and equity. In effect, the market recognizes that these companies are lower risk than other companies and rewards them accordingly. This finding alone should earn the issue of sustainability a prominent place in the office of the chief financial officer, if not the boardroom, of every company.
- 89 percent of the studies we examined show that companies with high ratings for ESG factors exhibit market-based outperformance, while 85 percent of the studies show these types of companies exhibit accounting-based outperformance. Here again, the market is showing correlation between financial performance of companies and what it perceives as advantageous ESG strategies, at least over the medium (three to five years) to long term (five to ten years).

The Collaborative Capitalism Pyramid

It is interesting to note that with the introduction of the term "impact investing" in 2007, many in the existing community of sustainable and socially responsible investing argued that impact had always been an aspect of their work.

We agree and would add that socially responsible investing has not only been a precursor to impact investing but also operates alongside impact investing as part of the same, larger body of activity we call Collaborative Capitalism. Put another way, Collaborative Capitalism brings together the two core practices that underpin socially responsible investing and impact investing, namely, risk mitigation and investing for outcomes.

The first practice of investing for *risk mitigation* in mainstream financial markets, especially in publicly owned securities, has expanded significantly in recent decades to include consideration of how extrafinancial factors affect an investor's ability to generate profits. Climate change, education, water, pandemics, and a host of other issues traditionally viewed as the purview of government and the nonprofit sector are increasingly understood to be legitimate objects of effective business management and investor interest. ESG factors are commonly included in the valuation of equity, real estate, corporations, and fixed-income investments. And many major global exchanges now require aspects of ESG reporting for listed securities.[16]

In the discussion led by Mercer on tackling climate risk, for example, we see how impact is present—though manifest differently—across asset classes and investment strategies. In addition to the effect of a firm's core operating practices, impact takes the form of corporate engagement and policy initiatives within a public equity strategy. This is not the direct outcomes-oriented impact of investing in, say, a microfinance fund; however, these are aspects of impact critical to asset allocation if an investor aims to generate social value across a total portfolio of capital investments.

The second practice is investing for *outcomes*. For decades, hundreds of individual asset owners, foundations, governmental actors, and others have been exploring how capital can be used to create positive social and environmental benefits. Government institutions have been doing this with grants and contracts; more recently, they also do it through investing.

The US government's Overseas Private Investment Corporation (OPIC), for example, is authorized to operate in 150 developing nations around the world, and it invests in projects across a range of industries, including energy, housing, agriculture, and financial services. OPIC focuses its work on "regions where the need is greatest and in sectors that can have the greatest developmental impact."[17] Individuals and institutions wielding purpose-driven capital of this kind have invested billions of dollars in the form of private, philanthropic, and public capital to drive social and environmental value creation in below-market-rate, near-market-rate, and market-rate return strategies. This explicit focus on outcomes is one of the key defining elements of an impact investment. You can inadvertently have impact (all investments have outcomes, both positive and negative), but when you are explicit about managing to achieve the specific positive outcomes you've articulated, *that's* impact investing—it is the intention to create and manage for optimizing impact that matters.

It should be noted these two approaches are often the primary entry points for investors into the realm of impact investing. Impact investors often start either with an orientation toward the outcomes they are trying to achieve, such as an interest in health or education, or by wanting to look across their portfolio to see whether they can align that portfolio with those interests in ways that mitigate risks. The two notions, of outcomes and risk mitigation, have very different histories, theories of practice, and practical steps in terms of how one realizes them through a set of investments.

But, and this is a critical step forward, the distinction between the results from these two practices—investing for risk mitigation and investing for outcomes—is becoming theoretical at best. They are really two sides of the same coin, as investors consider how to align more of their assets with the things they care about, and as the recipients of capital find themselves speaking to investors coming from both perspectives. The combination of the two practices is ushering in a new form of capitalism that integrates diverse stakeholder interests; recognizes the complex range of strategic, values-driven, and financial motivations that have always influenced why we invest in the first place; and generates blended value. The key elements of Collaborative Capitalism are shown in Figure 1.2.

The Collaborative Capital pyramid in Figure 1.2 is intended to be indicative, and certainly not exhaustive. It includes a range of business and investment approaches consistent with risk mitigation on the one hand, and an outcomes orientation on the other.

Starting at the bottom of the pyramid, we feature business practices with the primary objective of risk mitigation—namely, CSR, shared value, and operational and supply chain sustainability.

CSR has been developing quickly in recent years, pushing corporations into new territory consistent with the ideas of Collaborative Capitalism. For example, John Elkington, a leading advisor to companies integrating sustainability with CSR, has outlined a vision of the future of CSR and sustainability that moves toward new understandings of capitalism.[18] In this same vein, Professor Edward Freeman's vision of the future of capitalism has as its centerpiece a new understanding of corporations' engagement with stakeholders.[19]

Figure 1.2   The Collaborative Capitalism Pyramid

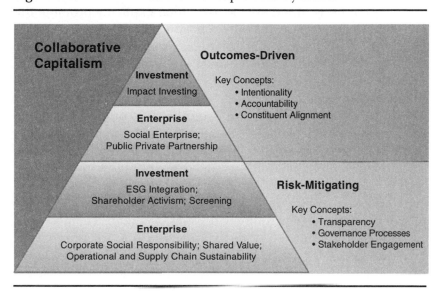

Shared value (introduced by Michael Porter of Harvard in 2006) builds on the concept of blended value introduced in 2000 and explores a similar theme in how companies can view their potential for creating value as being more than simply a function of pursuing shareholder returns. And operational and supply chain sustainability has been elevated as a core priority in recent years, as reflected in the work of Deloitte and others.[20]

The next tier in the Collaborative Capital pyramid consists of the investment strategies associated with risk mitigation, which we discussed previously in this chapter: ESG integration, shareholder activism, and positive and negative screening.

For all the diversity in risk-mitigating corporate and investment strategies, they share a number of key focal points: transparency, governance processes, and stakeholder engagement. In each case, a number of significant initiatives have arisen to advance these ideas.

On the issue of transparency, for example, there have been rapid developments in the effort to have companies report on their ESG practices and performance alongside financial data, led by groups including the Global Reporting Initiative and the Sustainability Accounting Standards Board, which explicitly promote the use of "integrated" sustainability reporting.

On the issue of governance processes, numerous networks have been developed, such as the Council on Institutional Investors, to bring the collective strength of investors to the table in an effort to influence the behavior of the largest public companies. And investors in their own right are being held accountable on their sustainability practices and governance through their participation in the UN Principles for Responsible Investment and its mandated disclosures.

On the question of stakeholder engagement, we see dozens of large advocacy organizations confronting companies with respect to specific social or environmental issues, sometimes combatively, sometimes in partnership with industry. Ceres is a community of investors interested in addressing climate change, for example. And companies are responding by developing platforms for engaging investors and other key constituencies on social and environmental issues. For example, the Sustainable Apparel Coalition is a trade organization comprising manufacturers, retailers, government, and nongovernmental organizations working to reduce the environmental and social impacts of apparel and footwear products around the world, representing about one-third of the global market.

The first layer of outcomes-driven activities in the Collaborative Capitalism pyramid is reserved for business approaches, specifically social enterprise and public-private partnership.

We have discussed social enterprise, which is broad in scope but has been aptly described by many leaders in Collaborative Capitalism, including Nick O'Donohoe, CEO of Big Society Capital in the United Kingdom:

> Do we really just have binary choices—between public or private
> provision of education, health and other social services; between
> charities and aid agencies focused only on dire needs or
> corporations focused only on maximizing profits; between investors
> who can choose only to maximize their returns or make
> philanthropic donations? Is there a middle way? Is there a model
> that embraces the financial disciplines of market capitalism but also

provides opportunity and support for the vulnerable, the dispossessed and the downright unfortunate? There is. Social enterprises balance a social mission with financial viability and sustainability, existing between the public sector and private markets in both the developed and developing world.[21]

Public-private partnerships are collaborative by definition. The term (and structure) spans everything from public service delivery by private enterprise through to sustainable infrastructure development.[22]

For its part, impact investing sits at the apex of the Collaborative Capitalism pyramid—as an investment strategy defined by (and illustrative of) the key concepts of outcomes-driven Collaborative Capitalism, including intentionality, accountability, and constituent alignment, each of which we discuss in some detail forthwith.

Before we leave the Collaborative Capitalism pyramid, it is important to note again that these different categories are by no means mutually exclusive, or exhaustive. On the contrary, many of the ideas and concepts may be seen as "rolling up" to a new understanding of the nature of value itself and the role of organizations (whether nonprofit or for-profit) and capital (whether philanthropic, near-market-rate or market-rate) managed with the intent of generating multiple returns and blended value, the previously referenced "meta" concept introduced at the turn of the century.

Similarly, impact investors are learning how to build on risk mitigation strategies, as we have discussed, and risk mitigators are learning to take external stakeholders' needs into consideration and to account for outcomes. And things change quickly. In the 1990s, the sustainability movement and ESG reporting were viewed by many in the mainstream business community as either irrelevant to fundamental business management or some type of neoliberal babble. They are now seen as a fundamental way to reduce long-term risks.

Three Core Elements of Collaborative Capitalism

Recognizing the distinction between the six key concepts in our pyramid is relatively nuanced, we have integrated and reworked the list into a more manageable number that can be readily translated and applied to business and finance writ large. The result is three core elements of Collaborative Capitalism: transparency, outcomes orientation, and attention to constituency.

Transparency

One of the requirements of Collaborative Capitalism is that people supplying capital and those receiving it know enough about each other to understand mutual strategic motivations. Disinterested and anonymous financial transactions executed globally through spreadsheets and wire transfers do not allow for this level of transparency. However, fund managers are exploring new structures to allow for increased transparency and for alignment of the strategic objectives of both parties. Many funds and transactions in the space, especially those that benefit from concessionary capital as part of the deal, include layered capital stacks in which different parties agree to certain kinds of risk and return in order to create an overall investment or fund. A good example of this is in our study: the Deutsche Bank Global Commercial Microfinance Consortium I contained five different capital "layers" (three debt layers and two equity layers), and each vehicle had a tranche of first loss or guarantee capital provided by a government agency.[23]

In a sense, all investments that have layered stacks of capital involve transparency to some degree. What is new in Collaborative Capitalism is that the trade-offs among different parties' interests involve more variables: they include impact, return, and risk.[24]

There is a tension in the notion of transparency as well; transactions that come with high-touch, customized, or idiosyncratic information are difficult to achieve at scale without friction and at low transaction costs. Many of the most successful impact investing deals require more effort in understanding and integrating the diverse objectives of both parties before transactions can be completed. A new field of intermediaries, including advisory firms such as CapRock Group, Enclude Solutions, and Imprint Capital, has arisen to coordinate the extra layers of critical information in such deals.

Outcomes Orientation

The second precept of Collaborative Capitalism is increased atten-tion to outcomes. Social and environmental outcomes are impor-tant in different ways to various stakeholders, and the increased attention and accountability related to producing measurable, understandable, attributable outcomes are core concepts.

All sorts of strategic goals become possible when there are measurement methods to determine whether and when one is succeeding. For example, a government agency such as OPIC can and does use its capital for multiple catalytic and risk mitigation purposes. Still, there are many challenges in this work. Efforts to standardize metrics across geographies, thematic areas, and indus-tries are making progress, but as yet the results are imperfect.[25] The field has concentrated primarily on outputs (quick measures of direct activities of a business or project, such as how many solar lanterns were sold) in the absence of rigor, energy, and capacity to track true outcomes (such as how much the purchaser's income increased due to the extra working hours that the solar lantern allows). We found in our study a combination of well-articulated "intentionality" (to achieve a particular social outcome) and care-fully operationalized "accountability" to those intentions. We call this "Mission First and Last."

Attention to Constituency

Constituency is an important aspect of nonprofit mission-related activity that is often overlooked. All US nonprofits, in order to remain designated as 501(c)(3) charitable organizations in the eyes of the IRS, must prove that they have a diverse set of donors and thus a diverse set of financial stakeholders. This is to prove that their purpose is public, not private. The translation of nonprofit activity to Collaborative Capitalism requires a similar sensibility, even if the implementation is different. Constituents are parties that have an interest in the organization's outcomes, not just those with a fiduciary relationship. The elements of constituent relation-ships, constituent feedback, constituent buy-in, and constituent accountability are all increasingly essential to the new model of Collaborative Capitalism.

In short, impact investing is about the convergence of interests and ideas that were previously viewed as distinct. This evolution in the understanding of our relative interests presents a historic opportunity—but also a multitude of challenges. Constituents are highly diverse and may include investors, governments, employees, community members, nonprofits, customers, suppliers, and others. Many of these groups may not communicate their desires effectively or efficiently. Thus key questions become challenging, such as: In an impact investment with multiple stakeholders, are the interests of investors more important than the interests of other stakeholders, such as beneficiaries or customers? If not, how can these interests be effectively balanced?

No norms exist to guide the answers yet, and mistakes are often clearer to discern than successes. The need to consider constituent accountability and alignment explains why a university can't toss out its president without consulting its key stakeholders, such as when the University of Virginia ousted President Teresa Sullivan in 2012, only to reinstate her several weeks later when key constituents protested their lack of involvement in the decision. It's why Mohammed Yunus, founder of Grameen Bank, argues that microfinance without ownership by its borrowers is prone to exploitation. (And, in at least one instance, he was proven right in India in the province of Andhra Pradesh in 2010; in other cases, his predictions have not come to pass.) And it's why B Lab, the nonprofit organization that certifies B Corporations, decided to pursue the legal strategy of creating a new corporate form that incorporates the needs of stakeholders into corporate charters. Once you posit the notion that an impact business is responsive to the needs of stakeholders, you set the expectation that these needs will be considered. A fundamental question for those engaged in Collaborative Capitalism is how to create the relationships and feedback loops that make the constituency engagement process feasible, actionable, and, of increasing importance, binding.

We also know there are potential downsides to Collaborative Capitalism. If, for example, there are not identifiable stakeholders who wish to purchase outcomes for a particular population or issue, it may be more difficult to attract *both* private capital and the public resources that may have been more readily available in the past.

Transparency is costly and can never be total in any market that depends on information asymmetry. Constituent feedback is often messy and expensive; sometimes you won't like what you hear. And decision making can be painfully slow, as we know from the political realm. Interpretation of constituent wishes may also be subjective, and political forces can seize power if relationships are not formalized. There is not yet a clear sense of the limitations and choices being made by and for stakeholders; however, we are certain that these limitations will make themselves more clear in the future and that we are now in a period of exploration, figuring out the potentials and limits of Collaborative Capitalism.

Examples of Collaborative Capitalism at the Enterprise Level

Transparency

Seventh Generation is a leading brand of green household and personal care products. The company remains an independent, privately held company distributing products to natural food stores, supermarkets, mass merchants, and online retailers across the United States and Canada.

Company highlights: More than 25 percent of managers are evaluated on the accomplishment of social and environmental targets. Seventh Generation publishes a transparent annual external report detailing mission-related activities, targets, and consistent measurements to allow for year-over-year comparisons.

Outcomes Orientation

IceStone is the world's "safest, most sustainable durable surface." Made from three core ingredients—100 percent recycled glass, Portland cement, and pigment—IceStone surfaces are used for everything from kitchen countertops to conference room tables to art installations. Since 2003, IceStone LLC has diverted over ten million pounds of glass from landfills.

Company highlights: 100 percent of products are certified "Gold level Cradle to Cradle"; IceStone uses 100 percent recycled glass in production; 100 percent of facilities are powered by renewable energy credits; 100 percent of water used in production is reused in the manufacturing process.

Attention to Constituency

Indigenous Designs is a leader in organic and fair trade clothing. Its clothing supports thousands of artisans in the most remote and impoverished regions of the world, and uses the finest organic materials and traditional skills passed down over thousands of years.

Company highlights: Supplier price controls are entirely democratically governed; more than 40 percent of suppliers are majority owned by women or minorities; Indigenous Designs builds direct and long-term relationships with artisans; and more than 5 percent of the company is owned by nonprofit organizations.

Note: These examples of award-winning certified B Corporations were accessed from B Corp. (2014). *Impact Reports.* http://www.bcorporation.net/.

Putting It All Together: Collaborative Capitalism in Action

Collaborative Capitalism is a relatively new idea—at least to the extent that it has been *intentionally* implemented—which makes any insight into the strategic approach that organizations are taking to address impact investing and Collaborative Capitalism invaluable. The following six real-world examples offer insight into the activities and approaches that Collaborative Capitalism encompasses, both within and beyond the twelve funds we studied.

1. Integrating an outcomes orientation into The California Endowment
2. Constituent alignment at Citi
3. Creating an investing platform for outcome-driven investors at Morgan Stanley
4. Aligning "outcome buyers" through social impact bonds
5. Transparency through RSF Prime
6. Stakeholders as investors at Calvert Foundation

Integrating an Outcomes Orientation into The California Endowment

Just as some philanthropic foundations have played a leading role in elevating and supporting business as a force for good, they also have the flexibility and strong incentive to turn principles into action. Endowed private foundations generally invest 95 percent of their capital purely for financial returns, enabling grantmakers to give away the remaining 5 percent for social impact. In effect, 100 percent of the charitable mission of a foundation is driven by just 5 percent of its capital (its grant making), while 95 percent of its assets are managed with no regard whatsoever for the purpose that the institution was created to pursue.[26] Although a small percentage of foundations use program-related investments (PRIs) to drive investment capital to "charitable" investments in social outcomes, these usually constitute a very small portion of the limited grant segment of their budgets.

With this situation in mind, on the urging of several thoughtful provocateurs (one of us [Jed] among them), over a decade ago foundations began considering whether it really made sense to invest most of their assets in a manner that was at best neutral and at worst undermining of their institutional mission.[27] A handful of pioneering foundations began to slowly change investment practice, even while acknowledging that strong financial performance was essential to sustain grant making. Among those leading the charge was Luther Ragin, now CEO of the Global Impact Investing Network and former vice president at the F. B. Heron Foundation, who asked: "Should a private foundation be more than a private investment company that uses some of its excess cash flow for charitable purposes?"[28]

The most explicit manner in which foundations responded was to create dedicated "mission-related investment" strategies, usually setting aside a small portion of their endowments for proactively advancing philanthropic goals through carefully selected investments earning competitive rates of financial return.

One of these is The California Endowment (TCE), a $3.5 billion foundation committed to supporting access to quality health care for underserved individuals in California. Since 2008, TCE has committed $101 million to investments in affordable housing, health clinics, community lending, and, most notably, the California FreshWorks

Fund, a $272 million initiative created by TCE (and launched in 2011 by Michelle Obama at the White House) for supporting healthy food retailing in low-income communities.

Like its peers, TCE had questioned how to broaden the set of tools available for achieving its mission. The foundation under-stood the necessity of adopting a systemic approach encompassing public policy, deep bottom-up perspectives from the communities in which TCE works, and a frontal assault on many of the upstream causes of health outcomes, including through the investment portfolio. The financial crisis of 2008 was also a clarifying moment. As Wall Street's supposedly clear understanding of risk and com-plex financial instruments unraveled, space was created in the boardroom to "hear and actually consider an alternative to the status quo," says Tina Castro, who was until late 2013 TCE's director of impact investing.

What's most interesting at TCE, however, is the way in which the conversation has moved beyond the financial crisis and evolved to complement the impact investing program—essentially socializ-ing internally what had been a niche initiative. TCE is discussing divesting from companies that undermine its mission, such as weapons manufacturers and heavy polluters, and Castro envisions a future in which the foundation is a more active shareholder, pushing companies to change their behavior, adding additional screens to the portfolio, deploying more dollars in structured funds like FreshWorks, and spending more time being a catalyst and advocate for impact investing—strategies that are consistent with the notion of sustainable investing discussed earlier. As recently as a few years ago, this might have sent the board of trustees and investment staff running for the hills, but the debate is now less hyperbolic. Explains Castro, "The Great Recession enabled a conversation, but there was also this increased fear and skepticism, and a sort of recoiling, retrenching and protecting of assets. Now it feels to me like a more rational conversation. We have a new set of board members with a different skillset. They are more multi-lingual. You have folks who are very investment savvy and sophisti-cated, but also who understand issues of public health, social justice, and these other things that are so core to our mission."

It helps that TCE has been doing impact investing for five years. Rather than wondering how to do something, TCE is looking at what has already been achieved and figuring out how to do it better. Although it is neither advisable nor possible for TCE to invest $3.4 billion in highly distressed communities in California, Castro believes there is a balance between investing in a manner consistent with fiduciary responsibility, with an eye to managing risk and targeting appropriate return, and dedicating resources to supporting California communities. This is not necessarily by investing in the communities directly, but in ways that support the work TCE is trying to do in those communities—an impact investing "wraparound" to their philanthropic investment strategy, as it were.

Constituent Alignment at Citi

The experience of foundation investors speaks to the idea of aligning investments with an explicitly social mission. And although the sector as a whole has been criticized for only recently taking baby steps to align their total capital with their institutional missions, it is clear why foundations would (or at least should) lead the charge in investing for impact.

For commercial financial institutions—including banks, insurers, and wealth and asset managers—it is a different question. Mission alignment is not the goal; rather, the goal is also responding to the changing political and regulatory environment in which they operate as key stakeholders.

In the United States, regulation has been the single most important driver of impact investing by the largest financial institutions. For example, the Federal Reserve System's supervisory mandate includes promoting development in low-income communities as an element of fair and impartial access to credit. And the most notable effort of this kind—the Community Reinvestment Act (CRA), which requires that depository banks make loans and investments in underserved places where they have branches—has created a $60 billion market for community finance, capitalizing some of the largest and most sophisticated impact investing intermediaries in the world.

In other words, all banks (certainly those in the United States) have at least some capacity for integrating elements of financial and social return through investment. But, as was the case for The

California Endowment, with its evolving embrace of investment strategies extending beyond the niche of mission-related investment, the developments that provide most insight are those that push beyond this more limited, mandated effort.

Citi is an interesting case in point. In recent years, the bank has reinvigorated its community development efforts in the United States, not just by building locally on the CRA's distinctively American and "nontransferable" platform, says Bob Annibale, global director of Citi community development and microfinance, but also by importing and adapting lessons from ten years of experience working in microfinance.

In fact, impact investing owes much to microfinance, which provides the best illustration of an investment market that has evolved from small and primarily philanthropic origins to being large and relatively commercial. In the years prior to Citi's foray, the microfinance sector grew about 12 percent annually, serving ninety-four million customers.[29] New intermediaries were launched, improving the availability and flow of information between microfinance institutions (MFIs) and other industry stakeholders. And as commercial funding became more abundant and grant funding scarcer, a greater number of MFIs became for-profits in order to access more capital. Roughly 50 percent of MFIs were nonprofits in 1997; by 2004, this was reduced to 24 percent.

Citi had been making grants in microfinance since 1982, consistent with its global footprint. And Annibale sees an important, ongoing role for a dynamic philanthropy in the sector, including through the Citi Foundation and Citi Microfinance, investing in research, innovation, new models for deepening financial education in the sector, and important microfinance networks like CGAP, SEEP, Women's World Banking, and Pro Mujer.

However, like many financial institutions, Citi thought it could add tremendous value by being much more a "part of the process" and treating MFIs like clients rather than beneficiaries, explains Annibale. "You could see in the work and what was happening in the market that there really were some impressive models coming out, some of which themselves had the potential to scale."

For Citi, that meant it was time *not* to create a separate fund or a separate "goodie bag" of proprietary assets to invest, but rather to fully integrate the idea of financial inclusion into existing business lines—extending a client service proposition to more far-flung locations. When he started the group in 2004, Annibale says that all of his colleagues came out of Citi's businesses and could bring relevant skills to the table. "We had worked with clients on solutions, on products, on risk management, on technology. We wanted to bring things of value to [microfinance] institutions, so much so that they think of us as a partner and banker."

Interestingly, even as Citi's total lending bottomed out in 2009 during the financial crisis, the microfinance business was growing—not by maximizing profit, which was never the objective, Annibale says, but by delivering sustainable rates of return through a portfolio that was stable and growing. Citi's work is well illustrated by an award-winning payment solution the bank created in the Dominican Republic, which allowed typically unbanked small grocery stores and other businesses to replace cash payments to their providers with mobile transactions. The service has now expanded to India, China, and South Korea.

Citi now works with 150 clients in the microfinance sector in nearly fifty countries, on financing, capital markets issues, foreign exchange hedging, fund administration, and transaction services. This includes a partnership with the US government's OPIC, which has provided $360 million directly to forty MFIs in the local currency, local language, and under the local law of twenty-two countries, reaching 975,000 borrowers, of which approximately 91 percent are women.

Annibale was handed responsibility for Citi's community development division in 2010, essentially representing the bank's CRA-driven work in the United States. Asked to approach that sector in the same way he had tackled international microfinance, Annibale transformed the community relations team into bankers, with "partners, clients, and goals," and soon made a mark when Citibank agreed in late 2010 to set up free bank accounts for all public school students and parents in San Francisco as part of a taxpayer-funded college savings plan.

The strategy at Citi goes so far as to include considerations of financial inclusion in any decision to close a bank branch. Annibale's role in the process is to ensure that the business is not thrown "out of balance" by eliminating a physical location that might be essential for reasons beyond just profit. "Some of that can go back to regulation and other stakeholder interests," he says. "But it's more than that. It's about how and where decisions are made, and their implications. If you're too far from the implications, you just can't be that effective. Others have to be the arbiters of whether we are impactful or not."

From the perspective of Collaborative Capitalism, Citi is in fact experimenting with new forms of constituent alignment and stakeholder-oriented governance.

Creating an Investing Platform for Outcome-Driven Investors at Morgan Stanley

Another institution pushing the boundaries is Morgan Stanley, the world's largest wealth manager, with over sixteen thousand financial advisors. But whereas Annibale's work at Citi focuses very intentionally on corporate and institutional partners, Morgan Stanley is laying foundations for impact investing primarily as a response to strong demand from a broad range of institutional, retail, and high-net-worth clients, including the new fiduciaries discussed earlier.

Morgan Stanley created an Investing with Impact platform in 2012 and, late in 2013, a new Institute for Sustainable Investment focused on product development, thought leadership, and capacity building. Announcing the Institute, together with a goal of managing $10 billion in client capital on the Investing with Impact platform, Morgan Stanley's chairman and CEO, James Gorman, said: "Our clients are increasingly turning their attention to what it takes to secure the lasting and safe supplies of food, energy, water, and shelter necessary for sustainable prosperity."[30]

Morgan Stanley sees the enthusiasm from younger investors that we discussed earlier, and the company believes that its efforts are enabling financial advisors to have more conversations with multigenerational clients. "The younger generation is clearly signaling that when they take over the reins to family offices and their own inheritances, they will not invest the same way," says Audrey Choi, CEO of the Institute and head of Morgan Stanley's Global Sustainable Finance group.

Choi's observation is also true in the institutional space, where young people are stoking interest in impact investing. It was Harvard students who unsuccessfully demanded that the university sell its stake in fossil fuel companies, through a divestment campaign that has been likened to earlier efforts to limit investment in South Africa during apartheid and in Sudan as fighting continued in Darfur.

In parallel with new client needs, however, Morgan Stanley has also been testing its own understanding of the changing social and economic landscape and seeing the business case for sustainability more clearly than ever. According to Choi, the challenge of resource scarcity demands not only that governments play a role through policy and public investment and that philanthropy provide catalytic financial support, but also that the power of capital markets is fully harnessed. "As a financial institution, we believe that private capital can and must play a role in driving innovation and investment to meet those challenges in the future," says Choi. "More than that, however, those challenges will represent a very powerful business opportunity."

Morgan Stanley is also focused on the full integration of this new perspective, as with Citi, culminating with the launch of the Institute, which provides a firmwide mandate for collaborating with core business units. Says Choi, "At the Institute, we really want to do something that is consistent with the quality and scale of opportunities that lie in the sweet spot for Morgan Stanley. Whether it's with our wealth management or investment management colleagues, we are increasingly turning our core skills to developing and distributing products with a focus on impact."

Morgan Stanley's Institute for Sustainable Investing aims to provide greater clarity and easier access to products that offer a risk-adjusted market rate of financial return, such that the core investment portfolios of clients can be mobilized. To this end, Morgan Stanley has structured the Investing with Impact platform to predominantly focus on a broad range of sustainable investing opportunities, from public markets to private equity. The implications for attracting talent are also clear to Morgan Stanley. Choi says that the best and brightest recruits, as well as the future leaders at the firm, care deeply about impact. "There is an increased desire and commitment to integrate what people do in their professional life with the values that they care most about," she affirms.

Aligning "Outcome Buyers" Through Social Impact Bonds

Using capital as a tool for social good means finding new ways to harness the power of transparency, outcomes orientation, and constituency to recalibrate the impact that finance has on society. If capital from impact investing is the fuel, building a strong, resilient society with it may depend on getting this right. According to the late J. Gregory Dees of Duke University, the value of social innovation and entrepreneurship is ambiguous at best, unless we as a society set out to use the power of continuous innovation properly. He called for using social enterprises as learning labs to help society more quickly identify solutions that work, reject those that don't, and create more resilient and effective social systems.[31]

This is the mind-set—which is appealing to even the casual observer—that is driving significant interest (and media attention) in new financial innovations like social impact bonds (SIBs), also called pay-for-success contracts. SIBs provide a new tool to help governments finance social outcomes through private investment in efforts to address homelessness, adult recidivism, juvenile delinquency, preschool readiness, environmental sustainability, and other issues.[32]

The mainstreaming of that idea received a significant boost when Goldman Sachs emerged as the sole investor in the first SIB in the United States as part of its strategic commitment, through its Urban Investment Group (UIG), to "invest the firm's capital through strategic partnerships with developers, nonprofits, and other local stakeholders to bring economic and social benefits to underserved urban areas."[33] In August 2012, UIG announced that its $9.6 million loan would support the delivery of therapeutic services to sixteen- to eighteen-year-olds incarcerated on Rikers Island, New York City's largest correctional facility, with the support of a guarantee provided by Bloomberg Philanthropies.

SIBs are on the march, particularly in the United Kingdom, where there are more than fourteen SIBs completed or in development, but also in at least nine other countries around the globe.[34] We think this is happening in part because SIBs embody Collaborative Capitalism, spreading risk for cash-strapped governments and allowing investors, especially those who care about social outcomes, to step into a new and formalized stakeholder relationship so as to achieve those outcomes.

Transparency Through RSF Prime

RSF Social Finance (RSF), a fund in our study, is an innovative public benefit financial service organization dedicated to transforming the way the world works with money. RSF offers investing, lending, and giving services to individuals and enterprises committed to improving society and the environment. Since 1984, RSF has made over $285 million in loans and over $100 million in grants.

RSF is both philosophically and functionally unique in the investment marketplace. Philosophically, RSF acts not just as a financial service organization but as a thought leader and field builder, inspired by the work of the famed economist and scientist Rudolf Steiner. Today RSF is dedicated to exploring how money can connect people and their values and strengthen the bonds of community. Functionally, RSF is also quite innovative. Through its mix of eight legal entities comprising both investment and grant vehicles, RSF offers its fifteen hundred investors, lenders, and donors the possibility to leverage investments, loans, and grants in order to create significant positive impact by working to align their money with their values.

The RSF Social Enterprise Lending Program is RSF's core investment product. The program, with $70 million in assets under management in January 2014, employs a disciplined risk management process, resulting in an extremely low default rate and leverage ratio. The team also employs a unique high-touch, transparent approach that allows borrowers and investors to interact with one another throughout the investment process.

In its lending activity, RSF funds its operating costs on the spread between the interest rate the borrower pays and the interest rate the investor receives. It calls the borrower rate "RSF Prime." Unlike other funds, it holds quarterly community pricing meetings for its borrowers and investors to discuss and have input into what

RSF Prime interest rates, investor interest rates, and RSF's operational cost rate should be.

The quarterly meetings began in 2009 after RSF decided to decouple its interest rates from LIBOR (the London Interbank Offered Rate, the interest rate charged by banks lending capital to each other), which is used as the basis for most short-term bank loan interest rates around the world. This was an important but challenging decision, and what made it possible was a study, conducted by RSF staff, of Rudolf Steiner's economics lectures, in which he speaks about setting price by bringing together all parties involved—producer, consumer, and distributor. According to John Bloom, RSF's senior director of organizational culture, "This struck a deep chord for [RSF staff,] as it is an essential part of our mission to build community through finance." At the pricing meetings, RSF asks each participant to discuss his or her interests, so as to bring all sides into alignment—investors talk about their motivations, borrowers talk about their use of the loan proceeds, and RSF staff discuss the resources needed for them to work in their unique way as an intermediary. Further, RSF asks participants to respond to how a change in interest rate would affect them. During this round of conversation, the group participants gain insight into one another's financial needs, priorities, and plans.

For example, at the December 2013 meeting, two borrowers indicated they had set their budgets for 2014 and that any upward change in interest rate would require reducing important program expenditures and potentially compromising business activities. As the intermediary, RSF brought to the table the fact that it had not changed the 4.0 percent margin it earns since 1991. It was clear from the meeting that because of the weak economy and historically low bank rates, everyone was operating on thin margins. Despite the initial tension, as a result of the discussions, there was a general desire to maintain the status quo for the first quarter of 2014. As John Bloom described in a recent blog post:

> A week following the pricing meeting, the RSF Pricing Committee met to set the interest rate for the quarter. After reflecting on what was shared at the pricing meeting, it was clear that a raise in rate for the borrowers would cause some financial hardship, and might potentially discourage other new borrowers from applying for loans,

as banks have a significantly lower cost of capital and more flexibility to negotiate rates. While none of the investors was enthusiastic about a lower interest rate, it seemed they were overall affected less by a change. Even a slightly reduced rate is still competitive with rates on bank savings accounts or CDs. The Pricing Committee needed to adjust somewhat for RSF's needs, at least for the near term. The result was a reduction of return to the investors by 25 basis points from the current rate of .50% to .25%, with RSF Prime (the rate for borrowers) remaining the same at 4.5%, [increasing RSF's margin to 4.25%].

This last gathering marked an important change in the nature of the pricing meetings. The associative [economics] picture that Rudolf Steiner gave was fully present as all parties outlined their needs and engaged in heart-felt learning. Though the resulting recommendation for status quo was not followed, the Pricing Committee believes the outcome respected the needs that were voiced at the meeting. RSF's purpose to transform the way the world works with money is exemplified in pricing meetings. We cannot imagine a more direct, transparent, and personal way to work with interest rates. Though the system may not be perfect for everyone, the participants in the meetings can assure you it is very real.[35]

Stakeholders as Investors at Calvert Foundation

Another financial innovation highlighting the core principles underpinning impact investing is the effort to integrate community lending more fully with local stakeholder communities. For example, Calvert Foundation, a longtime community development financial institution (CDFI) in the United States, launched in June 2014 an "Iconic Places Initiative" with support from the Kresge Foundation. The goal of the initiative is to connect local residents with investment opportunities that support redevelopment in their own backyards. Residents are able to invest with as little as $1,000 through a paper application or brokerage account, and in June 2014, Calvert Foundation also launched vested.org, an online platform to offer the investment in the underlying product, called a Community Investment Note, at a minimum of only $20.

The initiative set Calvert Foundation down the path of an entirely different theory of change, focused on the role of local investors in contributing to their own communities becoming more economically vibrant and sustainable—or what Calvert calls *place-making*. According to Jennifer Pryce, CEO of Calvert Foundation, the Iconic Places Initiative focuses not just on how money is deployed but also on how it can be raised. "We have an opportunity to engage local stakeholders in this work. We began to talk to nodes of connection within a city like Detroit—community foundations, other funds, initiatives—and all were passionate about finding a way for the local community to participate in the revitalization of the city. Our Community Investment Note fits that need without being philanthropy, but rather investment, so it can live on in the community," Pryce explains.

Calvert Foundation is not going into cities like Detroit with an economic development agenda. It is going in with the ability to raise capital and connect people to a conversation and movement about "the value of owning your community and owning the opportunity to invest in your community." "It's about civic pride and grassroots engagement," says Pryce.

Calvert Foundation is also doing similar work internationally and recently signed a partnership with the US Department of State and USAID to be a managing partner of the agencies' "IdEA" platform, which aims to create connections and opportunities for US investors to invest in their countries of origin or heritage, as part of the diaspora work initiated in 2011 by then secretary of state Hillary Clinton. Calvert Foundation is turning into a product development shop that specializes in Collaborative Capitalism—helping turn stakeholders into investors so they may invest in outcomes they care about.

Looking Ahead

Although many in the field of practice are talking about the growth of impact investing in the context of how to mainstream it—debating precisely where on the iceberg the waterline can be found—the transformation at hand is far more significant. We are witnessing both an opening up of investing itself—wherein financial markets are progressively internalizing new perspectives on value creation and asset management—and an expanded understanding of stakeholder relationships and the other factors that provide investors with what they really want:

fuller, more complete levels of accountability in that value creation process.

Put simply, impact investing and Collaborative Capitalism are a response to a changing world and shifting beneficiary preferences, in an era of unprecedented global growth, connectedness, and openness. In truth, investors have never cared only about financial performance. That was the means, but the end we all have in mind is the deep generation of true stakeholder and community value—blended value—through a capital system that truly "enriches" us all to live humanely and with dignity. And although we may differ on what we want or believe the path to that state to be, impact investing, by helping us clarify the essential elements of Collaborative Capitalism, may hold the key to its realization.

In chapter 2, we put the spotlight on impact investing; in chapters 3 through 6, we look at the specific practices of leadership and strategy that have underpinned the success of our twelve funds.

2

Raising the Curtain on Impact Investing

A movement is afoot. It reaches across sectors and across geographies, linking small business loans in Detroit with community development financing in Delhi. It has animated a generation of entrepreneurs and captured the imagination of world leaders. It links the social consciousness of philanthropy with the market principles of business. It's about how the power of markets can help to scale solutions to some of our most urgent problems. The movement is called impact investing.
—US National Advisory Board on Impact Investing
(http://www.nabimpactinvesting.org/
executive-summary/)

IN 2007, ON THE BANKS OF LAKE COMO in Bellagio, Italy, the term *impact investing* was coined at a Rockefeller Foundation meeting and defined as investing intentionally for measureable, positive social and/or environment outcomes.

After a second Bellagio gathering, in 2008, the Rockefeller Foundation's board of trustees approved $38 million in grants for field building through a dedicated Impact Investing Initiative, and the market as we know it began to take shape in earnest.[1]

To be sure, many of the pieces undergirding impact investing were already in place. As the Monitor Institute explained in a seminal 2009 report:[2]

- Prominent family offices were already actively seeking to source, vet, and execute investments to address a range of challenges, from the perils of climate change to the suffering of people living in US inner cities, African slums, or rural Indian villages.
- Clients of leading private banks were already calling on their investment managers to provide more choices than just traditional investment and pure philanthropy.
- Private foundations had been partnering with investment banks and development finance institutions to make investments in areas related to their social mission.
- Private equity funds were providing growth capital profitably to businesses that generate social and environmental returns.
- Pension funds were identifying how to deploy capital in ways that benefit the communities they serve.
- Corporations were already finding ways to materially improve the lives of the poor while creating products and services that generate a profit.
- Governments had invested in funds that support economic development in poor areas.

Rockefeller's leadership was about moving the field from a place of "uncoordinated innovation" to one of "marketplace building," according to the Monitor Institute. Among the entities funded to the tune of $1 million by the Rockefeller Foundation were the following grantees, illustrating the focus at the time of developing essential field-level "infrastructure":

- **The Global Impact Investing Network (GIIN).** GIIN is a community of investors and other service providers, an advocate for impact investing, and home of the Impact Reporting and Investment Standards (IRIS), a library of social and environmental outcomes metrics that help investors track their performance and are intended to spur greater comparability.
- **Global Impact Investing Rating System (GIIRS).** GIIRS has created a Morningstar-like social and environmental rating system for impact investors designed to standardize the tracking and reporting of impact and facilitate greater flows of capital.
- **B Lab.** B Lab certifies and supports B Corporations, the for-profit companies that deliver measurable social impacts, described in chapter 1.

- **Pacific Community Ventures (PCV).** PCV, a community development financial institution based in San Francisco, created the Impact Investing Policy Collaborative (IIPC) in partnership with the Initiative for Responsible Investment at Harvard University—an effort led by one of us [Ben]. The IIPC is an international network of researchers and government officials committed to growing impact investing, and provides guidance to this growing community through research and in-person meetings.

Even as impact investing emerged, however, the boundaries of the practice were not always clear. The idea of impact investing was unquestionably compelling—an action-oriented approach to maximizing the value of capital by investing for good. However, some of those who had been doing related work for decades were not always welcoming, particularly within socially responsible investing and US community finance circles, for different reasons.

In a March 2011 critique, Amy Domini, the founder and CEO of Domini Social Investments, wondered why "high impact" investing ("not to be confused with socially responsible investing") was being positioned as the only way to create impact through investment when she and her peers had been doing exactly that for decades. "What makes a manager a specialist in socially responsible investing? It's three things. One, they select investments by applying standards that include impacts on people and the planet. Two, they are activist owners and engage in issues either directly through filing shareholder resolutions or less directly through policy work. Three, they add investments into highly impactful entities such as community development loan funds for farmers, micro-credit funds and start-ups in positive change fields. . . . Mutual funds like Domini, Pax, and Calvert, for example, all do these three things."[3]

Leaders in community development worried that if impact investing stumbled or failed, it would undermine the credibility and brand of community development financial institutions (CDFIs, which we discuss in more detail later in this chapter), which are themselves significant impact investors, particularly in the United States. Mark Pinsky, president and CEO of Opportunity Finance Network (OFN), the trade group representing CDFIs in the United States, also worried in 2011 that impact investing was too broadly defined: "It is unbounded, requiring only self-determined good intent to qualify. By that standard, Angelo Mozilo, the failed former Countrywide mortgage mogul, and any number of predatory lenders, qualify as impact investors—many believed they were giving underserved people access to the American dream."[4]

Although no one would consider Countrywide an impact investor, the truth is the precise definition and ramifications of impact investing continue to be contested. Some, such as J.P. Morgan, have argued impact investing ought to be considered its own category of investment, or "asset class," because of its unique field-level needs and the way investment institutions have organized around it.[5] Others, such as the World Economic Forum and ImpactAssets through its Unified Investment framework, say impact investing is a "lens through which investment decisions are made," rather than a stand-alone asset class.[6] There has also been disagreement on what exactly constitutes "impact."[7] Finally, there are also contrasting understandings of impact investing in different countries. In the United Kingdom, for example, impact investing has been typically defined more narrowly, as investment in social enterprises developing innovative and sustainable ways to tackle entrenched social problems.[8]

Notwithstanding these nuances and disagreements, however, we now have the benefit of extensive practice on which to draw. On that basis, a consensus on impact investing is emerging among practitioners:

- The two key elements of impact investing are *intentionality* and *accountability* (through reported, measurable outcomes).
- Measurable outcomes can be delivered using an *impact lens* in every asset class.
- Different investors have different responsibilities and roles to play within an *ecosystem* of impact investing. For example, even when the focus of a fiduciary, such as a pension fund, is on sustainability in public markets, the higher standards of accountability that this drives have flow-on effects for downstream investors with more flexibility to pursue impact intentionally, such as high-net-worth individuals.

- The question of performance in impact investing is broadly about delivering *financial returns that are commensurate with an investment's asset class and stated strategy,* with *embedded positive social impacts* (including for strategies explicitly seeking "concessionary" financial returns, such as program-related investments by foundations).

Many of these ideas respond to earlier critiques. OFN's Pinsky had excluded the notion of accountability from his 2011 commentary. And the "impact lens" and "ecosystem" ideas are consistent with both the World Economic Forum and ImpactAsset's understanding of impact investing as a strategy rather than an asset class, and the perspective of Amy Domini.

Sizing the Market

Given the breadth of activity this more inclusive understanding of impact investing encompasses, it has been difficult to size the market. In the narrowest sense, 125 respondents to a J.P. Morgan/GIIN survey in 2014 self-reported that they had made $10.6 billion of impact investments in 2013 and intended to make $12.7 billion in 2014.[9]

Granted, this represents *new* investments in those two years. However, given J.P.Morgan's particularly large megaphone, the data has left the strong impression that impact investing is a smaller market than we know it to be.

Attempts at market sizing inevitably raise the question of definition—that is, what is in and what is out. We know as a part of Collaborative Capitalism, impact investing builds on and is inclusive in some measure of the very sizable market for integrated environmental, social, and governance (ESG) factors in investment, as detailed in chapter 1. In 2012, US SIF (the Forum for Sustainable and Responsible Investment) reported $3.31 trillion in US-domiciled assets held by 443 institutional investors, 272 money managers, and 1,043 community investment institutions applied various ESG criteria in their investment analysis and portfolio selection.[10]

Even with the high hurdles the concepts of intentionality and accountability put in place, the following five indicative sectors of the global impact investing market provide evidence of a much larger and entrenched set of activities.

Global Microfinance

Microfinance—the provision of small loans and other financial services to entrepreneurs and groups of entrepreneurs in places where access to banking is limited—has grown into a very significant market and is an essential mechanism for access to capital in many countries. Microfinance Information Exchange tracks data from over two thousand microfinance institutions (MFIs), the groups working with entrepreneurs on the ground, and in 2012 reported a cumulative gross loan portfolio of over $102 billion (from 1,337 reporting MFIs at the time).[11]

In 2012 alone, funders committed at least $29 billion to support the goal of financial inclusion, of which microfinance is the largest part, an increase of 12 percent compared to 2011, according to the Consultative Group to Assist the Poor, a global network of members including more than thirty development agencies, private foundations, and national governments.[12]

US Community Finance

Community finance is generally understood in the United States to encompass the work of CDFIs registered with, and subsidized by, the US Department of the Treasury for the purpose of providing banking, loans, and equity to designated low-income communities. The market is undergirded by the Community Reinvestment Act (CRA), which requires depository banks make loans and investments in underserved places where they have branches, providing a ready source of capital to CDFIs.

In recent years, however, researchers have noted a broadening of activity to encompass a range of place-based activities, including an expanded focus on such sectors as health, healthy and walkable communities, fresh food provision, and rural economic development.[13] According to US SIF, community investing generally encompasses one of three approaches: (1) supporting needed services—for example, food access, education, child care, access to transit, access to jobs, and affordable housing; (2) supporting economic development through quality job creation and by building infrastructure; and (3) creating sustainable communities through mixed-use and mixed-income smart growth and environmentally focused community investment.

Even when limited to special-purpose vehicles like CDFIs, the market is sizable. According to US SIF, a total of 1,043 community investment institutions collectively managed $61.4 billion in 2012.[14]

Economically Targeted Investment by US Public Pension Funds

US public pension funds, the retirement systems for state and federal government employees, are huge, influential institutions. Thirteen of the forty largest institutional investors in the world are US public pension funds.[15]

For more than twenty years, some of these funds have been making the extra effort to direct a small portion of their capital to sound investment opportunities in their local communities (that is, states where they and most of their beneficiaries reside), in an effort to generate economic development in addition to attractive financial returns—a practice known as economically targeted investment (ETI). For example, since 2008, a new law in Florida has allowed 1.5 percent of the Florida Retirement System's $130 billion fund to be invested in Florida-based businesses in technology and other growth sectors. Fully thirty US states have laws or pension fund policies that enable ETIs.[16] We estimate the total value of ETIs at between $10 billion and $20 billion in the United States.

Green Bonds

Green bonds—which link the capital raised by companies and financial institutions to environmental activities—have been attracting considerable attention and are expected to top $50 billion in 2015, according to Jim Kim, president of the World Bank.[17]

Kim should know. In 2008, the World Bank set aside a portion of its AAA-rated bonds to be used to mitigate climate change or help affected people adapt to it, giving them the name "green bonds," and has issued approximately $4 billion of the notes.[18]

Eligible uses include solar and wind installations; funding for new technologies that reduce greenhouse gas emissions; rehabilitation of power plants; initiatives improving the efficiency of transportation; waste management (methane emissions) and construction of energy-efficient buildings; carbon reduction through reforestation; food security improvement and stress-resilient agricultural systems; and sustainable forest management.

More recently, a 2014 *Economist* article noted the following green bond news:[19]

- On March 19, 2014, Unilever issued a £250m ($415 million) bond earmarked for reducing waste, water use, and greenhouse gas emissions.
- In November 2013, a French energy group, EDF, raised €1.4 billion ($1.9 billion), the first euro-denominated green bond from a large company.
- In 2014, Toyota is expected to raise $1.75 billion to help finance sales of car loans for hybrid and electric vehicles.

International Development

International development above and beyond the provision of direct aid, and in addition to microfinance, is a significant part of impact investing, led by private sector–facing national and multilateral development finance institutions (DFIs) such as the International Finance Corporation, the Inter-American Development Bank, Asian Development Bank, the Overseas Private Investment Corporation (United States), BNDES (Brazil), CDC Group (UK), DEG (Germany), and FMO (Netherlands).

These organizations typically provide long-term loans for large infrastructure projects and public-private partnerships, but also, increasingly, development through support for small and medium-sized enterprises (SMEs). The work of Overseas Private Investment Corporation (OPIC), in the United States, is prototypical of a recent surge of interest in impact investing.

In 2011, OPIC issued an impact investing request for proposals and, after having received eighty-eight responses from intermediaries, deployed $285 million to six funds. In 2014 OPIC reviewed its portfolio of investments in the period 2008–2012 through the lens

of impact investing—narrowly defined as "investments with partners whose very business models aim to address social or environmental problems while generating sustainable financial returns"—
and tagged 129 investments valued at $2.4 billion as impact
investments.[20]

Impact investments by all DFIs would easily be in the order of
tens of billions of dollars.

The Scale of Impact Investing in Indicative Markets

- Global microfinance: $102 billion
- US community finance: $61 billion
- US economically targeted investment: $10–$20 billion
- Green bonds: $50 billion
- International development: $20 billion

Taken together, investing intentionally for measureable, positive social and environmental outcomes represents a market in the
hundreds of billions of dollars—miniscule in the context of global
capital markets totaling hundreds of trillions of dollars, but significant nonetheless.

The growth trajectory of the market has also been a big draw for
the large institutions taking a greater interest in impact investing.
According to J.P.Morgan, the profit opportunity for investments in
housing, rural water delivery, maternal health, primary education,
and financial services for the portion of the global population
earning less than $3,000 per year will total from $183 billion to
$667 billion.[21]

Key Actors and Activities

As with any market, impact investing encompasses a tremendous
diversity of actors and activities, many of which we have already
touched on.

Actors include investors, such as high-net-worth individuals,
private foundations, impact investing fund intermediaries, and a
smaller number of large financial institutions, including banks,

Figure 2.1   Actors in the Impact Investing Industry

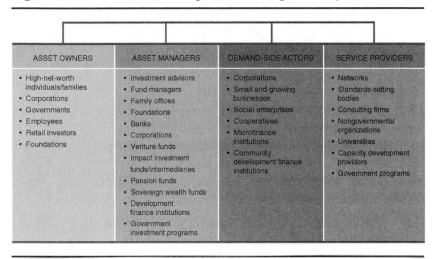

ASSET OWNERS	ASSET MANAGERS	DEMAND-SIDE ACTORS	SERVICE PROVIDERS
• High-net-worth individuals/families • Corporations • Governments • Employees • Retail investors • Foundations	• Investment advisors • Fund managers • Family offices • Foundations • Banks • Corporations • Venture funds • Impact investment funds/intermediaries • Pension funds • Sovereign wealth funds • Development finance institutions • Government investment programs	• Corporations • Small and growing businesses • Social enterprises • Cooperatives • Microfinance institutions • Community development finance institutions	• Networks • Standards-setting bodies • Consulting firms • Nongovernmental organizations • Universities • Capacity development providers • Government programs

Source: Jackson, E. T., and Associates. (2012, July). *Accelerating Impact: Achievements, Challenges and What's Next in Building the Impact Investing Industry.* Rockefeller Foundation. http://www.rockefellerfoundation.org/blog/accelerating-impact-achievements.

pension funds, and DFIs. Investment recipients include small businesses, social enterprises, and the myriad real estate and infrastructure projects that seek financial and social performance concurrently. There are also a wide range of service providers, government actors, networks, and standards-setting bodies. The full scope of participants was presented succinctly in a recent report from E.T. Jackson and Associates (see Figure 2.1).

This book focuses on a selection of high-performing impact investing *funds,* which we describe throughout. Here are some additional examples of *nonfund* actors in impact investing:

Foundations—Tony Elumelu Foundation. The Tony Elumelu Foundation, founded in 2010 by Nigerian businessman Tony O. Elumelu, has a primary objective of enhancing the competitiveness and growth of the African private sector, including through impact investing. In 2013, the foundation, together with the Rockefeller Foundation, created the Impact Economy Innovation Fund (IEIF). The IEIF is managed by GIIN and will support proposals "geared toward projects that seek to enable capital solutions, foster entrepreneurial ecosystems and promote impact investing industry infrastructure—ultimately aimed at impacting the lives of poor or vulnerable people throughout Africa."[22]

Retail investors—Investors' Circle. Investors' Circle is a US "angel network" that for more than twenty years has had a role in nurturing some of the brands and companies that now seem mainstream and nearly unrecognizable as the social ventures they started out as. Zipcar (sustainable car sharing), Honest Tea (iced tea with an ethical supply chain), and many others received capital from investors who recognized an enterprise model blending social impact and financial return. Investor members of the group have invested $166 million in more than 265 early-stage companies and funds.

Governments—Ghana Venture Capital Trust Fund. The Venture Capital Trust Fund (VCTF) was created by the government of Ghana in 2004 with the goal of providing "financial resources for the development and promotion of venture capital financing for small and medium-sized Enterprises (SMEs)." The VCTF has deployed $17 million, financing forty-eight SMEs through five intermediary funds, in addition to providing technical assistance for investors and entrepreneurs. The VCTF also received a $150,000 grant from the Rockefeller Foundation in 2012 to develop the impact investing market in Ghana, which was used to establish the Ghana Institute for Responsible Investment and to map the market.[23]

Corporations—General Electric. In 2013, GE provided a $1 million direct loan to Burn Manufacturing, maker of sustainable burning stoves for communities in Africa, under the auspices of GE's ecomagination program and in partnership with OPIC. GE has also created the ecomagination Accelerator, providing up to $20 million for scaling and commercializing ideas. The accelerator has partnered with five businesses on issues including carbon capture and efficiency in energy extraction and distribution.

Banks—Morgan Stanley. In addition to an active team of investment professionals directing capital to underserved parts of the

United States, consistent with its requirements under the Community Reinvestment Act, Morgan Stanley also created a new Investing with Impact platform for its clients in 2012 and, late last year, a new Institute for Sustainable Investment focused on product development and thought leadership, as highlighted earlier.[24]

Investment advisers—Veris Wealth Partners. Veris Wealth Partners is a US wealth management firm with $700 million in assets. The company believes that "superior investment performance and a positive impact are complementary parts of a holistic investment strategy." Veris applies an impact lens across all asset classes, including in cash and fixed income, where it has an "approved list" of community investment products, primarily from CDFIs. The approved list uses an established, third-party tool for tracking the financial quality of CDFIs, known as CARS (CDFI Assessment and Rating System).[25]

Pension funds—the General Board of Pension and Health Benefits of the United Methodist Church. The Board is a significant investor in CDFIs in the United States through its Positive Social Purpose (PSP) lending program, created in 1990. PSP has more than $725 million invested for the creation and preservation of affordable housing and other community development facilities. According to the Board, the PSP program has funded the construction, rehabilitation, or preservation of more than thirty thousand affordable housing units in all fifty states while receiving market-rate returns.[26] The Board also invests in microfinance.

Social enterprises

Etsy (www.etsy.com) is an online marketplace where people around the world connect to buy and sell unique goods. The for-profit company's mission is to reimagine commerce in ways that build a more fulfilling and lasting world. Brooklyn-based Etsy's global community is made up of nearly five hundred employees and thirty million buyers and sellers that list over twenty million items in more than one million shops in two hundred countries. Etsy is a certified B Corporation and has prominent venture capital investors, including Accel Partners and Union Square

Ventures. The company publishes an *Etsy Values & Impact Annual Report,* which details the company's efforts to improve its impact on employees, community, and the environment. In 2013, Etsy partnered with the nonprofit Kiva, which is now helping Etsy's artisan borrowers around the world access an open market by raising interest-free capital and opening Etsy shops through Kiva Zip.[27]

d.light (www.dlightdesign.com) is a for-profit social enterprise based in San Francisco, whose purpose is to create new freedoms for customers without access to reliable power, so that they can enjoy a "brighter future." d.light designs, manufactures, and distributes solar light and power products throughout the developing world. The company serves more than forty countries, through over ten thousand retail outlets, ten field offices, and four regional hubs. The company employs more than one hundred people directly, and indirectly employs hundreds more worldwide. d.light produces half a million solar lanterns every month, thanks to a significant customer: the French oil and gas company Total, which sells d.light's products as part of the Access to Energy Program throughout Africa on a business-to-consumer basis. d.light provides safe and reliable lighting to more than twenty million people worldwide and aims to increase this number fivefold by 2020.[28]

Riders for Health (www.ridersforhealth.org) is an international nonprofit organization that provides health care to rural African villages using motorcycles and motorcycle ambulances. As of January 2014, Riders has improved health care access for twelve million people across Africa. The nonprofit does this by ensuring that health workers and health facilities have access to reliable vehicles to carry out their work effectively. For example, Riders helped increase the proportion of fully immunized infants in the Gambia (62 percent pre-Riders, 73 percent post-Riders), and decrease malaria deaths in Zimbabwe (21 percent decline in the region served by motorcycles and supported by Riders, compared with a 44 percent increase in a neighboring region). The nonprofit is headquartered in the

United Kingdom and operates in seven African countries—the Gambia, Kenya, Lesotho, Malawi, Nigeria, Zambia, and Zimbabwe—employing three hundred people. Riders operates a nonprofit vehicle-leasing model in partnership with the Skoll Foundation, which provided a loan guarantee enabling the Ministry of Health in the Gambia to reach the entire population of 1.7 million with its public health services, including maternal health, immunization, and distribution of bed nets.

Evergreen Cooperatives (http://evergreencooperatives.com/) is an integrated network of for-profit cooperatives operating green businesses in the city of Cleveland, Ohio. The network includes a variety of ventures, such as a real estate unit, a shared business services unit, a revolving loan fund, and other for-profit ventures, such as a laundry company, a solar/eco-efficiency firm, and a sustainable greenhouse. Evergreen Cooperatives is based on the idea that "truly sustainable community economic development requires the creation of viable businesses broadly owned by community residents who can generate profits that can be recycled to catalyze further business opportunities and local wealth creation."[29] In addition to the ventures, the Evergreen network includes an impact investment fund providing capital to seed ventures owned by local community residents in the network.

Consulting and Investment Advisory firms—Social Finance. Social Finance was established in 2007 with the goal of building a social investment market in the United Kingdom. The firm offers a range of investment advisory and consulting services, from developing and managing social impact bonds and other financial instruments to providing advice to social enterprises seeking investment capital or procurement opportunities (http://www.socialfinance.org.uk/about/vision).

Universities—CASE at Duke University. CASE at Duke was already one of the pioneering programs providing education for the growing field of social entrepreneurship through a robust MBA program connecting business skills to social impact, when, in 2011, it launched the CASE i3 Initiative on Impact Investing.

CASE i3 aims to increase the awareness and effectiveness of social finance to catalyze new capital, talent, and initiatives dedicated to tackling social and environmental problems, and is led by one of us [Cathy].

Capacity development providers—REDF. REDF is a nonprofit organization based in San Francisco and formed in 1997 as a "venture philanthropy" to build the capacity of nonprofit social enterprises. REDF provides grants to a select portfolio of entrepreneurial nonprofits with revenue-generating and job-creating business units; along with that capital, REDF offers extensive business supports and mentorship.

Nongovernmental organizations—Indian Impact Investor Council. With nine founding members, including Aavishkaar and Elevar Equity, both of which are featured in this book, the Indian Impact Investor Council (IIIC) was created in 2013 to provide for self-regulation. The IIIC will develop a set of standards to which all of its members must adhere; the standards will address, among other topics, which sectors qualify for impact investments and how to measure returns.

There have been many commendable efforts to describe the activity on which all of these and other actors are focused, and we make our own contribution in the coming pages. One of the most recent was the bottom-up, market-oriented perspective provided by the Omidyar Network (ON), eBay cocreator Pierre Omidyar's "philanthropic investment firm." ON has invested about half of $630 million in the last ten years in for-profit businesses and half in nonprofit organizations, addressing financial inclusion, consumer Internet and mobile telecoms, education, property rights, and open government, and has a broad and holistic vision of market development.[30]

Focusing on the nonprofit grantees and for-profit investees working on the ground to deliver the social outcomes impact investors are seeking, ON describes three key categories of players, as illustrated in Figure 2.2:

- *Market innovators:* the entrepreneurs and teams that "believe in a product or service well before its profit potential is obvious to

Figure 2.2   Investment Continuum for Market Development

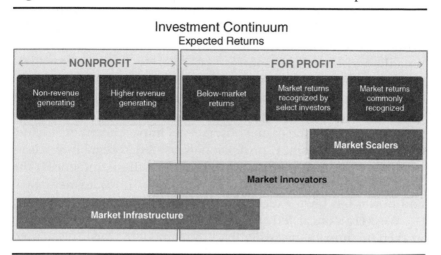

Source: Bannick, M., and Goldman, P. (2012, September). *Priming the Pump: The Case for a Sector Based Approach to Impact Investing.* Omidyar Network, http://www .omidyar.com/sites/default/files/file_archive/insights/Priming%20the% 20Pump_Omidyar%20Network_Sept_2012.pdf.

most established investors." According to ON, market innovators de-risk the generic model of an innovation or product. Some will scale; others will not be capable of doing so alone.

- *Market scalers:* these more mature enterprises enter a sector after market innovators have done their work de-risking the generic model. They refine and enhance the generic model and are capable of scaling individually.
- *Market infrastructure:* These enterprises fulfill common industry or sector needs in collective form, "helping to build a supportive ecosystem for entrepreneurial innovation."

The Fund Perspective

In 2011, as impact investing was gaining steam, the three of us began discussing some key challenges that had not yet been addressed—most notably the limited transparency that was characteristic of a field anchored in private market strategies, and the related lack of evidence on how investments were performing and what, precisely, was and was not working. Asset managers with private investors need not share their performance and lessons broadly, and most have not.

This research represented a kind of "inside baseball" objective—an effort to help practitioners understand what was going on broadly in their own field. However, we also had another audience in mind: the casual observers of impact investing, including finance and business professionals, as well as regular investors wondering what all the fuss was about. For these audiences, the need was simple: to demonstrate what impact investing actually is and how it has been executed.

We were concerned that insight into what had and had not worked in impact investing had remained in relatively closed circles; we called this early stage of development in impact investing the "1.0 era." In the 1.0 era, growth had been anchored in "observation" more than in "evidence." And even though observation had been sufficient to align key stakeholders, drive product development, and foment demand from new capital providers, we believed it was no longer enough.

For all the excitement about impact investing, it had not been growing as fast as many practitioners had projected, in part because the larger wealth advisors and institutional investors on whom growth depends were demanding a level of product and performance specificity that only time and experience can provide. So we set about orchestrating the largest-ever public release of detailed performance data and strategic insight into the way impact investing was being conducted.

We focused on funds, specifically, because they are at the heart of impact investing today, working and interacting directly with hundreds of enterprises, with the ultimate responsibility for delivering the blended performance of financial and social or environmental returns on which the case for impact investing rests.

As discussed in our introduction, when funds succeed, many important results follow that can have a positive impact on the development of the field: investors increase their investment, replicable financial structures emerge for new pools of fund capital, entrepreneurs have clear guideposts of what to expect of investment, and secondary markets more naturally emerge. Funds are also a crucible of accountability and, as with many investment markets, will continue to be the primary vehicle for deploying the largest volumes of capital. In a recent landscaping of the impact investing market, the World Economic Forum placed funds squarely at the center of the impact investing ecosystem (Figure 2.3).

Our idea was to identify a group of ten to fifteen privately owned funds (as opposed to funds that are government owned or run, whether for-profit or nonprofit) that invested directly in operating enterprises or development projects, had a shareable track record of more than five years of active investing, held a core objective of creating measurable social or environmental impact (whether as a primary or ancillary focus), and had tracked and reported on social impact over the years—and then to convince those funds to share their entire story publicly.

We remained agnostic with regard to such other factors as their sector or impact focus, geography, asset class, and performance objectives. It was important to recognize impact investors are a diverse group, located throughout the globe, using a variety of financial tools, from private debt and equity to real assets and guarantees, and with a diversity of impact objectives, from micro-finance and community development to agriculture, health care, and water.

We identified our final case study subjects by starting with a list of 350 funds internationally—including many from the community finance, microfinance, and international development sectors anchoring impact investing—and asking investors in these vehicles which of the funds had "exceptional performance," defined as meeting or exceeding the financial and social returns they had promised. In other words, we asked which funds had proven they were successful impact investors to their key stakeholders, regardless of geography, asset class, and blended return objective. Around thirty funds met our criteria. From these, we then selected twelve to study in detail.

Figure 2.3 The Impact Investment Ecosystem

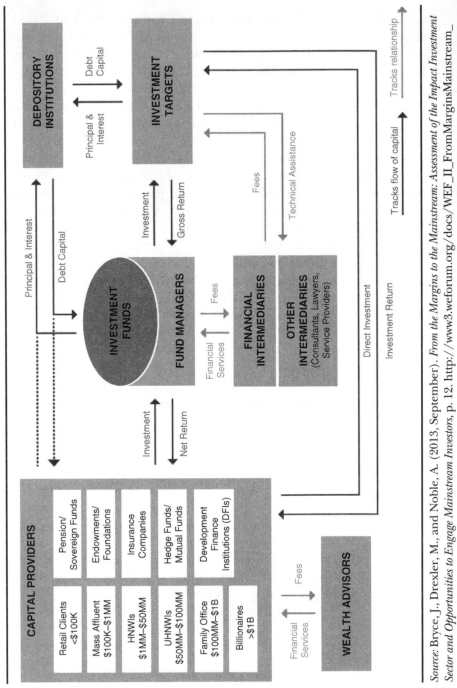

Source: Bryce, J., Drexler, M., and Noble, A. (2013, September). *From the Margins to the Mainstream: Assessment of the Impact Investment Sector and Opportunities to Engage Mainstream Investors*, p. 12. http://www3.weforum.org/docs/WEF_II_FromMarginsMainstream_Report_2013.pdf

The excerpt shown here is part of what we wrote to each of our research subjects:

> Our data-driven case studies will seek to illuminate the following aspects of successful impact investment funds:
>
> a. Fund Organization (governance, staffing, investment strategies)
> b. Fundraising and Limited Partner/General Partner Relationship
> c. Building a Portfolio for Impact (pipeline development, deal screening/due diligence)
> d. Structuring Deals (legal agreements, risk-mitigating strategies, flexibility in terms for social entrepreneurs)
> e. Adding Value—the GP/Investee Relationship (technical assistance, monitoring and adding value)
> f. Managing the Fund (impact metrics, defining success, aligning investor/investee purposes, collaborating with other private and public sector stakeholders)
> g. Financial Metrics
> h. Impact Metrics
>
> *Our Commitment to You*
> We are committed to protecting your proprietary insights and data as we work collaboratively to tell a compelling story of your success, backed up by evidence . . . We commit to signing a Non-Disclosure Agreement with your organization if requested . . .
>
> *Your Commitment to Us*
> As a subject of our case studies, you will be asked to share information about both your financial performance and your impact, recognizing that the benefits of the study are dependent upon the accuracy of the data you report.

Some of the research project's backers and peers were concerned that, as private organizations, funds would be reluctant to participate. However, nearly every one of the organizations we selected to study was a willing participant.

Building trust with funds was our top priority, holding fast to a process that would ensure their performance was revealed alongside the complete, detailed story of the fund's creation, governance, strategy, deployment, and relationship with investors and investees over its entire life—providing sufficient context for readers to understand how and why the fund had delivered the financial and social returns we were documenting. We signed an NDA with all twelve of our research subjects.

We developed a simple model of the ecosystem underpinning fund performance and growth (Figure 2.4) and were particularly interested in pressing on six impact investing dynamics we had identified early in our research within this ecosystem, through initial interviews with over thirty investors in funds.[31]

1. *The active investor.* We were aware that investors in funds— typically known as limited partners (LPs) in the private markets in which most impact investors operate—were playing an especially and increasingly active role in impact investing relative to conventional markets, where a clearly articulated financial return, and a known strategy for achieving it, are typically presented to LPs as faits accomplis. We wanted to explore the integral role of investors in fund creation and development, and the impact of the closeness of the relationship between LPs and fund managers in terms of strategies and performance.

2. *The pioneering fund.* Impact investing can be more difficult to perfect than traditional investing—operating as many impact investors do in newly forming markets, with financial tools and infrastructure that necessitate extreme creativity and collaboration. This makes the need for evidence about performance even more acute. Like a mainstream investor, the impact investor must find ways to define market offerings that can attract capital, can invest that capital, and enable the harvesting of financial returns in a reasonable time frame. Like foundation officers, impact investors must understand the drivers of change within the ecosystems in which they choose to work, and nurture the relationships that allow the desired impacts to flourish, creating new institutions or interactions if needed to get the work done. We wanted to know how impact investors paid attention to market development, from fund inception through investment and portfolio management.

3. *Financial ingenuity.* At the core of impact investing is an ability to use capital in pursuit of not only financial returns but also social and environmental impacts. By definition, this means

Figure 2.4 A Model of Fund Performance and Growth

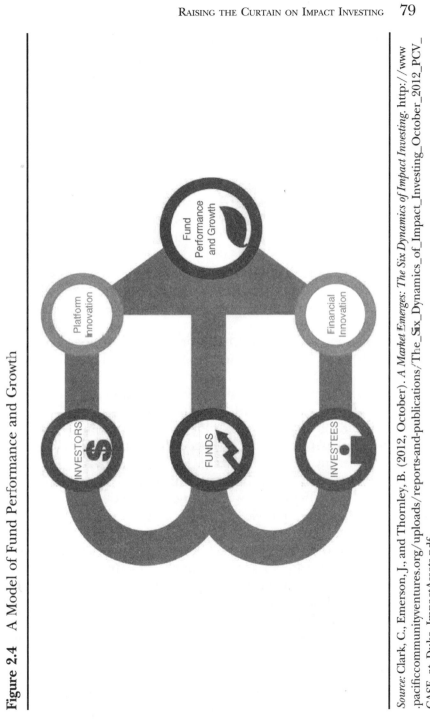

Source: Clark, C., Emerson, J., and Thornley, B. (2012, October). *A Market Emerges: The Six Dynamics of Impact Investing.* http://www
.pacificcommunityventures.org/uploads/reports-and-publications/The_Six_Dynamics_of_Impact_Investing_October_2012_PCV_
CASE_at_Duke_ImpactAssets.pdf.

that the traditional approach to capital structure and finance is simply a jumping-off point for the creation of new financial tools, new structures, and enhanced instruments capable of achieving this type of integrated performance. Many funds were experimenting with creative new approaches to capitalizing impact, and we wanted to know how.

4. *Platform influence.* With significant growth in the number of impact investing funds, we wanted to know how they were being used by investors and interacting with a new community of intermediaries dedicated to matching funds to a growing range of investor types, profiles, and risk tolerances. We wondered if there was a "retail imperative" changing fund structures and strategies and putting in place new responsibilities and calls for accountability. In other words, we expected that the emergence of impact investing distribution infrastructure was in and of itself influencing the creation of funds.

5. *The performance problem.* The critical issue for impact investing funds is to prove their success. As noted earlier, when funds have a clear track record of success in both social and financial scales, a number of positive things happen in the overall marketplace, and growth becomes more organic. However, the difficulty with the field of impact investing is that, for the most part, evidence of success does not always look like that of conventional investing. Some common practices had been emerging around how fund managers can communicate their achievements, but with a large portion of the marketplace dependent on equity-style returns, and still waiting for cash to come back from deals, there was significant uncertainty about the best way to assess track records and evaluate success. Perhaps most important, we wanted to explore the nuances of how funds establish the relative priority of financial and social goals and how this shapes the way they and we should perceive their success.

6. *Aligning purposes.* Aligning the very different and complex objectives and priorities that investors, funds, and investees bring to impact investing is very complicated. We expected that the ability of funds to clearly understand and leverage the blended goals of each stakeholder would be essential.

In addition to our work with the twelve funds directly—a 360-degree interview process that included the funds' key principals and staff, selected investors and investees, and a thorough desk review of agreements, presentations, and reports—our research team also embarked on a process of broad field engagement, leading discussions on performance and best practices that preceded the Skoll World Forum and were part of the SOCAP events in 2012 and 2013. The Skoll World Forum, held at the Saïd Business School at the University of Oxford, is an annual, invitation-only gathering of nearly one thousand of the world's most influential social entrepreneurs, key thought leaders, and strategic partners. The objective of the Skoll World Forum is to accelerate the impact of social entrepreneurs by shining a spotlight on best practices and new innovations, and connecting leaders to one another. SOCAP is a series of annual events, including a flagship conference in San Francisco, connecting investors, foundations, institutions, and social entrepreneurs operating at the "intersection of money and meaning."[32] At the four events, we hosted panels and small-group discussions, shared preliminary findings, and gauged the reaction of practitioners to the issues we raised, engaging directly with more than four hundred session participants and discussants.

The Twelve Funds

The twelve high-performing funds we studied account for more than $1.3 billion in assets. Taken together, they represent a rich and diverse cross section of impact investing, and they prove that concurrently delivering significant social impacts and financial returns meeting investor expectations is not only possible but also being done at significant scale. The funds operated in five countries, ranged in size from $9 million to $331 million, and employed a diversity of strategies, from providing microloans to investing through mezzanine debt and equity, as Table 2.1 illustrates.

One of the first things one might notice is that not all of the groups listed in Table 2.1 are funds per se. We realized we needed to have other key entities represented—most notably philanthropic foundations, which have played a crucial role in impact

Table 2.1 The Twelve Funds: Size and Strategy

Fund	Location	Size	Strategy
Aavishkaar: India Micro Venture Capital Fund	Mumbai, India	$9,428,270	Equity fund targeting early-stage rural enterprises
ACCIÓN Texas Inc.	San Antonio, TX, USA	$29,782,042	Community development financial institution providing microloans
Bridges Ventures: Sustainable Growth Funds I and II	London, UK	$184,575,000	Equity fund targeting high-growth, high-impact businesses
Business Partners Limited: Southern African SME Risk Finance Fund	Johannesburg, South Africa	$331,300,000	Equity and debt fund targeting small and medium-size enterprises
Calvert Foundation: Community Investment Note	Bethesda, MD, USA	$242,000,000	Fixed-income security available to retail investors that channels capital to community development in United States and abroad
Deutsche Bank: Global Commercial Microfinance Consortium I	New York, NY, USA	$80,600,000	Structured fund providing direct loans and other financial products to microfinance institutions

Elevar Equity: Unitus Equity Fund and Elevar Equity II	San Francisco, CA, and Seatle, WA, USA; Bangalore, India	$94,000,000	Equity funds supporting essential services for the "bottom of the pyramid"
Huntington Capital: Huntington Capital Fund II, LP	San Diego, CA, USA	$78,000,000	Mezzanine debt fund
The W.K. Kellogg Foundation: Mission Driven Investments	Battle Creek, MI, USA	$100,000,000	Diversified strategy including a portfolio of direct investments in impactful enterprises
MicroVest: MicroVest I, LP	Bethesda, MA, USA	$48,500,000	Hybrid low-income financial institution fund
RSF Social Finance: RSF Social Investment Fund	San Francisco, CA, USA	$101,000,000	Social enterprise loan fund
Small Enterprise Assistance Funds: Sichuan SME Investment Fund, LLC	Washington, DC, USA; Chengdu, China	$22,512,500	Equity fund targeting small and medium-size enterprises

investing, and the US community finance sector, which does not typically employ a fund structure.

Regardless, we will continue to use the term "funds" to describe the whole group together. And although we generally consider funds to be discrete pools of capital, often time bound, that aggregate third-party capital for the purpose of primarily making direct investments in enterprises and projects, we focused in our research on analogous activities for those entities that are not strictly "funds" yet are still operating as significant impact investing actors—specifically ACCIÓN Texas Inc., Business Partners Limited, Calvert Foundation, and the W.K. Kellogg Foundation.

A brief introduction to each of the twelve funds follows. At the outset, the sense that impact investors are doing things a little differently is inescapable, providing unique insight into Collaborative Capitalism.

Aavishkaar: India Micro Venture Capital Fund

Aavishkaar was founded in 2001 with the purpose of making early-stage equity investments in young businesses in order to stimulate economic activity and improve the quality of life in rural India. The founder, Vineet Rai, is a former executive at a paper conglomerate who was stationed in a remote forest village, and was the leader of India's first government-sponsored business incubator.

Rai and his team bootstrapped the operation for six years until successfully achieving a final close for the fund of roughly $12 million, proving that the Silicon Valley's venture capital model, modified and applied to the rural Indian context, could be financially sustainable and socially impactful. No equity investment firm focused on rural areas existed at that time in India—particularly with Aavishkaar's commitment to funding very early-stage businesses, often as the first external investor.

Aavishkaar succeeded by developing an ultra-low-cost yet staff-intensive operation that some investors believe is possibly the cheapest fund model in the world (in absolute terms). Aavishkaar relied on India's low cost of labor and the fund's charismatic partners and staff, who took substantially below-market salaries. Also critical to Aavishkaar's model was the team's early recognition that beyond cost considerations, early-stage equity investing in

India would need to be fundamentally different than venture capital in developed markets, specifically in regard to the type and degree of investors' risk tolerance.

Unlike venture capitalists in Silicon Valley, who rely on a few "winners" to compensate for the 80 percent of their companies that fail, Aavishkaar knew that even highly successful Indian rural businesses were not likely to generate as much upside as top-performing, early-stage technology businesses in the United States. This realization led Aavishkaar to target a 30 to 40 percent failure rate, with a focus on businesses whose risk of failure was primarily driven by execution rather than technology or market discovery.

ACCIÓN Texas Inc

Since the launch of ACCIÓN Texas Inc. (ATI) in 1994, the CDFI based in San Antonio, Texas, has grown into the largest micro-finance institution in the United States (in terms of gross loan portfolio), serving entrepreneurs throughout eight states in the Mississippi Delta region: Alabama, Arkansas, Kentucky, Louisiana, Mississippi, Missouri, Tennessee, and Texas.

Microfinance institutions in the United States, both for-profit and nonprofit, are defined as organizations that "seek to empower self-employed individuals with affordable and accessible business capital" through loans typically ranging from $500 to $35,000.[33]

ATI attracts investment predominantly by way of the US Community Reinvestment Act (CRA). Furthermore, ATI is a certified CDFI, meaning it can apply for grant funding from the US Treasury's CDFI Fund.

ATI has emerged as a leader in the US microfinance sector both by embracing entrepreneurial innovation in its product development and diversification and by taking full advantage of community development policy in its fundraising.

Bridges Ventures: Sustainable Growth Funds I and II

Founded in 2002, Bridges Ventures is a London-based private investment firm majority-owned and managed by its executive directors and the Bridges Charitable Trust. It is a founding principle of the firm that all the funds that it raises aim to achieve dedicated social and/or environmental goals as well as financial returns for investors.[34] Within that goal, each fund raised by Bridges Ventures has specific strategies to achieve a positive social and/or environmental impact.

The two initial sustainable growth funds (SGFs), the investment vehicles we profiled within the larger Bridges Ventures family of funds, had approximately $184,575,000 under management in 2014 and invest in high-impact businesses pursuing a range of growth strategies (in such sectors as education, health, and environment), consumer-champion businesses serving underserved markets, and companies building economic dynamism in under-invested parts of the country.

In addition to investing in seed- to mezzanine-stage companies, SGFs work to incubate a small number of early-stage deals in each fund, and the firm has built a sophisticated thought leadership and consulting practice around impact measurement and field development.

A self-defined "thematic" investor, Bridges Ventures' SGFs aim to drive the development of the impact investing field at large, by showing that investors can achieve dedicated social and/or environmental goals while also aiming to achieve market-rate financial returns for their investors.

Business Partners Limited: Southern African SME Risk Finance Fund

Business Partners Limited (BPL) was created in 1981 with $24 million of invested capital from the philanthropic sector—father-and-son team Anton and Johann Rupert, owners of the large investment holding company Remgro Limited—the government of South Africa, and other large South African corporations. It has since grown into an investment company with over $331 million, not through the solicitation of additional capital from multiple rounds of new investors, but rather by structuring its investment approach as one that invests in the long-term growth of its invest-ees—enabling the business to steer clear of forcing strategic liquidity events in order to meet the traditional limited lifetime of private funds.

Traditional investors had been reluctant to enter a particularly underdeveloped market segment in South Africa—the provision of debt to small businesses at all stages, from start-up to expansion, with loans ranging from $5,000 to $100,000—and BPL stepped up.

In 1996, BPL shifted from being a lending entity, or banklike firm, to being a venture and growth firm, making direct quasi-equity and equity investments in a portfolio of companies, while utilizing some debt instruments to maintain flexibility. As part of this shift, BPL returned the government's initial lending capital, plus earnings (a total of $100 million)—earmarked for supporting microenterprises and start-ups—and reduced the state's equity share from 50 to 25 percent. With the introduction of an equity investment structure, BPL's transaction size became $50,000 to $3 million.

The transition was also marked by the adoption of new impact-oriented goals targeting black-owned small businesses in South Africa, gender parity within its portfolio of companies, and the full integration of environmental and social factors into its considerations. BPL has made a name for itself internationally as a leader in the support and development of SMEs.

Calvert Foundation: Community Investment Note

Calvert Foundation was founded in 1988 as a nonprofit 501(c)3 when Calvert Investments, a mutual fund family, found strong interest among its clients to invest directly in underserved communities. Today, through its Community Investment Note—the first impact investment available to everyday, nonaccredited investors online and in their brokerage accounts—Calvert Foundation works to empower communities around the world. It has more than $220 million invested in roughly 140 nonprofits and social enterprises working in approximately 80 countries on behalf of more than 4,000 investors.

Calvert Foundation's portfolio partners are a diversified mix of high-impact organizations working in affordable housing development, microfinance, women's empowerment, fair trade and sustainable agriculture, small business development, and critical community services, and Calvert Foundation itself is a registered Community Development Finance Institution.

With a twenty-year history of 100 percent principal and interest repayment to over 13,500 investors, Calvert Foundation holds an important position in the impact investing space as a democratizer and product innovator of impact investing.

Deutsche Bank: Global Commercial Microfinance Consortium I

Deutsche Bank was one of a number of institutions to recognize, a decade ago, that the microfinance sector had fundamentally changed. With a diversity of high-performing microfinance institutions, the field was ready for new financial products.

Led by a tenacious managing director, Asad Mahmood, Deutsche Bank launched a new $80 million structured fund in 2005 that represented a breakthrough for the microfinance sector on a couple of fronts. Most important, with "subordination" (that is, risk protection for senior lenders) of just 40 percent, considerably less than the 80 to 100 percent credit guarantees provided to similar funds at the time, the Global Commercial Microfinance Consortium I exposed institutional investors to the true risks of microfinance for the first time, forcing them to begin the process of developing their own internal impact investing capabilities. The fund also made loans in local currency, which was unusual in 2005.

Key to the fund's success was Mahmood's "intrapreneurialism"—leveraging Deutsche Bank's institutional muscle, including no- or reduced-cost services from the firm's trustee department and swaps desk, external legal counsel, and some choice introductions to prospective investors.

Thirteen institutions signed on as noteholders in the fund, including State Street Bank and Trust, AXA Financial, and the General Board of Pensions and Health of the United Methodist Church, United States. The fund's subsequent performance revealed the power of structured products to respond to the diverse needs and priorities of investors in new, impactful markets.

Elevar Equity: Unitus Equity Fund and Elevar Equity II

Elevar Equity was created in 2006 by four individuals, three of whom had worked at the nonprofit organization Unitus, which provided capital and expertise to microfinance institutions in developing countries from 2000 to 2010, with staff and field offices in Bangalore, India, and Nairobi, Kenya.

Led by a group of talented partners, each of whom brought an average of more than fifteen years of experience in investing and emerging markets, Elevar Equity has built a set of funds that are accomplishing what many thought was an impossible task: using equity investments to build early-stage, high-growth, scalable businesses for underserved customers in bottom of the pyramid (BoP) markets.

Through microfinance, the partners had gained unique insights into the needs of BoP customers in adjacent services, such as financial services, housing, payment networks, and rural health care. Much of the progression of Elevar from its first fund, Unitus Equity Fund, to its second fund, Elevar Equity II, was based on leveraging this understanding, together with a core expertise in entrepreneurial business models that scale profitably serving BoP customers.

Elevar prides itself on a culture that enables its team to be geographically dispersed: some are based in India and Latin America, in order to be close to portfolio companies, and some are in the United States, in order to access other investors. The team has developed strong connections over many years of working together and in the markets that their companies serve.

The funds together have invested in sixteen early- to growth-stage companies serving close to eleven million households in Asia and Latin America through such services as microcredit, savings accounts, rural health care, housing loans, convenient payment access, small business credit, migrant (housing) services, and information services.

Huntington Capital: Huntington Capital Fund II, LP

Huntington Capital launched its second fund (HC II) in 2008 as the continuation of a proven investment strategy—providing $2 million to $5 million of mezzanine debt, per deal, to lower-middle-market companies in a range of non-high-technology industries, in the racially diverse southwest area of the United States—but with a clearer articulation and accountability for the social impacts that had been generated by the firm for many years.

These impacts included access to finance for underserved SMEs, job creation (with health and retirement benefits) in low-income communities, and support for businesses owned by women and ethnic minorities, and were consistent with the economic development goals of some banks and other large institutional investors, including pension funds, insurers, and foundations.

Commercial banks were attracted to HC II because their investment in the fund, with its anticipated social impacts, qualified for credit under the CRA. For insurers, HC II met the requirements of the California Organized Investment Network, a California Department of Insurance program modeled after the CRA that requires insurers to invest in underserved communities on a voluntary but closely monitored basis.

Huntington's first fund was also a Small Business Investment Company (SBIC), registered with the US Small Business Administration, illustrating the importance of the broad, enabling policy environment for impact investing. The SBIC program has been in operation since 1958 and provides publicly guaranteed leverage to privately owned and managed investment funds for the purpose of capitalizing small businesses.

Huntington's partners had backgrounds almost entirely in banking and finance, but with an economic development twist, working for state government funds with job creation as a primary objective, or in emerging international markets, identifying ways to stimulate growth.

The W.K. Kellogg Foundation: Mission Driven Investments

W.K. Kellogg Foundation's (WKKF's) $100 million Mission Driven Investments (MDI) initiative, created in 2008, stands as an especially innovative example of a large institution aligning endowment preservation with programmatic objectives, particularly because of its core commitment to investing directly in for-profit companies.

MDI made six direct investments from 2009 through mid-2013 anchored firmly in WKKF's singular goal of supporting the "whole development" of vulnerable children through education and learning; food, health, and well-being; and family economic security, including building skills and income, asset preservation, and wealth creation. WKKF's investments of $500,000 to $6 million have focused on growth-stage enterprises with imbedded relationships, policy influence, and deep knowledge of scalable business models that can be leveraged organization wide.

The MDI portfolio is also invested with two overarching screens in mind: place and diversity. WKKF has a target of investing more than 50 percent of its assets in Michigan, where it is headquartered, and in New Mexico, Mississippi, and New Orleans, which are identified priority places for WKKF, where entrenched issues of poverty were made a high priority decades ago, and long-standing relationships and initiatives remain. The concerted effort to invest in companies and intermediaries led by racial minorities and women is ongoing.

Embracing direct investments was key to developing the MDI program at WKKF, connecting the idea of impact investing directly to the language of philanthropy and the mission-critical ideas of innovation, growth, and impact. The strategy has been enabled by a governance structure that provides sufficient discretion; the leadership of senior staff with the right mix of skills, interests, and institutional and market credibility; and a deep and enduring relationship with a boutique third-party impact investing advisor, Imprint Capital.

MicroVest: MicroVest I, LP

MicroVest Capital Management was created in 2003 by the global NGO Cooperative for Assistance and Relief Everywhere (CARE), as one of the first dedicated US-based asset managers to invest in low-income financial institutions (LIFIs) in emerging markets. CARE had identified the scarcity of capital as the principal barrier facing microfinance institutions and, after five years of research and planning, launched a first fund, MicroVest I (MV I), with the mission of extending capital markets to reach a greater number of developing world entrepreneurs.

Even with social sector roots, however, MicroVest takes a decidedly commercial approach to its work and has mainstream credentials. Founding chair W. Bowman Cutter was managing director of the private equity firm Warburg Pincus. The firm's financial due diligence process is so widely recognized and admired that MicroVest investments often attract other institutions to invest at the same time or subsequently.

The seamless balancing of financial and social interests undergirds MicroVest's success. The firm was governed exclusively by

CARE and its other nonprofit owners at the board level throughout the life of MicroVest's first fund (MV I). Yet management was encouraged to replicate the structure and processes of an "institutional quality" investment manager, solely seeking risk-adjusted financial returns, even while targeting the bottom economic quartile of the world's population.

Using a hybrid strategy of investing debt and equity, and with a mission to prove that the working poor represent an excellent credit risk, MV I deployed over $160 million to sixty-six LIFIs from thirty countries before closing in September 2011.

RSF Social Finance: RSF Social Investment Fund

RSF Social Finance (RSF) is an innovative public benefit financial service organization that offers investing, lending, and giving services to individuals and enterprises committed to improving society and the environment. Since 1984, RSF has made more than $285 million in loans and over $100 million in grants, on behalf of more than fifteen hundred client investors, lenders, and donors.

The RSF Social Investment Fund (SIF) is RSF's core investment product. It provides loans to US-based nonprofit social enterprises whose work focuses in one of three areas: food and agriculture, education and the arts, and ecological stewardship. Through another 100 percent–owned RSF for-profit subsidiary, Social Enterprise Inc. (SEI), RSF also lends to for-profit social enterprises in the same areas with the same investment criteria. Loans in both SIF and SEI constitute RSF's social enterprise lending program, which has a goal of enhancing the financial services available to viable social enterprises.

RSF is known for a disciplined risk management process, resulting in an extremely low default rate and leverage ratio, and a uniquely high-touch, transparent approach, in which borrowers, lenders, and donors can interact with one another throughout the investment process. Most notably, RSF's loan instrument may be the only one in the world that allows investors to influence the interest rates they receive based on input from quarterly face-to-face meetings with the funds' borrowers. RSF has also started to integrate stakeholder alignment more formally into its deal structures, finding ways for stakeholders to bring in layers of catalytic capital (i.e., grants and concessionary investments), which RSF calls "integrated capital." These practices allow RSF to provide solutions that reduce risk, amplify impact, and differentiate the fund from other lenders.

SEAF: Sichuan SME Investment Fund, LLC

The Sichuan SME Investment Fund (SSIF) represented an enormous milestone for SEAF and for direct equity investing in China more broadly, when it was created in 1989 as an experimental attempt by CARE to spur SME development.

With the launch of SSIF in 2000, SEAF became the first global SME equity investor; SEAF had previously invested in Latin America and Eastern Europe. SSIF was also the first private equity fund in the province of Sichuan (where the population exceeds that of Germany) and one of the first funds targeting inland China.

SSIF was capitalized primarily by development finance institutions (DFIs), which had invested in other SEAF funds and were pleased with their financial and social performance. This institutional and brand support enabled SEAF not only to attract investment from New York Life, one of the world's largest insurers, but also to complete fundraising in a remarkably short eight months and persuade the Chinese government to approve the creation of the fund.

The goal of SSIF was to create jobs and economic development in Sichuan, one of the most underserved provinces in China, which resulted in investments of common equity and debt of $540,000 to $4.2 million in nine growth-stage companies in the manufacturing and food industries between 2003 and 2006. The fund's portfolio companies have created jobs and improved staff income levels faster than the broader Chinese economy.

Performance Numbers

High performance was a prerequisite for being selected as one of our twelve funds. We make no claims, therefore, that the field as a whole is delivering results that are nearly as impressive as those of this group, though there are undoubtedly other funds that are. Our list of funds is exclusive but not exhaustive. The funds have also had various challenges and some setbacks, which we dissect in coming chapters.

More broadly, it is important to note that performance is not linear in impact investing; rather, it is consistent with the types of markets that funds invest in and the strategies they implement— all elements that are known to investors at the time they commit capital. This is why, in narrowing our selection to 12 funds from 350, we relied primarily on investors to tell us which had been "successful," defined as satisfying the objectives that had been promised—incorporating and blending both financial and social returns. We were agnostic on the balance between financial and social outcomes. And in a new field characterized by scant public data, the insights of investors who had seen financial and social disclosures firsthand were even more essential.

Seven of the twelve funds have commercial investors and were seeking a risk-adjusted market rate of financial return. They usually had market benchmarks against which to judge their performance and were expected to exceed them. For the other five funds, the accountabilities were no less stringent: providing to investors the interest rates they had promised and maintaining the appropriate risk and capital profile in order to enable that outcome.

Table 2.2. describes the financial and social performance of each of the funds. The funds can be separated into three broad categories for the purposes of examining their performance. In the aggregate, developed market equity and hybrid funds returned up to 14 percent, emerging market equity and hybrid funds returned 3 to 21 percent, and social debt funds returned 0 to 3 percent, without ever losing their investors a dime. Social performance is more difficult to aggregate, as each of the funds seeks different outcomes. Where there were common measures at some funds, aggregated social impacts include the following:

- 1.3 million jobs were created or sustained.
- 17 million people were provided with access to finance.
- 40 percent of all enterprises receiving finance were led by women.
- 67 percent of all enterprises receiving finance were led by a disadvantaged ethnic group.

Table 2.2 The Twelve Funds: Financial and Social Performance

Fund	Financial Performance	Social Performance
Developed Market Equity and Hybrid Funds		
Bridges Ventures: Sustainable Growth Funds I and II	Successful exits have generated multiples ranging from 1.6 to 22x.	Has placed over 80% of portfolio in underserved areas, catalyzing more than £435M in investment and creating more than fifteen hundred jobs (40% in underserved areas).
Huntington Capital: Huntington Capital Fund II, LP	13.78% net internal rate of return (IRR) at March 31, 2013	352 total jobs created; of the 2,811 total portfolio company employees at December 31, 2012, 78% reside in low- to moderate- income areas; nine of sixteen portfolio companies (56%) are owned or operated by an ethnic minority individual or female.
The W.K. Kellogg Foundation: Mission Driven Investments	Two realized exits out of six total direct investments, delivering IRRs of 46% and 65%.	The MDI program's investments support WKKF's theory of change, which addresses social conditions, such as improving the quality of and equitable access to food, education, and health care for vulnerable families; 53,300 vulnerable kids were supported through direct investments, which accounted for 75% of the MDI total.
Emerging Market Equity and Hybrid Funds		
Aavishkaar: India Micro Venture Capital Fund	20% IRR on investments and 13% IRR net of fees. Six complete exits: three with IRRs between 12% and 39% and three at discount to principal; two partial exits with 45% and 63% IRRs and three write-offs.	Varies by company. Highlights include 101,817MT of CO_2 emissions reduced; 10.5 million dairy farmers with increased incomes; 145,500 people with disabilities gaining access to computer/web services; and 344,925 people accessing financial services through rural ATMs.

Table 2.2 (*Continued*)

Fund	Financial Performance	Social Performance
Business Partners Limited: Southern African SME Risk Finance Fund	In excess of 2.5× original capitalization returned to shareholders via dividends between 2005 and 2013; 7% average ROE from 2003 to 2013	Since 1981, total of over $1.5 billion invested in more than 69,500 SMEs, creating or sustaining more than 550,000 jobs.
Deutsche Bank: Global Commercial Microfinance Consortium I	Targets met for all investors (3%–7% IRR) in 2010, except Class B Equity (3.5% IRR, met in 2012, below 12% IRR target)	Active clients served by investees: 2.6 million. Estimated number of loans to entrepreneurs: 732,146.
Elevar Equity: Unitus Equity Fund and Elevar Equity II	UEF: 21% realized IRR, net to LPs	Sixteen companies introduced more than twelve essential services to eleven million households.
MicroVest: MicroVest I, LP	7.6% net IRR to LP investors, within 7.5% to 8% IRR target; full interest paid to note/debt investors	Clients receiving financial services (at MV I's largest size): roughly 3.5 million microentrepreneurs. Women clients for LIFIs in the MicroVest I portfolio: 52% on average.
SEAF: Sichuan SME Investment Fund, LLC	11.38% net IRR and 22.73% gross IRR as of June 30, 2013	21% average annual increase in employment and 17% average annual increase in wages at each portfolio company since SSIF investment; 58% of jobs created for low-skilled workers.

Social Debt Funds

ACCIÓN Texas Inc.	2%–3% return to investors	Since inception, the organization has made over 13,400 loans totaling $145 million, and has preserved or created thirteen thousand jobs. In 2012 alone, ATI disbursed 919 loans totaling $18 million.
Calvert Foundation: Community Investment Note	Investors select from available rate and term combinations, currently ranging from one year at 0.5% to ten years at 3.0%. 100% principal and interest repayment to more than 13,500 investors over twenty years.	Since 1995, more than 13,500 investors have invested nearly $1 billion in the portfolio of nonprofits and social enterprises worldwide. Metrics are tracked through IRIS and CARS.
RSF Social Finance: RSF Social Investment Fund	1.26% average interest rate (2009–2013). No investor has lost money, and the loan fund has less than 2% default rate over twenty–eight years.	Impact differs within each focus area, but overall, borrower impact increased by a normalized average of 7 points on the B Impact Rating System from 2011 to 2012, meaning they increased their impact even as they expanded their business as a result of loans received from a mission-aligned lender.

The Impact Investing Fund Landscape

Our research on the twelve funds has delivered two important outputs. The first comprises the separate, highly textured stories of each of the funds in their own right—the most detailed public release of data on strategy, execution, and performance in impact investing to date. We will be delving deeply into the discrete experiences of the twelve investors throughout the remainder of the book. Full case studies are available on our project website.[35] There is much to learn from their successes and the challenges they have overcome.

The second is the insights into the group as a whole: market-level data, such as the aggregated social impacts mentioned previously, and key characteristics and practices that were common across all funds. By selecting a "sample" of funds that is relatively representative of activity in the market to date, we are able to present a rough sketch of the field of impact investing as a whole and, as important, how it differs from traditional investing.

By examining the funds as a group, we were also able to synthesize the best practices we will be sharing throughout this book, and attempt to answer a critical question posited at the beginning of this chapter:

What, precisely, is impact investing?

We know that impact investing constitutes a diverse group of strategies, ranging from microfinance to community finance, markets for social enterprise, economically targeted investment, and international development. It is still too early to conclusively ring-fence a practice that is growing quickly and in a multitude of innovative directions.

Yet with access to data from the twelve funds, we have been able to ask and answer the foundational question of what purpose they each serve, bringing together disparate practices and painting a cohesive picture for the first time.

This analysis—or "market landscaping"—is anchored in two data points that best describe each of the funds. The first focuses on the capital flowing *into* the fund—that is, who and what kinds of institutions are investing in the fund, and why. The second focuses on the capital flowing *out*—that is, what type and scale of enterprises the fund is supporting.

We approach the first question by looking at the range of investors engaged in impact investing—government entities (including development finance institutions), investors motivated by public policy (for example, US banks fulfilling their CRA obligations), private foundations, commercial and fiduciary institutions broadly, and individuals—and then analyzing the particular mix present in each of the twelve funds.

Investors engage in impact investing for myriad reasons, informed by deeply held values and convictions, strategic institutional and mission priorities, rules and regulations, and, of course, risk-and-return objectives. However, our landscaping makes use of a single, particularly important distinction: whether investors are primarily motivated by "public policy" (the priorities and activities of government) or by "private interest" (operating without the influence of government). This distinction speaks directly to an important element of impact investing: Policy Symbiosis, which is one of our four key practices and the subject of chapter 4. We discovered that the specific mix of investors in any single fund provides clues as to the types of sectors they operate in and the extent to which these markets are characterized by failure and deep government involvement. We then categorized the funds as being supported by institutions that are predominantly motivated by either public policy or private interest—and all of the points on a continuum that connects the two.

We approach the second question—focused on where the fund invests—by examining the maturity of the enterprises receiving capital. All twelve funds have an explicit strategy of investing in companies at either an earlier, "blueprint," stage, with its related strategic implications and challenges, or at a later growth, or "scale," stage. This is specified in policy statements and partnership agreements. And with access to data on the size and nature of each of the fund's actual deals, we were able to confirm that the reality matched the rhetoric. It should be noted that the funds we classify as investing at a later growth stage are still making much smaller investments in companies, at much earlier stages, than the typical mainstream investor in similar investment categories.

The "blueprint" and "scale" terminology builds on excellent research from the Monitor Institute that explored the particular challenges of early-stage impact investing.[36]

Fund Landscaping

1. Capital in: Who are the fund's investors? What do they tell us about the markets in which the funds are operating?
2. Capital out: Do the funds invest in earlier-stage or later-stage businesses? What does this tell us about the maturity of the markets in which they operate?

Table 2.3 describes each of the funds according to the composition of its investors and the nature of its investees.

Table 2.3   The Twelve Funds, Capital In and Capital Out

Fund	Capital In: Investor Base	Capital Out: Investment Recipients
Aavishkaar: India Micro Venture Capital Fund	• Primarily individuals • Some tax-advantaged foundations • One investment from a government entity late in the day	Early stage
ACCIÓN Texas Inc.	• Government (through subsidies provided to CDFIs) • Banks motivated by regulation • Large investments and significant grant support from private foundations	Early stage
Bridges Ventures: Sustainable Growth Funds I and II	• Seed investment from government • Institutional and foundation capital, deployed independently, but also motivated by government partnership • Individuals	Growth stage
Business Partners Limited: Southern African SME Risk Finance Fund	• Seed investments from government, philanthropy, and corporations	Early stage

Table 2.3 (*Continued*)

Fund	Capital In: Investor Base	Capital Out: Investment Recipients
Calvert Foundation: Community Investment Note	• Core investments from thousands of individuals • Many faith-based, foundation, and other institutional investments	Growth stage
Deutsche Bank: Global Commercial Microfinance Consortium I	• Catalytic support from DFIs • Institutional investors as senior noteholders • Foundations and individuals in high-risk equity tranches	Growth stage
Elevar Equity: Unitus Equity Fund and Elevar Equity II	• Foundations • Individuals • Endowments • Emerging Markets Funds	Early and growth stage
Huntington Capital: Huntington Capital Fund II, LP	• Core of institutions making economically targeted investment, including pension funds, and banks motivated by regulation • Foundation mission-related investments	Later growth stage
The W.K. Kellogg Foundation: Mission Driven Investments	• Capital sourced entirely from the foundation's endowment	Later growth stage
MicroVest: MicroVest I, LP	• Core of private foundation, individual, and commercial investors • Late investment from a DFI in senior notes	Later growth stage
RSF Social Finance: RSF Social Investment Fund	• Core of individual investors • Associated philanthropic resources	Early to growth stage

Table 2.3   (*Continued*)

Fund	Capital In: Investor Base	Capital Out: Investment Recipients
SEAF: Sichuan SME Investment Fund, LLC	• Core investor base includes one DFI and one institution motivated by policy-oriented economic development obligations	Growth stage

The landscape takes shape when we place the funds on a simple chart, as shown in Figure 2.5. The vertical axis represents capital in—that is, the investor base of the funds, ranging from individuals and institutions that are entirely driven by public policy to investors driven entirely by private interest. The horizontal axis represents capital out—the investment strategy of the funds, ranging from "blueprint," the earliest stages of a company's development, to "scale," the later stages of a company's initial growth.

Figure 2.5   Investor Base and Investment Strategy of the Twelve Funds

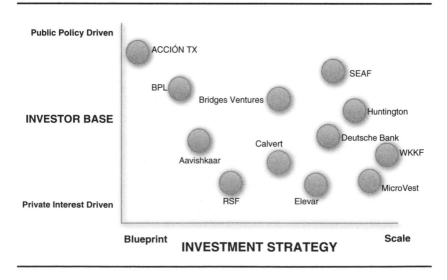

Figure 2.6   The Four Types of Investment Funds

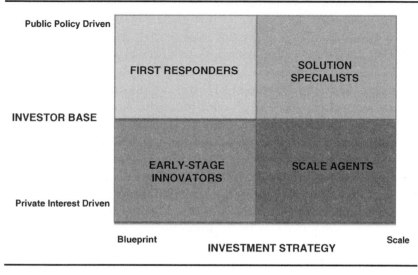

The chart allows us to readily compare the funds. MicroVest, for example, is worlds apart from ACCIÓN Texas Inc. (ATI); whereas MicroVest makes larger investments on behalf of primarily commercial, privately driven investors, ATI provides microloans to start-up businesses, supported by significant subsidies from the public and philanthropic sectors.

The analysis becomes more useful, however, when we generalize the landscape and create four quadrants of funds, each with its own unique set of characteristics, as Figure 2.6 illustrates. Let's examine each fund "type" in turn.

First Responders

First responders like ATI and Business Partners Limited (BPL) operate in underserved, generally low-income markets that have been relatively devoid of mainstream capital. More important, due to endemic market failure and the associated lack of business skills, economic infrastructure, networks, experience, and data that make capital markets function effectively, mainstream investors are unlikely to play a direct role in providing needed capital anytime soon.

This does not mean intermediaries operating in the space are any less sustainable, only that catalytic and concessionary capital in the form of public sector, philanthropic, and policy-driven private sector funding will continue to be essential. And because intermediaries must be structured to receive and manage these kinds of funds, they tend to be created as special-purpose entities—a prime example being US CDFIs like ATI that are registered with the US Department of the Treasury and required to work in designated, underserved places.

ATI and BPL provide useful counterpoints. ATI operates in low-income communities, providing microloans to start-up businesses. Both the geographic places in which ATI operates and the types of enterprises it supports mean the high-impact work it does is essential, but will likely never be profitable. As a result, half of ATI's $14 million budget comes from philanthropic grants. BPL started out this way—as a public-private partnership, with the government's half of BPL's seed investment specifically earmarked for microenterprises. And although BPL has developed economies of scale in order to make the investment process more profitable, it has also moved into more mature markets; BPL's average deal size has increased accordingly: it began at a range of $5,000 to $100,000 and has moved to deals from $50,000 to $3 million in size.

Solution Specialists

Solution specialists, such as Bridges Ventures, SEAF, and Huntington Capital, implement investment strategies that satisfy the very particular needs of investors, often tied to political or policy imperatives. As a result, solution specialists are often created (or designed) in very close collaboration with their investors, in order to ensure clear alignment.

To be sure, the "solution" that is provided by the funds usually has mainstream credentials. After all, investors in solution specialists include large institutions. For example, Bridges Ventures and Huntington Capital take a "thematic" approach to their investing, identifying mature, competitive market sectors, but with the potential to generate the imbedded impacts that their investors desire, including creating quality jobs for low-income populations. We will discuss these investment strategies in more detail in chapter 3.

SEAF's Sichuan SME Investment Fund provides a prototypical example in this category. The fund was created at the request of the International Finance Corporation (IFC), which, together with the Chinese government, was interested in driving economic development in a particularly underserved part of China. The fund also served the discrete purposes of New York Life Insurance, which was eager to demonstrate its commitment to creating jobs in China while seeking a license to offer insurance in the country. Together, the IFC and New York Life account for 60 percent of the capital invested in the SEAF fund.

Early-Stage Innovators

Early-stage innovators like Aavishkaar and RSF are expert at attracting capital primarily from socially motivated individual and foundation investors, for the purpose of funding newer, mission-driven businesses. In order to do so sustainably (addressing the inherent difficulties of investing in earlier-stage businesses or sectors), innovation is critical.

Aavishkaar pioneered an ultra-low-cost operational model that made possible small investment sizes in rural areas where investments carry high transaction costs, and a very hands-on provision of business support services to investees. RSF cleverly blends different types of financial and philanthropic capital to make more businesses "investable," and has a strong brand associated with funding enterprises that deliver socially beneficial products and services that individual investors find appealing.

The capital provided to early-stage innovators is often explicitly concessionary (that is, it does not always provide investors with a risk-adjusted market rate of return). However, when this happens, it is provided freely (without government influence) because its deployment is perceived to be so impactful and so well targeted to an individual's or foundation's discrete social objectives.

Scale Agents

Scale agents like Deutsche Bank, MicroVest, the W.K. Kellogg Foundation, Elevar, and Calvert Foundation find ways to make impact investing more commercial—attracting mainstream investors to the field by proving the case that, in some markets, it is possible to generate attractive, risk-adjusted market rates of financial return alongside significant social and/or environmental benefits.

This usually means scale agents invest in more mature enterprises and markets, for the simple reason that risks and returns are more predictable and transaction costs are not prohibitive. At the same time, scale agents may be as innovative as other impact investors, and, because they are still operating in relatively new markets (by the standards of most mainstream investors), they must work just as hard to educate investors and bring a range of individuals and commercial, philanthropic, and even public sector institutions to the table.

The microfinance market is typical of the sectors in which scale agents operate. In the mid-2000s when MicroVest's and Deutsche Bank's funds were taking shape, the sector had been growing by about 12 percent annually, serving ninety-four million customers.[37] New intermediaries were launched, improving the availability and flow of information between microfinance institutions (MFIs) and other industry stakeholders. As commercial funding became more abundant and grant funding scarcer, a greater number of MFIs became for-profits in order to access more capital. Roughly 50 percent of MFIs were nonprofits in 1997, compared to 24 percent by 2004.

Calvert Foundation's Community Investment Note is more accessible to individual investors and their advisors than almost any other product on the market. It invests primarily in scalable intermediaries to more efficiently drive capital to players in established sectors such as community development and microfinance.

Elevar invests in markets where the potential for scale is understood because of very large unmet demand at the customer level in BoP markets. They have the ability to go in early (first-time investments are $1 million or less) and take a company through to scale, bringing in larger institutional capital along the way. We placed them in scale agents because of that larger institutional capital focus and their focus on market rate returns.

The W.K. Kellogg Foundation (WKKF) invests directly in larger social enterprises—the same types of businesses that RSF Social Finance supports, but at a slightly later stage of development. In fact, WKKF has invested subsequent to RSF in some deals.

What Is Impact Investing (What Role Does It Typically Play)?

The landscaping and four categories of funds provide a useful way to think about impact investing on the whole. Investors and funds are

- Providing capital through subsidized, special-purpose intermediaries to places that are stubbornly underserved
- Using capital to solve very particular challenges related to regulatory or strategic and institutional imperatives
- Creatively blending capital sources and strategies to fund innovative business models that address the specific social impacts investors care about most
- Finding ways to scale capital markets that are inherently impactful, and bringing an impact lens to more mainstream investment opportunities

The market-level perspective we've described shows us that, although inherently diverse in its application, impact investing is in fact more developed and coherent than might have been assumed—representing a new "2.0" era in the market's evolution, grounded in evidence of what does and does not work.

In the chapters of part 2, we focus on four key practices:

1. Mission First and Last
2. Policy Symbiosis
3. Catalytic Capital
4. Multilingual Leadership

The experiences of the impact investing funds we researched make these practices concrete—and demonstrate the power of impact investing as a harbinger of Collaborative Capitalism.

Together, the four practices recognize that all businesses serve a purpose higher than simply earning profits, and demonstrate that teams and strategies may be cultivated to successfully implement this more integrated approach.

PART TWO

FOUR KEY ELEMENTS OF SUCCESSFUL IMPACT INVESTING

3

Impact DNA

The most important part of the ecosystem is when somebody down the line of a company, let's say a field officer or customer officer, interacts with the customer; that's where the magic happens.
—Sandeep Farias, Elevar Equity

AGAINST SIGNIFICANT ODDS, ELEVAR EQUITY HAS INVESTED $94 million of capital under management in scalable businesses for underserved customers in bottom of the pyramid (BoP) markets, delivering a market rate of return of 21.4 percent.

Elevar's efforts to connect underserved communities to global networks have resulted in equity investments in sixteen early- to growth-stage companies, serving close to eleven million households in Asia and Latin America, through such services as microcredit, savings accounts, rural health care, housing loans, convenient payment access, small business credit, migrant (housing) services, and information services.

This ability to achieve such a high level of impact within such a challenging context may sound like an art in many respects—after all, these are new markets with almost no guideposts—but Elevar's particular strength is in designing the sort of analytical devices and rules of thumb that make it more like a science.

The "Elevar method" contains numerous parts, from identifying large and undervalued, disconnected groups, to recognizing their needs and creating an investment hypothesis, evaluating and analyzing economic systems, and ultimately supporting customer-centric business models. But one of the most interesting and important criteria to emerge after seven years of operations has been a focus largely on the quality of the entrepreneurs in which they invest.

There are two facets of an entrepreneur's skill in execution and professional maturity that Elevar has determined are essential. The first will strike a chord with any mainstream investor: the individual's commercial experience in managing large organizations. Entrepreneurs leading Elevar portfolio companies are seasoned, long-term professionals averaging approximately twenty years of prior professional experience. Most have held C-level positions in their prior careers in large companies in their home markets. Cofounder and managing director Sandeep Farias explains:

> It's much easier to socialize a commercial person than to commercialize a social person. It's quite a controversial statement because of the word *socialize*. Based on our track record, we are capable of both, but we make an explicit choice to focus on one. With all of our backgrounds . . . we actually worked with a bunch of social guys to commercialize. I, for example, did a lot of work in helping [microfinance institutions] transform from nonprofits to for-profits. But what we realized was, if we have to back successful companies, the entrepreneur needs to be able to build large organizations. And to build large organizations, this is not a twenty-four-year-old who's never had a job, and it's not like building an Internet company. You are going to have thousands of people working for the organization, and you need someone who has real experience in building them, from within a multinational or a large corporation.

The second facet is more unusual: the entrepreneur's mind-set, which must incorporate an understanding of target customer markets at a deep level. Elevar examines whether, for example, CEOs spend time in the field, disavow creature comforts—"Are they able to work in a non-air-conditioned environment in India?" asks Farias—and spend time really interacting, authentically, with customers. "We ask to go into the field with potential CEOs and meet some customers," says Farias, "and while they talk to the customers, we watch them. Are they going to sit in their car and go two feet in, or are they actually walking in and spending time talking to people? That is critical. I wouldn't invest otherwise."

This may not be rocket science, but the fact this is considered make or break is something Elevar deeply understands.

Like many impact investors, Elevar is pioneering a new model of capitalism in its chosen market, which requires courage and disciplined creativity, but also a particular set of experiences and characteristics. In examining funds like Elevar, we asked ourselves the following question: What are the right indicators of the same commitment to mission in impact investors (the funds) that they expect themselves from their own investees?

Elevar credits its success directly to the fact that each of its partners bring an average of more than fifteen years of investing and emerging markets experience, including deep knowledge of the systems and processes needed for distributing services en masse in developing markets. Their microfinance backgrounds, before Elevar, also provided the ability to understand and identify with customer needs in adjacent services, such as financial services, housing, and rural health care. The partners are of diverse nationalities and ethnic backgrounds and are dispersed, investing out of three locations: Bangalore, San Francisco, and Seattle. However, they have also all known each other and been working together for an average of eight years.

This is Elevar's particular DNA. But it is also representative of what we call "Impact DNA," the structural and strategic approach of impact investors to integrating two core elements of impact investing: intentionality and accountability.

Intentionality refers to a fund's commitment to seeking social and/or environmental outcomes through investment. *Accountability* refers to the tracking and reporting of these measureable, positive social benefits.

For all the complexities of this integration, which we discuss in this chapter, successful impact investors actually make the process seamless and fully embedded in all facets of their design and operations.

Surprisingly, the approach that funds take is relatively consistent across the set of funds we examined. We call it "Mission First and Last," where mission refers to the fund's core objective of pursuing specific intentional social or environmental impacts through a particular practice of investment. We discovered through our research that the key to implementing a successful impact investing strategy was to put financial and social objectives on an equal footing by developing a clear, integrated strategy and structure for achieving mission *prior* to investment (sometimes called "mission lock"), which enables the fund to maintain financial objectives as the priority during deployment.

Knowing early and explicitly that impact is contained in a fund's DNA allows all parties (investors, investees, and the fund itself) to move forward with an investment discipline akin to any other financial transaction, confident that mission drift is unlikely.

We will return to the specifics of mission lock. For now, DNA is the ideal analog: a complicated molecule that encodes the genetic instructions for the development of all living things. We explore some key strands of impact investing DNA in later chapters: an approach to soliciting and deploying capital that is multifaceted rather than one-dimensionally focused on "best use" and ROI; a deep awareness of the role of public policy in impact investing; and the "multilingual," cross-sector skillset that underpins impact investing.

In chapter 2 we talked about what impact investing is. Here we ask, how and why do impact investors do what they do in the first place?

A Means to an End

It may seem obvious, but an important idea bears repeating at this point: impact investing is not, by any measure, the solution to all or even most of the deep and intractable problems we face as a society.

The governments we ourselves have created, and often elected, retain ultimate responsibility for our collective welfare. Even as impact investors see opportunities in the retreat of government from some areas of social service provision in developed countries, or in the general lack of public resources and capacity in emerging markets, the truth is that governments are always likely to be best positioned to provide many social services, for reasons of collective action, equity, and efficiency.

Similarly, there are impacts that only the most "concessionary" of investments—philanthropic, nonrepayable grants—can sustain, focused on the earliest stages of systemic social innovation, the most underserved populations, and the "big moral questions of our day." As president of the Rockefeller Foundation, Judith Rodin, wrote in 2013: "Strategic philanthropy can continue to transform by serving as the risk capital that oils the wheels of progress, speaking truth to power, listening and valuing the input and ideas of our grantees and those populations we serve, and by striving to build their individual capacity to create their own transformation."[1]

Impact investing is only applicable, in other words, when there is a clear market-based solution to a problem, or a clear path to that solution.

For example, with the goal of providing health care at the BoP in emerging markets, a purely grant- or aid-based solution may be needed to provide vaccines and other services to the poorest populations. However, to target beneficiaries with more resources, it may be more sustainable and scalable to encourage the development of a market-based solution with a modest cost to users, but with a more limited subsidy, or even none at all.

Acumen Fund, one of the world's most well-recognized impact investors, uses a method for understanding its impact that attempts to quantify the distinction between a charitable approach and an entrepreneurial approach to tackling social challenges, which it refers to as the "best available charitable option" (BACO) ratio. The BACO ratio compares the total cost per the social impact of Acumen's investments to the charitable options for addressing the same explicit social issue. Acumen uses the example of a $325,000 loan to a textile mill in Tanzania for manufacturing particularly innovative insecticide-treated bed nets, with the goal of reducing the incidence of malaria, compared to providing a grant of the same amount to UNICEF or an international NGO to distribute traditional insecticide-treated bed nets for free. According to Acumen, the investment approach would cost less than $0.02 to protect one individual from malaria for one year, compared to $0.84 through the charitable option.[2] The evidence indicates that this particular method for treating malaria may be well suited to impact investing.

So although impact investing is clearly focused on producing desirable solutions to social and environmental problems—what we call being "outcomes driven"—it should not be considered an end in itself in most cases, but simply a means, alongside other means that may be more efficacious. The idea that different kinds of investment strategies are considered for the same ends is far from unique to impact investing. Consider pension funds, for example, the overarching goal of which is not to generate attractive rates of financial return per se, but ultimately to provide for the retirement of their beneficiaries, through investment practices that integrate various risk-and-return profiles. Some argue that defined-benefit plans are the best approach, pooling the risks of all members and paying out a predetermined retirement benefit. Others believe defined-contribution funds do a better job, giving individuals control over their own risks and rewards in the investment of their retirement funds. Each side may be right in different circumstances, in the same way impact investing may be a useful tool for addressing certain social challenges, but ill-suited to others.

Of course, determining the range of problems for which impact investing might be applicable is just the first step. Further analysis to understand the practical and ethical suitability of a market-based approach, the specific financial tools that might be appropriate, and the need for subsidy encompasses an entirely more complex set of calculations.

In some cases, funds may be alone in making that determination. At the same time, entire markets have been developed on the basis of years of carefully researching and calibrating the appropriate financial responses to social challenges. Microfinance globally and community finance in the United States are but two examples of decades-old impact investing markets. A new fund in these sectors will have a wealth of practices and practitioners on which to draw, numerous fund structures and investment strategies to adapt, and access to a network of professional service providers geared up to support their work at every turn, including through established tools for tracking and reporting impact. Funds in other, less developed spaces within impact investing will need to work harder to align intention and accountability from scratch.

This book touches on the many complexities inherent in determining the appropriateness of impact investing in particular markets—but in an admittedly abbreviated fashion. In truth, the sheer magnitude of decision-making criteria needed to assess the financial viability of even a single business solution to a difficult social problem makes it impossible to present the full scope of these variables with any confidence. In any case, the attempt would limit our understanding of the breadth of impact investing and its approaches.

Instead, in our own analysis of successful impact investing, we used the proxy of a fund's *preparedness* to tackle complexity, asking the question: What is it about a fund's structure, disposition, and general approach to impact investing that gives investors the confidence to provide capital, and the proof that their investments are having the impact they were counting on?

The Need for Clarity

If impact investing is complex and outcomes driven—indicative of a bottom-up form of Collaborative Capitalism that necessitates the type of transparency and attention to constituency described earlier—then it follows that those doing it well have mastered the most important antidote: clarity.

This is the crux of Mission First and Last: clearly seeing the social problem being addressed and clearly seeing the need for and limitations of capital as one solution to that problem, then making the clear connection to outcomes.

The way in which the community development financial institution (CDFI) ACCIÓN Texas Inc. describes its impact is illustrative:

> The economic impact of small businesses in the U.S. is profound: $11 trillion a year, according to the most recent figures available from the U.S. Small Business Administration. The SBA reports that 99.7 percent of ALL employer firms are small businesses! So the chances are good that you, your family and your friends work for small enterprises. There are almost 30 million small businesses in America and they employ nearly 57 million people.
>
> . . . But starting and sustaining a small business is hard work—and there are often enormous obstacles that keep people from succeeding . . . They need access to capital, education and a support system to realize their potential and increase their chances for success. We provide those things.
>
> - We've made 14,438 loans totaling more than $159 million. And we've grown to include lending in eight states—enabling us to reach more and more people with each passing year.

- We have helped thousands of people achieve the financial stability and growth they so richly deserve as a result of their vision and hard work.
- ACCIÓN financing increased the probability of a firm's survival by 44 percent and doubled the number of employees at firms."[3]

What impact investors are doing is blending two key ideas: the *theory of change,* a concept borrowed from social science, which provides a construct of the key assumptions that are believed to lead from activity to impact; and the *investment thesis,* or investment policy, a concept borrowed from finance, which provides a clear statement of where and how an investor proposes to add value.

The Impact Value Chain and Theories of Change

Two key tools used by social scientists to unpack and define the social impact of enterprise-level solutions are the logic model and the theories of change analysis.[4] If the logic model is what you use to define your desired end state, the theories of change analysis is what you use to guide your progress toward those goals. The logic model is like a snapshot. The theories of change is a map.

Logic models were developed in the 1970s by the United Way, and gained popularity in the 1990s when United Way started using them with its agency partners. The United Way logic model was renamed the Impact Value Chain by one of us (Cathy) in a paper, which applied the model for the first time to investment in mission-driven ventures.[5] The model has since been replicated throughout the sphere of market-driven solutions, social entrepreneurship, and impact investing. It has been published in guides by the World Economic Forum and used in seminars across the globe to help social enterprises define their goals and approach.

The Impact Value Chain (see Figure 3.1) delineates four main elements of a social enterprise's or program's efforts:

- *Inputs,* which are what you put into the activity, including hard assets, human talent, and financial or intellectual capital.
- *Activities,* which are the core processes you undertake as a venture (for example, recruit and select students in an

Figure 3.1   Impact Value Chain/Logic Model

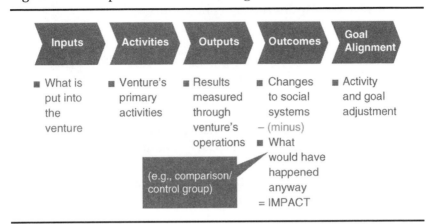

Source: Adapted from Clark, C., Rosenzweig, W., Long, D., and Olsen, S. (2004). *Double Bottom Line Project Report: Assessing Social Impact in Double Bottom Line Ventures,* http://www.riseproject.org/DBL_Methods_Catalog.pdf.

afterschool program). These include not only the processes that lead to a sale of a product or service but all the processes that affect outside stakeholders.

- *Outputs,* which are the measurable results that an associated nonprofit or project manager can measure or assess directly through his or her operations. Outputs for an afterschool program, for example, could include the number of children participating in the program, the percentage who drop out, and the percentage enrolled in the following year.

- *Outcomes,* which are the ultimate changes the funds are trying to make in the world. For the afterschool program, desired outcomes could include higher self-esteem or higher educational achievement for participants. Outcomes are always expressed as an increase or decrease in some social system variable, such as income, educational achievement, GDP, disease prevalence, and the like. Commonly the organization running the program may not have the expertise or resources to evaluate whether all outcomes have been achieved at the broader community level, but that organization should be able to define desired outcomes and figure out which internal output measures it can directly control are most likely to be correlated with desired outcomes.

Impact has a very specific definition inside the Impact Value Chain. The social science definition refers to the portion of the total outcomes that happened as a result of the activity of the venture, above and beyond what would have happened anyway. In social science, we need a *counterfactual* to compare to the experimental state in order to discern the dependent variable from all other factors that could be causing a change. In our afterschool program, for example, to discern real impact, a social scientist might randomly assign children to the program under evaluation and to another control program similar in most respects, and measure the differences in the children's educational achievement after both programs have been completed. The program's impact would then be defined as the statistically significant difference in educational achievement between the program group and the control group, or the results "but for" the intervention. This is a sophisticated definition of impact and one that can be costly to prove with certainty.

To be sure, very few for-profit social ventures have the time and money to create true experiments in which third parties come to validate their impact. The idea behind theories of change analysis is to help delineate impact in situations where the implementation of a comparison or control group is infeasible or unethical. For example, you cannot randomly assign some battered women to a shelter with services and leave some to fend on their own. A theories of change analysis allows us to understand the series of assumptions that are made between the output of a program or an intervention and the outcomes that you desire. There are two kinds of theories of change analysis. One recaptures the primary elements of the Impact Value Chain in a simple "if-then" sentence:

Enterprise theory of change: If more people use solar lanterns than burn kerosene in their homes in rural Tanzania, then there will be fewer deaths from home fires.

Lender theory of change: If peer groups of women are given access to small loans as a group and asked to pay in small weekly installments, then their collective incomes will increase, and their children will achieve higher levels of education.

The more complete theories of change recognize there are multiple dependencies and assumptions that relate any output to any desired outcome; they also recognize that there are often multiple levels of outcomes desired and that some may be dependent on others. The idea of this analysis is that you articulate those assumptions explicitly and then map them in a logical manner to determine which are progressing the way you expected, what the interdependencies are, and what kinds of things you can do to improve your theories and ultimately prove your impact. Theories of change in the social science literature are always plural (as opposed to the vernacular "theory of change") because there is always an interweaving of different theories in the analysis. Then, over time, data is collected and the theories are updated to reflect various lessons learned. The analysis is a living map that is especially useful to the practice of socially oriented entrepreneurs, because it reflects the "iterate, test, refine" practice that most entrepreneurs employ naturally.

For example, if we assume the microfinance example listed earlier represents a theory for Grameen Bank, Figure 3.2 is a sample initial theories of change chart, which breaks down the ultimate outcome into component parts that can be tested.

In the example shown in Figure 3.2, we see how Grameen as a lender is entering into a complex system of interrelated parts, where one of its most desired ultimate outcomes, increased educational achievement for children, depends on many others factors outside of its direct control as a lender. But at the bottom is something it can control, and does: the belief that the borrower should be encouraged to send her children to school. Grameen Bank has a cultural component designed to help spread this message strongly among its borrowers. Sophisticated impact enterprises and funds often address these assumptions as risk factors and start to pinpoint them one by one, even building partnerships with other organizations with complementary offerings to try to eliminate them. Coastal Enterprises in Maine is another good example. As a CDFI, its theories of change are about using investments to create jobs for underprivileged people. Coastal made some

Figure 3.2 Theories of Change Example, Constructed for Grameen Bank

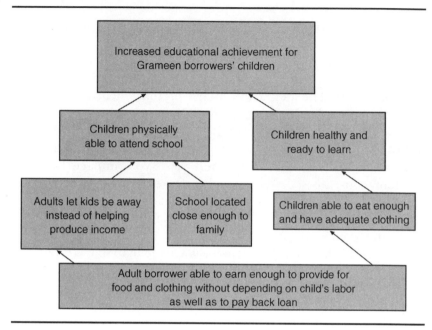

investments and started to track the tenure and turnover of people who were given new jobs at its investee companies. The fund found really high turnover in the first year, even among employees who were performing very well. It spot-surveyed the employees and learned that the number-one reason for quitting the job among women was lack of adequate, low-cost child care. Coastal set up partnerships between investee companies and child-care providers and watched its own outputs and outcomes improve.

A plan to create outcomes through the practice of investing and a strong theories of change analysis are the building blocks of an impact investing thesis. Of course, they are not all you need. Successful funds of any sort have to make a case to potential investors about the overall strength of their investment thesis. The investment policy, or stated investment strategy, is fundamentally an agreement between fund intermediaries and their investors, although there have been efforts to better standardize that relationship. One example is the Institutional Limited Partners Association (representing LPs in *all* private equity funds), whose "private equity principles" recommend the minimum elements that should be included in investment strategies:

- An investment purpose clause that clearly and narrowly outlines the investment strategy
- A statement on any authority to invest in debt instruments, publicly traded securities, and pooled investment vehicles
- Appropriate limitations on investment and industry concentration, and consideration of investment pace limitations if appropriate
- Accommodations of an LP's "exclusions policy," which may proscribe the use of its capital in certain sectors and/or jurisdictions, mindful of increased concentration effects on remaining LPs and the need for transparency of process and policies

The objective is to ensure that when committing capital to funds within the context of a broad portfolio of investments, investors have clarity on the specific fund strategy and value proposition it presents, which must be "well defined and consistent."[6]

But the impact investor has to add to this clear articulation of its financial strategy a compelling and convincing argument about the outcomes their investment will drive, or what we call an "investment thesis of change." This is the tangible expression of the mission concept discussed earlier and the precise steps by which a particular investment strategy will create the outcomes that are needed and anticipated.

We discuss the investment thesis of change (ITC) in more detail in the tool kit section at the end of this chapter. In short, it should include the following parts:

1. The "change," or social outcome, that is being pursued (that is, the overarching fund objectives and intentions)
2. The source of capital for pursuing that change (for example, some funds, such as Acumen, use charitable contributions; most solicit debt or equity investments from individuals and institutions)

3. The fund's investment approach (by financial instrument, size of deployments, and so on)
4. The fund's investment recipients (by type, size, sector, and so on)
5. The activities (outputs) of investment recipients made possible by the provision of capital (for example, hiring, purchasing from suppliers, delivering goods and services)
6. The outcomes that these outputs will lead to, and how they will be measured

Every fund seeks different positive social outcomes. These are often at both the level of investees and the individuals they service, and the level of entire sectors (and by implication the impact investing field as a whole). Our research included examples of funds more heavily weighted to each. For example, let's explore the ITCs of two funds that have different units of change:

1. Enterprise/individual focus. The Aavishkaar India Micro Venture Capital Fund was created to improve the quality of life in rural and underserved communities in India. The fund targeted businesses that either created livelihood opportunities for communities in rural India or were able to serve individuals' basic needs (for example, providing low-cost health care, education, or access to energy). The vision is primarily about transforming the lives of individuals. Aavishkaar also hoped that the fund would encourage systemic change—incentivizing aspiring entrepreneurs to launch businesses, and demonstrating to investors that profits and positive social change could be generated concurrently.

2. Sector focus. Deutsche Bank's Global Commercial Microfinance Consortium I had an explicit goal of proving the case for microfinance as a viable investment strategy for large fiduciary investors, together with the provision of capital to the poor. The fund used a number of tools for attracting thirteen institutional investors to the table: financial innovation in the form of a grant, a guarantee and two layers of equity investment that struck the balance between protecting senior noteholders and exposing them to the true risks of microfinance; a highly transparent process that transferred knowledge to the fund's investors, encouraging at least two to create specialist microfinance teams within their institutions on the back of the knowledge they had gained; and a direct marketing pitch to the C-suite, conveniently avoiding the bemusement of CSR units unfamiliar with investment, and the suspicions of investment units of anything socially motivated.

The high-level ITCs for the two funds might look as illustrated in Table 3.1—vis-à-vis their enterprise-level and sector objectives respectively, notwithstanding their interest in a more holistic impact.

Omidyar Network, an influential impact investor (including in the Deutsche Bank fund), emphasizes sector-level impact, arguing that "though investing in firms is an essential component to driving sector-level change, it is ultimately sector development that matters most" because it drives capital to early-stage innovations and the infrastructure needed to create entire new markets. In the 2012 report *Priming the Pump,* Omidyar argues for an approach to calculating the total impact of a firm by adding its direct impact to its sector-level impact.[7]

Whatever the level of proposed impact, the most important and often intangible attribute regarding a clear ITC is that prospective investors recognize the fund's managers have some unique experience that makes their thesis, and unique skills and capacities for delivering on that thesis, believable. For impact investors, *the credibility of a fund's ITC is often just as important as the credibility of its financial return thesis.*

Many of our fund managers had prior experience working in enterprises or financial intermediaries closely connected to the ITC of their first funds. Elevar's principals were active in microfinance for years, and saw the opportunity to provide equity to the emerging for-profit models; principals at Bridges had experience in real estate, which translated directly to the low-income, asset-backed businesses they focused on in the first fund. These examples abound even outside our research studies: SJF Ventures was started by founders who had been in the recycling business for years, and their first fund's thesis was about the provision of jobs in environmentally friendly companies; the Managing Partner at Pacific Community Management (PCM), Eduardo Rallo, is a restaurateur. It make senses that PCM's equity investments in

Table 3.1 Investment Thesis of Change Examples

	Social Objective	Source of Capital	Investment Approach	Investment Targets	Outputs	Outcomes
Aavishkaar	Improve the quality of life in rural and underserved communities in India	Primarily individuals and socially motivated institutions	Early-stage equity	Enterprises in agriculture, health, water and sanitation, education, information and communication technology	Production of goods and services; hiring	Varies by company: creating local livelihoods, and products and services that reduce the vulnerabilities of low-income and rural populations
Deutsche Bank	Attract fiduciary investors to microfinance	Public sector, impact investors, and institutions	Structured product to reduce risk, making primarily direct loans	Balanced portfolio of microfinance institutions at different stages of growth and in different places	Loans to underserved entrepreneurs	Access to capital in underserved communities; proof of concept for LPs, through financial success

for-profit companies intended explicitly to create jobs for low-income people are often in the food services industry.

Impact investing funds need to do the math and balance all the factors of size, stage, geography, and vehicle that any fund manager has to in order to come up with an investable fund proposition and a risk-and-return profile that an investor can understand and trust; but they must also convey some sort of unique expertise around their ITC, be it a related professional background or some other special insight that can translate in the LP's mind into a competitive barrier to entry and a way to actually reduce the risk of the investment, rather than increase it.

Getting Everyone Aligned

There are many reasons clarity is essential, not least for knowing the addressable market and designing the right investment strategy for tackling it, as the ITC makes plain. But perhaps the most important is the need to align the diverse interests that are necessarily present when an inherently collaborative endeavor engages multiple stakeholders. If disparate perspectives are not reconciled—or, better still, coordinated and leveraged—across LPs, funds, and investees, success in impact investing is likely to be more elusive.

Interview subjects in 2012 and 2013 shared stories of companies poorly positioning themselves in the market, funds struggling to remain focused in order to showcase competitive advantages, and impact investing programs within large institutions that missed the mark and failed to attract either the support of internal stakeholders or the coinvestment of other large asset owners—all because of insufficient clarity.

Jessica Matthews, manager of the Mission Related Investment Group at Cambridge Associates, a US consultant, reiterates the importance of a statement or policy regarding impact investing goals and objectives: "We observe clients having a harder time initiating their impact investing programs if they have not clearly articulated the goal or purpose of the program," she says.

Clarity was on the mind of Rosemary Addis, then social innovation strategist at the Australian government's Department of Education, Employment and Workplace Relations, when she approached the market in December 2010 to invite applications for seed funding to establish at least two new social enterprise and development funds. "If we couldn't explain our intentions and objectives and set out clearly what we expected fund managers to address, how could we expect others to come forward with robust ideas?" Addis asks.

The examples noted here primarily concern what we call "external alignment," or the engagement of multiple stakeholders in a collaborative endeavor. It is just as important to understand the implications of clarity for "internal alignment," or the actual governance, management, and operations of a fund.

Looking at internal alignment, MicroVest believes that the governance of its firm has played a critical role in its growth to over $210 million in assets under management, and uses a nautical analogy to describe the way in which it navigates impact investing "waters."

The firm's board of directors and nonprofit owners, including CARE, provide social ballast in addition to deep financial expertise. However, the sail is clearly commercial, with a for-profit structure and focus. Too much ballast would mean the ship would not go anywhere. Too much sail would mean the ship capsizes when the seas get rough. It is a constant challenge to keep the ship steady. CEO Gil Crawford explains, "On any given day I can get it wrong, but the blend of our board and our staff has allowed us to often get that balance correct." Crawford represents the firm's managers on the board of directors, but does not have an executive role, underscoring the management company's commitment to absolute independence. Crawford argues it is very important that management and owners respect their proper roles: "Inside MicroVest, as long as I am acting in an ethical manner and in the interest of the shareholders, I have authority. Meanwhile, the executive committee and the board provide guidance and know our social balance. For instance, if we were just a for-profit firm before 2008, we might have taken advantage of a lot of tempting, high-growth initiatives that were not right for the future of MicroVest."

In the Mission First and Last tool kit, we discuss one other opportunity to build internal alignment, through incentive structures for fund managers tied directly to social performance.

Finally, clarity is also important because it is inclusive. Impact may be generated by investors using any number of strategies, in a diversity of markets, for a multitude of ends. What matters is not which approach is "better" or "more impactful" but that with intentionality and accountability as touchstones, investors see a clear path to outcomes.

An ITC can be developed for each and every scenario. Whether it holds water should not depend on the superficial characteristics of the market in question—for example, whether it is public or private—but on the very nuanced investment approach and the specific audience weighing the diffuse or targeted outcomes on offer. A large investor actively engaging or pressuring a public company in its portfolio on ESG issues may be just as likely to influence the behavior and subsequent impact of that business as a fund with a larger stake in a private enterprise.

From First to Last: Measurement and Reporting

For impact investing insiders, there is no subject that has been more preoccupying than the question of performance tracking and reporting. Impact performance measurement is both essential and ubiquitous. When the Global Impact Investing Network (GIIN) and J.P. Morgan released their 2014 annual survey of global impact investors in May 2014, 95 percent of respondents reported they use metrics to measure the social and/or environmental impact of their investments, and over two-thirds also stated that standardized impact metrics are important to the growth of impact investing.[8]

Rigorous impact measurement is an essential prerequisite for impact investing integrity and success, yet very challenging in many respects. Most ventures can count their outputs but have very little opportunity to measure outcomes in any convincing way. Sometimes attributing your impact in a complex system is next to impossible. And there are many different options for impact reporting within most fund structures, but very little extra cash to do it well.

The impact fund manager faces some choices, then, with regard to how best to navigate this challenge. She must answer a specific question: what priorities, attention, and resources should she place on measuring social outputs or outcomes?

First, a note about the complexity inherent in really strong impact assessment and reporting and how different this is for people coming from commercial backgrounds. Every business has performance metrics, and many build robust and sophisticated systems to help track not just the ultimate ends (usually financial success) but all sorts of interim measures to help take the temperature of what's working and help make management of the organization effective. But commercial ventures almost never have to report on outcomes, only on outputs. The challenge for social ventures is getting from outputs to outcomes. Even if they can't truly measure outcomes, they need to make a convincing case for how they are having an impact on real outcomes over time.

Consider a business that spends a great deal of time and money studying how to promote a sale and what conditions lead people to change their behavior enough to make a purchase. In most cases, the business need not worry about whether the sale led to a behavior change the next day, the next month, the next year, or the next decade. For social ventures, however, there is a need to understand how short-term outputs (measurable parts of business operations and customer interactions, like the sale) lead to long-term outcomes (which could occur years later). For investors in social ventures, there is also the need to make a convincing case about how much of those ultimate outcomes can be attributed to their investment.

In the realm of social or environmental change, getting the product in the hands of the customer at the right time is 75 percent of the battle, as with all businesses. Yet it is only by studying closely what happens postsale that you understand if you succeeded. Some clear examples of this are in the health care domain:

Embrace, a baby warmer technology in India. The problem Embrace solves is the lack of a low-cost, portable, non-electricity-reliant baby incubator outside of major medical institutions in the developing world. The impact of someone using a baby warmer for a premature or low-birth-weight baby is clear: warmer babies fare better, and infant mortality rates go down. The trouble is, it turns out newborn babies in need of heat don't look cold. So even when you have sold a clinic a set of Embrace baby warmers, they often sit unused because the nurses or other workers in the clinics do not understand *why* they must be used.[9] Sales as an output measure is highly misleading. What investors in Embrace have learned is that the Embrace solution is more effectively used in hospital and clinical settings where education can take place regarding the needs of premature and low-birth-weight babies.

Changamka's Linda Jamii, a mobile microinsurance product in Kenya. Linda Jamii is a new microinsurance product that allows users to store money on a mobile phone and, once they reach half of the annual premium, a year's worth of health insurance for an individual or a family kicks in. Again, the output of number of subscriptions completed is the sales point that makes the company money. But the impact of this product comes only when the person knows she has insurance and acts differently as a result, such as by taking her baby to the doctor for preventive visits or by getting the care she needs without waiting too long. Otherwise you're just wrenching more money from a poor person for the same care she would have gotten anyway.

For impact investors, there's an art to identifying a convincing set of metrics and methods (in addition to sales metrics) that can help paint a fuller picture.

For example, Elevar's ITC relates to the belief that many communities in BoP markets are underserved (for reasons including poverty, discrimination, distance, and so on), which is an impediment to development. These communities often contain thriving informal sectors in which a variety of services are being demanded and offered, though generally of low quality and at high prices. Elevar invests in companies that deliver products and services to these communities in ways that develop a thriving market, where the company can both scale to millions of customers and ensure its own financial sustainability by delivering products and services that simultaneously maintain quality and reach. The overall thesis is one of financial and economic inclusion, and Elevar's impact metrics reflect as much.

A good example of this is a company in Elevar's portfolio that trains small shopkeepers in Peru to become financial service agents. The agents help with deposits and withdrawals, facilitate loan and credit card repayments, enable utility bill payments, and fulfill other basic financial needs. Elevar has created a detailed set of measures, listed in Table 3.2, to help answer critical questions

Table 3.2 Elevar Equity's Core Impact Themes

Theme	Question	Subquestions	Sample Indicative Metrics
Customer Demographics	Is the business centered on the target customer?	What percentage of customers do not otherwise have access to services or are unable to afford services at currently available price points?	• Increase in percentage of customers without credit score/records • Increase in average income of borrowers • Increase in number of RSBY[10] insurance customers • Increase in numbers of underserved districts in which hospitals or bank/MFI branches have been set up • Increase in number of customers with no prior banking products
Customer Financial Strength	Does the product or service help strengthen the customer's balance sheet?	Does it help reduce expenses or increase income? Does it help build a long-term asset?	• Reduction in borrowing, rental, and transaction costs compared to status quo • Increase in value of asset (such as land or a building) • Improvement in health (long-term asset creation)

Product/Service Quality (as Measured by Customer Satisfaction)	Does the business offer significant improvement in quality or reduction in price as compared to the current alternatives? Is the customer satisfied?	How satisfied is the customer as compared to next best alternative? How strong is demand for and uptake of products and services?	• Increase in average tenure and occupancy levels at hostels • Increase in word-of-mouth customer referrals • Increase in staff productivity (ease of customer acquisition)
Scale	Is the business able to scale and cater to large, unmet customer demand?	How is the number of customers growing? What is the value of products sold? What kind of presence does the business have, in terms of locations covered, number of units set up, etc.	• Increase in # of loans disbursed • Increase in # of hospital beds or patients treated • Increase in # of customers with better homes • Increase in # of homes sold to migrant workers
Capital Leverage	Are our investments attracting capital to this space?	How much debt/equity capital has the company raised?	• Amount raised for every dollar invested by Elevar • Mix of commercial versus social sources of capital

about the depth and breadth of interaction that the agents have with their customers. The data that is collected at the customer level can be used by the company and by Elevar to tell the story of whether the agent is really being trusted by the customer and whether the customer is moving from low-threshold transactions to higher ones that indicate a raise in income. By piecing together the right kinds of output data, you *can* get very close to a picture of outcomes, but you need to build the systems carefully.

The implications of this kind of system are clear. If Elevar wants to track a range of variables for its own reporting to stakeholders, it has to figure out how to encourage its investees to share the data in a trusted manner. There is no one-size-fits-all approach. Some funds have covenants in their investment agreements; some have jettisoned them after years of seeing that they do not help if a company is in trouble, "so why bother." All of our case study subjects also emphasized the importance of being aligned with the ethics and moral outlook of the investee as an equally critical measure.

Overall, there are still many tensions in the marketplace around impact evaluation, especially if funds have many different stakeholders asking for different kinds of metrics. Many funds are trying to figure out ways to shortcut this process, make measurement easier, integrate it into their overall reporting from investees, and find ways to benchmark themselves against other funds, in order to show their comparative performance on impact. It was concern about these issues that led some practitioners in the field, associated with Acumen and Investors' Circle, and with funding from the Rockefeller Foundation, to contemplate and then create some new standards for impact reporting. The Impact Reporting and Investment Standards (IRIS) project arose as a way to try to standardize the metrics that different businesses and funds were reporting, so that, for example, a job in Nairobi meant the same number of hours as one in Bombay. The IRIS catalog now encompasses over 490 different generally accepted performance metrics that impact investors can use to measure social, environmental, and financial success; evaluate deals; and grow the credibility of the impact investing industry.

The ratings platform B Analytics has also emerged, to allow investors and their stakeholders to measure, benchmark, and report on impact performance by either defining their own metrics, using IRIS metrics, or combining them. And for those investors who want to compare the social performance of impact funds, there is also the Global Impact Investing Rating System (GIIRS), a holistic and transparent rating system that provides funds with a Morningstar-like star rating on their impact. These systems are increasingly widely used and seem to have helped many investors get a handle on reporting, although our research shows that many of the first-generation funds that we studied felt they needed to customize the assessment around their ITC, and were exploring standard reporting as a second step. That may change as new funds get started and more mature systems are in place. It will change even faster if the fund's investors start to require use of these standard systems, which some large development finance institutions and institutional investors are starting to do.

RSF Social Finance is one fund that has balanced custom and standard metrics. According to president and CEO Don Shaffer:

> The specific challenge that we faced was that our role as intermediary does not easily lend itself to impact assessment. Yet we know that we affect our donors and investors and our borrowers through *how* we do our work. That quality is often one of the primary reasons that others seek us out. As a financial services organization, we create a whole system of interdependent relationships through transactions—money coming in as well as money deployed. In our research with investors and donors about what impact information would be meaningful for them, they indicated that our values and operating principles were as important to them as the extraordinary projects we fund. Our approach to finance has a quality that we wanted to be able to assess without the ethical challenge of claiming the good work of our borrowers or our donors and investors as ours directly.

The team agreed a multifaceted approach would be necessary to assess how well RSF fulfills its purpose of transforming the way the world works with money. Building on the Steiner concept of associative economics, RSF has taken a stakeholder approach to social impact assessment, by dividing its core constituents into common groups and using different tools and processes to assess the value and impact created for each cohort. As of December 2013, these were in different stages of development, but the core concepts and some summary information on each is described here:

For borrowers: the annual Portfolio Audit is meant to show the impact RSF's portfolio of borrowers has had in the aggregate and over time, and has two years' worth of data. RSF also requires its borrowers to take the B Impact Assessment, which provides a broader field-level benchmark for reported impact.

For investors/clients: the annual Client Impact Survey consists of just one year of data, but presents an important baseline.

For RSF employees: the annual Organizational Culture Survey includes a compilation of three years of data.

For the field at large: the Field Building assessment includes some early third-party data, along with clear indicators of how RSF will be developing a Partner Audit instrument for next year. The data is focused on how RSF has influenced the emerging field of social finance.

Overall, we are enthusiastic about the Impact Investing Spectrum in the "Short Guide to Impact Investing," published by the Case Foundation in April 2014.[11] Investors have to choose the level of commitment they and their stakeholders have to impact reporting and then adjust their assessment activities accordingly. The guide lays out three levels of commitment: Impact Motivated, Impact Committed, and Impact Certified, as shown in Figure 3.3.

All the funds in our study were in the Impact Committed or Impact Certified categories, as our criteria included evidence that they had been measuring and reporting impact. Elevar is an example of Impact Committed; RSF is Impact Certified. RSF not only asks its own borrowers to use third-party metrics but also uses such metrics itself. The for-profit lending arm of RSF is a certified B Corporation (an independent impact rating system at the enterprise level) and also changed its corporate form to become a Delaware-based benefit corporation.

Just as Goldilocks discovered the perfect bowl of porridge, impact investors are realizing there is such a thing as too much information and reporting, and too little. So what lessons can we take from the choices made by these and the other funds?

Figure 3.3   Impact Investing Impact Commitment Spectrum

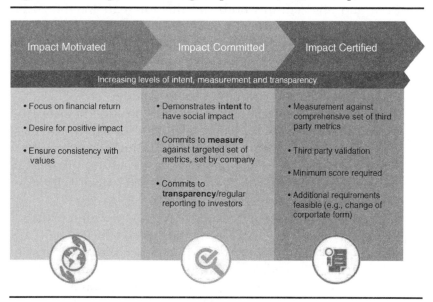

Source: Case Foundation. (n.d). "A Short Guide to Impact Investing." http://casefoundation.org/impact-investing/short-guide.

- Attribution of impact to an intermediary such as a fund is always hard. Most funds and standard rating systems for funds depend on the rollup of metrics from investees and other stakeholders, which is a practice that needs to be communicated and agreed on up front.
- When you are not able to set the terms of impact assessment, you are often much more limited in the credit you can take from the work. The W.K. Kellogg Foundation's Mission Driven Investment program, for example, prorates the portion of the impact it gives itself "credit" for, as it has generally made later stage investments in companies with clear impact propositions for the communities that the foundation aims to serve.
- Fund managers need to identify stakeholders who are explicit about the level of impact reporting they want to see, and then meet them where they are. Some funds set up a nonprofit arm to do this reporting, as their LPs actually want much more information than the funds can afford to track and provide,

and this allows the funds to subsidize the assessment activity. PCM and SJF Ventures both did this for years for their LPs. PCM's efforts led to the creation of a highly respected, stand-alone impact advisory practice within its affiliated non-profit organization, Pacific Community Ventures, providing a consulting service to third-party investors, including the largest pension fund in the United States, CalPERS.

• Data should be collected with enough granularity to expose weaknesses and underlying assumptions, especially if you have philanthropic or government investors. Generally these investors specialize in analyzing theories of change and will want to see you match their sophistication in regard to how well you're meeting your impact goals.

• And the best data will be actionable for you as a fund manager as well. Try to create systems that help you focus on what's working and what might need help before an investment goes off the track. This means taking the time to define up front what the most important social metrics are to you and to the investee for each investment. The field is littered with stories of investors who looked away and then suddenly found that the company was no longer meeting the needs of its target beneficiary. Use metrics as a communications tool, not a paper-pushing exercise.

Bringing It Together: Sequencing the DNA of Impact Investors

When impact investing was quickly converging into a more distinct practice in 2009, an important report from the Monitor Institute coined the terms *financial-first* and *impact-first* to describe the different approaches of investors to impact investing. Financial-first impact investors give high priority to competitive rates of financial return and seek ancillary social benefits. Impact-first impact investors are concerned primarily about the delivery of social outcomes, with a financial floor.[12]

The distinction became a default barometer for good reason. For the first time, impact investors were able to describe themselves in a way others understood. This enabled them to identify the right peers and products more quickly, and also provided for a more segmented and, therefore, actionable conversation. However, in recent years, it has become clear that the objectives of investors are more multifaceted than this initial dichotomy allowed—a reality reinforced by our fund case studies. Mission First and Last is in part a response to the limits of financial-first and impact-first as categories, and representative of a more complicated blending of objectives throughout the life cycle of an investment.

For funds, in particular, financial and impact priorities tend to ebb and flow over time, in a relatively consistent fashion, as illustrated in Figure 3.4.

The development of an ITC comes early, and recognizes the primacy of the social outcomes that the fund is seeking. This is where intentionality is formulated. And impact resurges as the most important consideration again when the fund is reporting on its performance and focused on accountability. As Figure 3.4 illustrates, for impact investing to succeed, financial discipline is paramount. Enterprises deliver impact only if they are sustainable.

Figure 3.4   The Impact Investing Fund Life Cycle: Mission First and Last

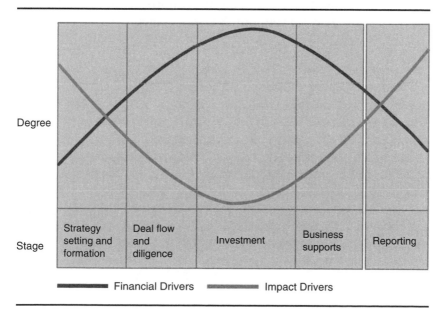

Calvert Foundation, ("the foundation"), one of the largest impact lenders in the world focused on nonprofits and social intermediaries, is a good case in point. The foundation has more than $220 million invested in roughly one hundred forty nonprofits and social enterprises working in approximately eighty countries. Its portfolio partners are a diversified mix of high-impact organizations working in affordable housing development, microfinance, women's empowerment, fair trade and sustainable agriculture, small business development, and critical community services.

Although the organization has a very strong impact proposition and attracts investors because of its accessible product and commitment to impact, its internal systems emphasize discipline and rigor around reducing risk. For each proposed loan, Calvert foundation fully assesses social performance through customized metrics that incorporate industry metrics and best practices for each sector. All applicants are expected to provide three years of financial information for analysts to produce due diligence reports prior to the investment committee's review of prospective investments. In addition, the foundation analyzes the organization's operational and management track record, capital structure, loan portfolio quality, mission focus on underserved populations, and compatibility with the foundation's strategic goals. The foundation risk rates each loan, which determines the level of loan loss reserves, and screens each loan through a pricing model to establish whether the proposed investment requires subsidy. The foundation's lending is governed by a comprehensive lending policy manual, addressing loan and product parameters, single exposure limits, pricing, approval authorities, reserving, portfolio monitoring, and reporting. Loans are monitored based on quarterly reporting as an early warning tool to identify any negative trends, and each loan is reviewed annually. Investors are protected by $30 million in loss reserves, net assets, and subordinate debt.

As a result of these practices, Calvert Foundation has maintained a 100 percent repayment rate to its investors, even while investing in some of the most underserved communities around the globe.

Given financial discipline is a must—as it is for any traditional investor—the element that really distinguishes impact investing is this idea of mission lock. Impact investors will inevitably be faced with tough financial decisions—saying no to plainly impactful opportunities, hiring and firing management, knowing when to cut losses, and moving aggressively to exit even when the timing is not ideal. How will investors know, therefore, that when funds are faced with these decisions, their social mission will inform an approach that is balanced and holistic, even while being unremittingly disciplined? Again, it comes down to the DNA and character of the firm.

Kate Starr, vice president of capital deployment at F.B. Heron Foundation, says that character has been a big draw for the foundation's $2 million mission-related investment in Huntington Capital II, which seeks concurrent market-rate financial returns and social impacts: "Character makes a huge difference—not only in ensuring good LP/GP [general partner] relations, but in the relationship between GPs and their portfolio companies. You have to know that the symbiosis goes all the way through and that the GP will take seriously the role of social impacts in working with management. If social impact is part of the ethos, GPs and management will think about the consequences of any financial event on the enterprise and its workers. We only want to take the risk of investing in private partnerships so that GPs can create real long-term value."

Mission First and Last Approaches

Funds are a powerful locus of research because they boil many complex ideas—and the incredible diversity of their investors' motivations—down to the cut-and-dried decision of whether to green-light or set aside a deal. Whereas investors often lack clarity in their motivations, funds themselves do not have the luxury of ambiguity—which makes their work especially illustrative of what it takes, day in and day out, to activate a very distilled form of Collaborative Capitalism. Moreover, funds naturally link intentionality and accountability: they first lay out an ITC—that is, a map of their intentions—that attracts investors; they then commit, through binding partnership agreements and side letters, to seeking goals that are measureable and will be reported in a very prescribed fashion—their accountabilities.

In our research initiative, we were searching for nuggets of insight into the way the twelve funds weave together intention and accountability. What we found were four distinct approaches to Mission First and Last, or mission lock.

Structural. Mission is locked into the DNA of the fund through an external designation, registration, or special-purpose corporate form. The performance of a fund is assumed to be consistent with this structure. Accountability is by design.

Strategic. Mission is embedded in an investment strategy that targets certain enterprises or populations, often with defined attributes, that are generally understood to have embedded impacts, lessening the depth of required accountability.

Investor driven. These funds are created in close collaboration with LPs, for whom the fund is meeting a very specific mission objective. Demonstrating impact against this objective is an important element of accountability.

Thematic. Mission is embedded in an investment strategy targeted to sectors with the potential for social or environmental impact, though the sector may include other nonimpact investments. Accountability relates to demonstrating that investments within these sectors have been impactful.

Let's look at each of these approaches in more detail.

Structural

Some funds embed their mission through structure—literally a legal construct or some other binding form of third-party commitment that standardizes, to some degree, the type of impact desired. This might include being registered as a philanthropic foundation or public charity, where fidelity to mission is paramount in investment programs that are established explicitly to invest for financial and social outcomes. Another approach is to earn designation as a community finance institution or some other special-purpose entity created or certified by the government (such as a CDFI or an SBIC in the United States). A fund could also provide a registered security required to invest in a very specific, impactful fashion. Four of our funds met these criteria: the W.K. Kellogg Foundation (WKKF), RSF Social Finance, ACCIÓN Texas Inc. (ATI), and Calvert Foundation.

The "structural" approach to Mission First and Last is the purest demonstration of what we call mission lock. Investors in these funds are confident that they are making an impact investment because the fund has agreed to adhere to some generally recognized standards of impact. The performance of a fund is assumed to be consistent with this structural requirement, which may include reporting standards. Because their accountability must be aligned to the standard requirements of the form, these funds have less motivation to define and implement their own accountability systems.

WKKF is an independent, private foundation operating under a clear mission: to support children, families, and communities by creating conditions that propel vulnerable children to achieve success as individuals and as contributors to the larger community and society. Investments that do not explicitly meet this mission are not even considered for investment by the foundation's Mission Driven Investments (MDI) program, the subject of our case study. MDI's primary accountabilities are external, to the IRS (adhering to guidelines for endowment investing by private foundations), and internal, to an investment committee and board of trustees. Nonetheless, the internal tracking that MDI does is innovative, focused on determining the proportion of a company's impact for which WKKF's investment is responsible.

ATI is registered as a CDFI with the US Department of Treasury's CDFI Fund. CDFIs are required to have community development as a primary mission and provide 60 percent of their financial services in low- to moderate-income areas. As a result, CDFIs collect critical information about the income levels of their borrowers. Moreover, investments in CDFIs automatically provide other US investors with "credit" for making impactful investments under the terms of related legislation.

Calvert Foundation's Community Investment Note is a security available in nearly all fifty US states. CIN's prospectus describes in detail the investments that Calvert Foundation, a nonprofit organization, is permitted to make. As discussed earlier, Calvert Foundation also collects social and environmental performance data from each of its portfolio partners annually, using a custom social performance measurement report template that incorporates industry-aligned metrics and best practices, based on IRIS, GIIRS, the CDFI Assessment and Ratings System (CARS), and metrics from the US Department of Housing and Urban Development. Calvert Foundation has been a powerful influencer in promoting the use of third-party standards.

Strategic

Funds categorized as "strategic" address Mission First and Last primarily through their stated investment strategy. However, although sectors of interest are a priority for these funds, they also target a very particular type of organization that is viewed by investors and the funds as inherently impactful (for example, SMEs in rural areas or social enterprises).

In practice, this means the accountability of funds with a strategic approach is similar to those funds we categorize as having a structural approach: any investment they make is assumed to be impactful, as long as it is consistent with their stated investment strategy. Although funds report primarily on outputs rather than outcomes as a social metric, it is important to note that this does not reflect a diminished commitment to impact, or a lessening of the rigor with which they track nonfinancial performance. On the contrary, all the funds we studied thought deeply about the change they were making through investment. A strategic form of Mission First and Last merely reflects a different approach to accountability focused on outputs.

The funds we place in the strategic category are Aavishkaar, Business Partners Limited, and Elevar Equity.

Aavishkaar focused on the extremely difficult challenge of making venture-capital investments in SMEs in rural India from the outset—an unheard of proposition at the time. For this reason, and especially during Aavishkaar's early years, there was relatively limited scrutiny of the impact of Aavishkaar's portfolio companies, which was considered self-evident. As a result, Aavishkaar was not required by investors to report as extensively on impact as some of the other funds in our study. Through 2012, Aavishkaar's first fund used a range of metrics to assess the fund's nonfinancial performance, which were determined jointly by the team and its investees to be the closest proxies to the positive social and environmental outcomes generated by each portfolio company. Examples include the amount of abated CO_2 emissions, and increased access to health care, drinking water, financial services, and education.

However, as the nascent impact investing industry that is focused on rural India has grown substantially over the life of Aavishkaar's first fund, the firm is now taking a leadership role in the development of increasingly sophisticated impact assessment tools for fund managers. In October 2013, the firm announced the launch of a tool named Prabhav, which was developed because Aavishkaar and Intellecap senior managers believed that fund-level impact reporting should track not only the nonfinancial performance of investee companies but also the approach taken by fund managers to achieve this impact. The tool analyzes this second component of fund impact by assessing the risks undertaken by impact funds, based on the location of investments, stage of investments, and financial instruments utilized. Whereas Aavishkaar's early impact assessments included "snapshots" of companies' social outputs, Prabhav now measures social outputs and outcomes generated by investees in terms of the change between pre- and post-investment.

Investor Driven

One of the six "dynamics" we were eager to explore in our research, and that we mentioned in chapter 2, is what we called the "active investor," noting that limited partners (LPs) in the private markets in which most impact investors operate were playing an especially and increasingly active role in impact investing relative to conventional markets.

Funds that embed and are accountable to their mission through an "investor-driven" practice grow out of this dynamic. They are conceived of to meet the very specific, strategic objectives of investors, and created in close collaboration with those very same institutions. We also described some of these funds as "Solution Specialists" in chapter 2.

There is one fund in our study which met that definition squarely: SEAF's Sichuan SME Investment Fund (SSIF). In early 2000, the International Finance Corporation (IFC) approached SEAF with a novel proposition: with the IFC's support, would SEAF be interested in launching a fund in the Sichuan Province of West China? Despite China's strong economic growth, the region was highly underdeveloped, with income disparities five times as large as those in East China. At that time, no private equity or risk capital providers were in Sichuan—or any part of China, outside of its major cities; bank lending was the only formal source of capital for SMEs. The central Chinese government was acutely aware of this growing economic inequity, SEAF learned, and it was the government's desire to incentivize the growth of underdeveloped provinces that was the driving force behind the IFC's request and, ultimately, the formation of the fund.

SEAF prepared environmental and social impact reports on potential investees and tracked several social metrics during the life of the fund. Examples of these metrics include average annual rates of portfolio company employment and wage growth, the percentage of new jobs going to unskilled and semiskilled workers, and the percentage of employees receiving health and pension benefits—a robust approach consistent with the need to measure the extent to which the fund's investments were aligned with SEAF's, LPs', and the government's development objectives.

Accountability is complicated in the investor-driven approach to Mission First and Last. Funds are answerable to the purpose of their creation, which may require anything from a more narrative and strategic form of impact reporting, to the disclosure of detailed impact metrics. In any case, reporting is likely to be relatively rigorous. To be sure, even if investors do not demand robust impact tracking and reporting, investor-driven funds are incentivized to provide a level of detail sufficient to broaden their appeal beyond a limited group of LPs.

Thematic

The "thematic" approach to addressing Mission First and Last is grounded less in the origins or institutional characteristics of funds (as is the case with structural and investor-driven practices) and more directly in a fund's stated investment strategy, similar to strategic funds. This approach is embodied in a fund's legal under-pinnings (including offer documents, side letters with investors, and partnership agreements) and, of course, in its deployment.

Specifically, these funds (including from Bridges Ventures, Deutsche Bank, Huntington Capital, and MicroVest) are explicitly and intentionally committed to an investment strategy that is, quite literally, thematic: focused on a particular place, market sector, or industry that has the potential to deliver embedded social or environmental outcomes, alongside financial returns. What mat-ters most in signaling alignment with the social objectives of prospective investors is the inherent impact within the targeted sector (for example, education or health). Yet it remains to be proven that the enterprises in which the fund invests are delivering the social or environmental benefits that have been promised. Therefore, strong accountabilities and a rigorous process for tracking and reporting impact are characteristics of funds that address Mission First and Last using a thematic approach.

Bridges Ventures' Sustainable Growth Funds I and II self-identify as taking a thematic approach, providing growth capital for SMEs that create impact either through the products they sell within certain sectors (health and well-being, education and skills, or the environment) or the economic growth they generate in underserved areas (80 percent of investments are located in the most deprived 25 percent of the United Kingdom, with over a third in the most deprived 10 percent). They focus closely on a cluster of issue areas where a social or environmental need creates a com-mercial growth opportunity for market-rate or market-beating returns, insisting that each investment must demonstrate that its mission is "in lockstep" with growth. In addition to its IMPACT Scorecard, which is applied across all its funds, Bridges Ventures has professional staff dedicated to sharing best practices around integrating impact throughout the investment cycle (from invest-ment selection, to engagement, to tracking and reporting).

■   ■   ■

It is important to recognize the four categories we've discussed in this chapter, together with those that relate to our other three key practices in coming chapters, have been constructed primarily as analytical devices. They are not exhaustive by any measure, and certainly not mutually exclusive.

In truth, the balance between intentionality and accountability is often very fluid in response to the evolving needs of investors, even when a core concept of mission is unwavering, as the example of SJF Ventures, a double-bottom-line private equity fund in North Carolina, illustrates.

At first, SJF was focused on sustainability, defined primarily as recycling companies. However, the fund could not find enough investable deal flow. SJF leaders realized they needed a broader conception of their mission as focusing on "sustainable jobs," blending environmental goals relating to a company's product, and social goals relating to workforce and employment practices. The reconfiguration provided them with enough room to focus on deal flow and to begin to track outputs effectively, and it helped SJF raise a first fund. Although the flavor of the fund's branding has changed along with its institutional partners—Fund I was a registered CDFI; Fund II was also a CDFI, but dropped the word "social" from all branding; and Fund III became a registered "impact investing fund" under a program of the US Small Business Administration instead—the underlying intentionality has been strong and consistent, enabling SJF to maintain mission and accountability across all three funds. The core of SJF's intentionality is an engaged workforce in businesses that help the environment. This has been a difficult dual mission to brand and articulate over time; however, in 2014, after ten years, SJF's annual impact reports show metrics that have been tracked consistently over that period, and the results speak for themselves. After thirty-six investments across all three funds, SJF portfolio companies employ more than 8,310 individuals, with 80 percent of these jobs created after SJF investment. More than 81 percent of SJF I and II portfolio company jobs are characterized as green jobs, and 75 percent of employees from the companies surveyed were low to moderate income. During 2012, the average portfolio company entry-level wage was $17. For permanent non-management employees, median average hourly wages of full-time and part-time employees were $34 and $18 respectively.[13]

SJF has also been able to track mission alignment through portfolio company exits. When Ryla Teleservices, a minority-owned call-center company based in rural Pennsylvania, sold to Alorica in California and kept all its employee practices in place as a competitive advantage compared to offshore call centers, it proved out SJF's ITC to investors, including banks, foundations, and individuals—namely, that there is a material connection between social and financial performance. SJF believes that its clearly defined and actionable mission had made its accountability to investors easier, not harder.

The Mission First and Last Tool Kit

We have described some very specific actions of successful funds that bring clarity to the complexity of impact investing. And although these funds may have been created with a more inherently collaborative set of "genes" than other funds, these genes only mutate into organizational DNA—and create the conditions for success—over time. The specific practices are discernible, in other words, and can be learned.

In this section, we describe a set of tools that funds—and all businesses, for that matter—can use to lock in mission for Collaborative Capitalism, focusing on four steps:

1. **Gaining clarity.** Use the ITC as an anchor for understanding, internalizing, and communicating precisely the value you propose to add.
2. **Aligning internally.** The way you structure, govern, and manage your fund speaks volumes to mission.
3. **Aligning externally with investors and other stakeholders.** Tune in to the motivations of investors, and the needs of a broader set of stakeholders, including your investees, the markets you operate in, and your users or customers.
4. **Tracking and reporting impact.** Tap a range of resources to develop robust accountabilities.

Let's explore each of these in turn.

Gaining Clarity

The general idea in gaining clarity is to think hard about how, precisely, your investment is making an impact, compared to others. This analysis can be grounded in any number of methods, including, for example, extensive research, internal reflection, and engagement with peers.

The ITC is designed to intuitively articulate and present your mission to a range of stakeholders, essentially providing a vision and platform for soliciting broad engagement and buy-in.

As noted earlier, the ITC includes six elements, each of which is discussed briefly here:

1. The "change," or social outcome, being pursued (that is, the overarching fund objectives and intentions). What is it you are ultimately trying to achieve? What is it you intend to create that is different from the current state of affairs?
2. The source of capital for pursuing that change (for example, some funds, such as Acumen, use charitable contributions; most solicit debt or equity investments from individuals and institutions). What is the capital structure of the fund? Do you use diverse types of capital (grants with debt or "stacking" of various types of capital provided by investors seeking various types of returns)?
3. The fund's investment approach (by financial instrument, size of deployments, and so on). How does the fund intend to structure its own investments? Are there particular types of investment strategies and approaches you will use?
4. The fund's investment recipients (by type, size, sector, and so on). What stage of development will fund ventures attain? What is their profile?
5. The activities (outputs) of investment recipients made possible by the provision of capital (for example, hiring, purchasing from suppliers, delivering goods and services). What will the venture bring to market as a result of this investment? What is the set of outputs generated by virtue of the investment?
6. The outcomes these outputs will lead to, and how they will be measured. Outputs describe how many individuals are affected by any given strategy, whereas outcomes speak to how they will be affected. Outputs speak to the number of people served,

whereas outcomes speak to the number of lives changed—and *how* they are changed.

Aligning Internally

Internal alignment refers to the operational and ownership strategies which ensure that a fund's entire staff, board, and any other affiliated parties are on the same page and working collaboratively toward shared goals. There are some very concrete ways to do this—for example, with the governance of the fund or impact-based incentive schemes.

Bridges Ventures very intentionally designed a governance structure to better align its work with key, primarily charitable stakeholders. The funds was founded in 2002 by Sir Ronald Cohen along with Philip Newborough and Michele Giddens, who believed that market forces and entrepreneurship can be harnessed to do well by doing good. Currently Bridges is majority owned by its senior management team, with the nonprofit Bridges Ventures Charitable Trust holding a substantial minority ownership interest with control over any change to the firm's founding commitment to raise only funds with both financial and social goals. The Bridges Ventures team also donates 10 percent of their own profits to the trust's philanthropic activities, which are targeted at financial support for social issues that cannot be resolved by market-type investment capital.

Funds should think clearly about the messages that their particular governance strategy sends, and the incentives it creates. In a recent paper on impact-based incentives, the Global Impact Investing Network highlights the work of some impact investors in tying a portion of general partner (GP) compensation to social and environmental performance. According to GIIN, for example, Core Innovation, a venture capital firm focused on financial services for the underbanked in the United States, ties 100 percent of its GP bonus and 10 percent of fund management's carry fee of 20 percent (that is, 2 percent of the portfolio's profit) to impact.[14]

The following five questions point to some broad opportunities to strengthen mission alignment internally:

1. Does your governance structure include a mission perspective?
2. How strong and resilient are your internal feedback loops? Do they incorporate feedback from external stakeholders?

3. Are there concrete opportunities to embed mission in compensation strategies and through other operational policies and practices?
4. What resources do you commit to tracking and reporting impact? Does the effort feel cursory or foundational?
5. What learning resources are available to staff and other direct stakeholders—for example, through formal training, participation in field-building events, or peer groups?

Aligning Externally

External alignment refers to a fund's relationship with stakeholders not directly related to the management and operation of the fund. These stakeholders might include policymakers, investors, investees, beneficiaries and the communities in which they live and work.

Again, there are formal paths to strengthening external alignment, most obviously through the structure of term sheets. There are funds that build reporting requirements and expectations into term sheets; milestones around impact, at which time interest rates decrease; or even hurdles for specific outcomes.

Funds rated by GIIRS use a variety of methods to build external alignment, including putting mission language into their placement memoranda or side letters, defining their mission intention publicly with all stakeholders, and working to ensure mission friendly exits. In fact, using a third-party standard and being public about the results can also be an external alignment strategy, as it may protect the company from some stakeholders wanting the company to change its impact practices affecting other stakeholders.

Here are another five questions to help diagnose your performance:

1. Are you familiar with what others are doing? Which funds are at the top of their game on alignment, and what does best practice look like? Is anything missing from your ITC that peers are incorporating into their own?
2. Is there external buy-in for your internal practices and policies? Have you tested the market or socialized ideas on alignment with key constituencies?

3. Have investors rallied around a relatively targeted set of social performance indicators that are consistent with your ITC? If not, it may be advisable to wrestle with investors on a more consolidated set of metrics, which will provide a deep insight into the motivations of LPs and force an important conversation on alignment.

4. Do investees clearly understand your mission, and vice versa? Are you supporting the mission-oriented needs of investees, and do you report to your investors and other key constituencies not just on fund *performance*—that is, social outcomes—but on the fund *process* of engaging externally?

5. Do you actively engage in field building and work with peers on issues related to alignment?

Tracking and Reporting Impact

Rigorous but efficient and value-added performance measurement in impact investing is a must, both as a tracking mechanism and as a tool to strengthen asset management strategies and operational practices.

In 2013, GIIN reaffirmed that the core characteristics of impact investing include intentionality, investment with return expectations across a range of asset classes, and impact measurement. It also laid down some markers, asserting that quality impact evaluation must include clearly established and stated social and environmental objectives; performance metrics and targets related to these objectives, using standardized metrics wherever possible; monitoring and management of the performance of investees against these targets; and reporting on social and environmental performance to relevant stakeholders.[15]

These are process standards, of course—and ought to be. In terms of the specifics—that is, which metrics to track and which evaluation methods to use—the possibilities are extensive, ranging from relatively standardized approaches, through to highly customized strategies. The following resources should be of use in deciding how to track impact. For some highly accessible insights into the subject:

- Bridges Ventures' *Shifting the Lens* report usefully contextualizes impact evaluation as one of an important group of activities that de-risk impact investments.[16]

- Root Capital's *A Roadmap for Impact* report is a prime example of reporting by a significant impact investor.[17]
- An excellent 2013 article by Ted Jackson in the *Journal of Sustainable Finance and Investment,* "Interrogating the Theory of Change: Evaluating Impact Investing Where It Matters Most," highlights a range of fund and institutional best practices in tracking impact.[18]
- The *Toniic eGuide to Early Stage Global Impact Investing* and *The Toniic eGuide to Impact Assessment* both include discussions on how to build effective impact tracking into your investments.[19]
- The Aspen Network of Development Entrepreneurs (ANDE) report, *The State of Measurement Practice in the SGB Sector,* provides an excellent overview of the current state of affairs in tracking and reporting impact for those investors focused on capitalizing the growth of SMEs in emerging markets.[20]
- The "Getting Started with IRIS [Impact Reporting and Investment Standards]" guide is arguably the most useful read for any funds considering tracking social and environmental outcomes for the first time.[21]

4

Symbiosis as Strategy

SEAF's Sichuan SME Investment Fund (SSIF) shows the value of bringing an equity finance model to frontier markets. Not only does this approach bring much-needed patient capital for SMEs, but it serves as a powerful demonstration effect for local governments, local financial institutions, and local entrepreneurs. They see firsthand the benefits of an equity partnership model based on an equation that is not simply about repayment of a loan but about growth of the enterprise—growth that allows the SME to scale up, gain efficiency, become more profitable, and create social impact through jobs and community benefits.

—Mildred Callear, Small Enterprise Assistance
Funds (SEAF)

In 2000, a small but influential group of private sector and civil society leaders came together in the United Kingdom as the Social Investment Task Force. Convened under the auspices of the Social Investment Forum, an independent association with more than 250 members (now known as the Sustainable Investment and Finance Association), the goal of the task force was to understand how "entrepreneurial practices could be applied to obtain higher social and financial returns from social investment, to harness new talents and skills, to address economic regeneration and to unleash new sources of private and institutional investment."[1] The seven-member task force comprised a number of social entrepreneurs, experts in philanthropy, the former editor of a prominent magazine (*New Statesman*), a community banker from the United States, and, as chairman, one of Britain's most revered venture capitalists, Sir Ronald Cohen.

Seeing an opportunity to advance the UK government's own agenda through the work of the task force, the UK Treasury endorsed the task force as a formal "observer" and charged it with making an "urgent but considered assessment of ways in which the UK could achieve a radical improvement in its capacity to create wealth, economic growth, employment and an improved social fabric."[2]

A number of recommendations emerged from the task force's seminal 2000 report, *Enterprising Communities: Wealth Beyond Welfare*, including a discussion of the need in the United Kingdom for what the task force called community development venture (CDV) funds—entities providing long-term equity investment and business support to entrepreneurs, much like traditional venture capital funds, but in lower-income communities. CDV funds had been experiencing a period of rapid growth in the United States (where they are referred to as community development venture capital funds, or CDVCs), and the United Kingdom was eager to emulate this experience.[3]

Due to the British government's involvement in the process— demonstrating precisely the sort of symbiotic relationship we explore in this chapter—policymakers were primed to receive the recommendations from the task force and acted quickly in response. The UK government provided the first half of capital for a £40 million CDV fund created by a new intermediary, Bridges Ventures, with the goal of directing capital to businesses in the most deprived 25 percent of England. In effect, the UK government had made possible the creation of Bridges Ventures, now one of the world's largest impact investors, with £400 million under management.

The Practice of Policy Symbiosis

Knowing government has a significant stake in the success of impact investing and, more broadly, in the types of markets in which impact investors operate (markets often characterized by failure or particularly notable negative or positive externalities), we expected to find some direct public sector interest in the twelve funds in our study—and perhaps a few outliers as especially significant beneficiaries of public policy. Instead, we discovered the influence of government is far more prevalent; in fact, fully eight of the twelve funds had been direct *recipients* of public sector investment, whether through grants, equity, loans, or guarantees.

What this indicated was two things. First, governments have recognized that beyond redressing specific market failures, the *mechanism* itself—impact investing—has an inherent value and potential for scaling social innovation, not least through the business models, relationships, and networks that impact investors are pioneering. Second, in contrast to much of the rhetoric regarding impact investing being a market-based, free-enterprise strategy, the role of government in creating the right enabling environment and supports has been significant, as is true in traditional business and investing. The public sector does not drive outcomes or determine winners, but it has certainly been critical to the rational development of the impact investing industry.

The approach of government has also been notable. Rather than simply being a service that is commissioned by public agencies in a one-dimensional "client-and-vendor" relationship, government clearly sees the potential for learning in impact investing and the opportunity to pioneer new, proactive forms of social value creation.

This is what we mean by "symbiosis as strategy"—the chicken-and-egg interplay between the public and private sectors, anchored in growing relationships of trust and mutual interest. Impact investors and policymakers increasingly realize they share common goals and each has something powerful to contribute in achieving these goals. Governments are recognizing that social enterprises, in particular, offer sustainable and effective solutions to social and environmental problems; investment practitioners are becoming more aware of the opportunities to engage with policymakers, and the risks of not doing so. From the perspective of funds, it is clear that impact investing is in fact a form of cross-sector partnership, with public officials among the key actors, and that what we call "Policy Symbiosis" is a core element of success in impact investing.

As Matt Bannick and Paula Goldman write in the Omidyar Network report *Priming the Pump*:

> Impact investors cannot afford to ignore critical political
> considerations. Enlightened politicians and policymakers

have the potential to dramatically speed up the rate at which an industry can scale to responsibly serve hundreds of millions. Conversely, when impact investors fail to align with policymakers, we will find ourselves at risk of double jeopardy. We can fail because the companies we invest in may have a hard time growing in the most challenging of markets. Or we can fail because these same companies may eventually be seen as too successful and profitable—inviting a powerful and potentially destructive backlash from public opinion, threatened incumbent commercial interests and/or politicians.[4]

Public Sector Innovation in Alignment with the Private Sector

By their nature, impact investors represent a marriage of public and private interests. They combine a commitment to improving public welfare with the power and efficiency of capital markets. Policymakers—who have a vested interest in maximizing the social and environmental well-being of their constituencies and hold massive power to influence the market through laws, regulations, and resources—are natural partners for impact investors.

Although our understanding of the appropriate role for government in capital markets falls too easily into one of two camps (either with the private sector in the lead and ultimately winning the endorsement of government, or with the government setting rules behind which private actors fall into line), Policy Symbiosis is in neither. Instead, Policy Symbiosis is the innovative attempt to appropriately bridge private and public sector approaches.

In this context, innovation is key. Bridges Ventures was not created through cumbersome procurement processes or formal legislation, for example, although these have their uses even in impact investing, but rather through the entrepreneurial and symbiotic act of recognizing a clear market failure and capitalizing on a fresh solution in the offing, balancing the public sector's own risks with those of its coinvestors.

Cocreation of funds and coinvestment by government do not guarantee programmatic success by any measure. Had Bridges Ventures not delivered, history might have judged the UK government's gamble as another failed attempt to pick winners. And critics argue that direct government investments often crowd out the private market.

However, the evidence shows instead that as a prime example of Collaborative Capitalism and Policy Symbiosis, early interventions in impact investing have succeeded in powerfully aligning incentives and in crowding *in* private investors, who bring all of their smarts and relationships to the table to ensure that their capital is deployed wisely and that a new model of economic development is proven to be effective.

Government support for Bridges Ventures attracted three of the United Kingdom's most prominent private equity firms: Apax Partners, 3i, and Doughty Hanson. The UK government certainly was taking both financial and political risks in investing in Bridges Ventures, but the unprecedented depth of the public-private sector collaboration mitigated these.

The Public Case for Impact Investing

In the broadest sense, beyond simply the various symbiotic roles for government described in more detail in this chapter, public officials see in impact investing an opportunity to maximize the delivery of social and environmental benefits to society, at a time when government has fewer resources to address social problems that are more complex and entrenched than ever.

This is not a pipe dream. On the contrary, the expectation that impact investing presents one of the most important new tools for amplifying the social outcomes of public resources is completely consistent with the track record of the "first responders" with the longest histories of engaging with government, among them the more than eight hundred community development financial institutions (CDFIs) in the United States.

CDFIs were created in the United States specifically as a rejection of failed, one-size-fits-all approaches to community development and as an outgrowth instead of new alliances among the public, private, and nonprofit sectors—in other words, Collaborative Capitalism.

Reflecting on this history in 2009, then chairman of the US Federal Reserve, Ben Bernanke, described how the CDFI Fund, an arm of the US Department of the Treasury that certifies and subsidizes CDFIs, had attracted $15 in nonfederal investments to CDFIs for every $1 it had invested.[5] The community development finance sector in the United States would not exist without policies driving private capital to it, creating intermediary infrastructure, and ensuring that impactful investments make financial sense through tax credits and other incentives. However, this take on the market—as a highly subsidized client of the state—vastly understates the impact of the true Policy Symbiosis at hand.

While many of those within mainstream finance may believe the contrary, CDFIs are, in a very real sense, nothing less than an essential part of the fabric of US financial services—providing a benefit to society that goes far beyond the specific products underwritten by government. Bernanke's comments in 2009 clarified the extent to which the government was counting on CDFIs at the height of the Great Recession:

> While community development finance is a small part of our overall capital and credit markets, the Federal Reserve recognizes that these financial flows are critically important for many low- and moderate-income communities . . . The current crisis points to the importance of a strong network of healthy community-based organizations and lenders. As many communities struggle with rising unemployment, high rates of foreclosures, and vacant homes and stores, these organizations lead efforts to stabilize their neighborhoods. Rather than pulling back, CDFIs are introducing new products and programs to help communities respond to the crisis. For instance, a number of groups are purchasing homes, which might otherwise sit vacant, from loan servicers who take possession of foreclosed properties. These homes are repaired and then sold or rented to families. Because foreclosures and resulting vacancies impose costs on neighborhoods and local governments, facilitating occupancy can help maintain neighborhood stability . . . Indeed, this community stabilization work is important for the overall economic recovery. Healthy and vibrant neighborhoods are a source of economic growth and social stability.[6]

More recently, the new chair of the Federal Reserve, Janet Yellen, chose the 2014 National Interagency Community Reinvestment Conference for her first public address, commenting that the Fed supports the work of community finance institutions because they "make a difference": "You help ensure that credit is available for families to buy homes and for small businesses to expand. Your organizations sponsor programs that help make communities safer and families healthier and more financially secure. One of the most important things you do is to help people meet the demands of finding a job in what remains a challenging economy."[7]

Yellen also highlighted a number of important recent research initiatives led by divisions of the Federal Reserve System, including the following:

- Investing in What Works for America's Communities, a partnership between the Federal Reserve Bank of San Francisco and Low Income Investment Fund (LIIF), a CDFI, which showcased innovative, effective, and collaborative community development initiatives across the United States. The effort advocated for a "Community Quarterback" model to coordinate initiatives and better leverage funding among groups with similar goals.[8]
- The Federal Reserve Bank of Boston's Working Cities Challenge, focused on cities striving to diversify away from a declining, manufacturing-based economy, in part through "collaborative leadership," whereby governments, businesses, and nonprofits unite behind one focused approach.[9]

In 2013, CDFIs originated more than 24,285 loans totaling $2 billion, including over 8,000 small business loans and financing for nearly 18,000 affordable housing units. Those loans helped create an estimated 35,000 jobs. In addition, CDFIs also provided about 294,000 individuals with financial literacy or training that year.[10] According to Opportunity Finance Network, in 2011 CDFI customers were 52 percent racial minorities, 49 percent female, and 68 percent low-income.[11] In recent years, the CDFI Fund has enjoyed bipartisan support, as has the New Markets Tax Credit for investments in low-income communities, which the CDFI Fund administers.

It is this same innovative spirit—born from a realization that established methods for addressing entrenched social challenges are no longer sufficient—that has driven heightened interest in impact investing from dozens of governments in recent years, most recently through the G7 (formerly the G8) process. Under the United Kingdom's presidency of the G8 in 2013, a dedicated Social Impact Investment Taskforce was created and chaired by Sir Ronald Cohen, who personifies Policy Symbiosis. On June 6, 2013, in London, at a special G8 meeting on impact investing, UK prime minister David Cameron emphasized his administration's collaborative approach, focusing particularly on public procurement from social enterprise as a powerful guarantee for investors:

> We've got a great idea here that can transform our societies, by using the power of finance to tackle the most difficult social problems. Problems that have frustrated government after government, country after country, generation after generation. Issues like drug abuse, youth unemployment, homelessness and even global poverty. The potential for social investment is that big . . .
>
> So how does it work? Businesses need finance to grow and make profit. Governments need finance to fund big infrastructure projects. That's why we have banks, bonds, investment markets and all the rest. The idea here is just as simple and just as powerful. Social enterprises, charities and voluntary bodies have the knowledge, human touch and personal commitment to succeed where governments often fail. But they need finance too. They can get it from socially minded investors. So we need social investment markets, social investment bonds and social investment banks. And here government needs to help. Government needs to be more creative and innovative— saying to social entrepreneurs: "if you can solve the problem we'll give you money." As soon as government says that, social entrepreneurs can go out and raise capital.[12]

Interest at the highest levels of government will undoubtedly create a more enabling environment for impact investing in years to come. In the meantime, funds are busy raising and deploying capital day in and day out, and partnering with government in very practical ways.

The twelve funds in our study demonstrated Policy Symbiosis— utilizing, benefiting from, and influencing public policy at the investee, market, and field levels—in a variety of forms: foundational, financial, regulatory, advocacy driven, and opportunistic.

The Forms of Policy Symbiosis

Foundational: The origins of the fund or firm are deeply rooted in a partnership with government, above and beyond the provision of any financial or other assistance.

Financial: Government entities are direct investors in the fund.

Regulatory: Government regulations directly and heavily influence the structure, operations, and investments in and of the fund.

Advocacy driven: The fund works directly with government to shape the broader, systemic policy environment in which it and its investees operate.

Opportunistic: The fund makes a dedicated effort to identify and leverage the discrete, nonsystemic opportunities for government to support the success of portfolio companies, as do many traditional investors.

Foundational

In 1981, father and son Anton and Johann Rupert, from one of the wealthiest families in South Africa (Johann is the current CEO of Richemont, the luxury goods company that his father Anton [now deceased] founded, with brands including Cartier and Montblanc), approached the national government and other large South African corporations regarding the creation of the Small Business Development Corporation, now called Business Partners Limited (BPL). After several months of negotiation, the government agreed to join the endeavor as a cofounder, matching what the corporations and the Rupert family collectively contributed and providing 50 percent of the funding to launch BPL as a debt fund. The government's contribution to BPL's lending capital took the form of quasi-guaranteed fees that allowed the firm to support businesses with the highest prospects for creating social and economic impacts: microenterprises and riskier start-up companies.

The South African government maintained a 50 percent ownership position in BPL for fifteen years. In 1996, in an effort to narrow its target market and begin offering equity and quasi equity, the firm returned all of the government's initial lending capital and reduced its equity share to 21 percent. Although its stake in the firm has been significantly reduced, the government had helped build the foundations that allowed BPL to grow and thrive in its impactful market niche: risk finance for underserved small and medium-sized enterprises (SMEs). BPL has deployed a total of $1.5 billion to more than 69,500 SMEs since inception, creating more than 550,000 jobs in the process.

BPL is illustrative of a foundational form of Policy Symbiosis in impact investing, where a fund is cocreated through a partnership that recognizes shared public and private sector objectives in delivering particular impacts. In these instances, governments may play a significant role in influencing the fund's initial and ongoing practices; bring attention to the market and attract additional investors; and contribute other public expertise, policy supports, and high-level relationships.

The Foundational Role of Development Finance Institutions

Sichuan, in the west of China, is one of that country's poorest provinces, identified by China's banking regulator as lacking even basic access to financial services as recently as 2009.[a] Sichuan was even more under-developed in early 2000, with income levels five times lower than in eastern China, where a majority of the country's economy and wealth is concentrated. There were certainly no formal private equity or risk capital providers.

Into this environment arrived the International Finance Corporation (IFC), the World Bank agency focused on development through private sector activity, at the behest of the central Chinese government, which was acutely aware of the growing inequity.

Before long, the IFC had partnered with another lead investor, New York Life Insurance (which was eager to demonstrate its support for economic activity in underdeveloped provinces while obtaining a license to sell insurance in China), and set about catalyzing the creation of a new fund for providing growth capital to SMEs, managed by Small Enterprise Assistance Funds (SEAF).

SEAF was the ideal partner. Since launching its first fund in Poland in 1992 with funding from the US Agency for International Development (USAID), the European Bank for Reconstruction and Development, and the Foundation for the Development of Agriculture, SEAF had become a specialist equity investor in formerly socialist countries seeking to transition from state-run to market-driven economies.

As a result of the IFC's explicit (and the Chinese government's implicit) support, SEAF went on in Sichuan to invest $16.9 million in nine companies in the manufacturing and food industries, supporting five thousand jobs and generating annual employment growth of 21 percent for its portfolio companies.

This was Policy Symbiosis at work. Without the IFC, SEAF's Sichuan Fund would not exist. And without SEAF and the other third-party investment funds like it, the IFC would have far fewer tools at its disposal.

Other development finance institutions like IFC also played a critical role supporting the creation of Deutsche Bank's Global Commercial Microfinance Consortium I. When Deutsche Bank was raising capital for the fund, among the first calls then managing director Asad Mahmood made were to the UK and US governments. This ultimately led to symbiotic support from the UK's Department for International Development (DFID) and USAID.

DFID's $1.5 million grant provided essential operating capital to the consortium. A $15 million guarantee from USAID provided the critical risk mitigation that enabled Deutsche Bank to secure more than $60 million of senior debt from commercial and fiduciary institutions. USAID's support not only reduced investment risks but also, as with all guarantees, allowed Deutsche Bank to offer noteholders an increased estimated risk-adjusted return. If all of the noteholders' $63.35 million were at risk, the return was expected to have been 6.6 percent. Because only $48.35 million was actually at risk, Deutsche Bank offered noteholders an estimated 16 percent risk-adjusted rate of return.

To be sure, the IFC, DFID, USAID, and other similar agencies have been designed by governments over the course of decades precisely to operate with the discretion needed to partner symbiotically with private investors. For example, the US government's development finance institution, the Overseas Private Investment Corporation (OPIC), is authorized to operate in 150 developing nations around the world, and invests alongside private institutions in projects across a range of industries, including energy, housing, agriculture, and financial services. It focuses its work on "regions where the need is greatest and in sectors that can have the greatest developmental impact."[b] OPIC made an explicit $333 million commitment to impact investing in 2012, issuing an RFP to the very funds, like SEAF, that OPIC counts on to realize the impact that US taxpayers are counting on.

Overall, OPIC has estimated that it made 129 impact investments—defined by the agency as investments with partners whose very business models aim to address social or environmental problems while generating sustainable financial returns—totaling $2.4 billion since 2008.[c]

[a] Tobin, D. (2011, June 29). "Inequality in China: Rural Poverty Persists as Urban Wealth Balloons." *BBC News.* http://www.bbc.co.uk/news/business-13945072.
[b] Overseas Private Investment Corporation (OPIC). (2014). "OPIC in Action." http://www.opic.gov/opic-action/overview.
[c] World Economic Forum Investors Industries. (2013, December). *From Ideas to Practice, Pilots to Strategy: Practical Solutions and Actionable Insights on How to Do Impact Investing.* http://www3.weforum.org/docs/WEF_II_SolutionsInsights_ImpactInvesting_Report_2013.pdf, 12.

In the case of Bridges Ventures, the UK government doubled down by also investing in the firm's Social Entrepreneurs Fund, which was launched in 2009 and is intended to scale innovative social enterprise models—such as social impact bonds—that cannot support commercial investment for now.

Perhaps it should come as no surprise that Bridges Ventures is such a notable example of foundational Policy Symbiosis. Business, finance, and political leaders can regularly gather in one location, London, creating a uniquely conducive environment for this deep form of partnership in impact investing, where a foundational approach to Policy Symbiosis necessitates long-standing professional connections and relationships.

In fact, some of the most notable global policy innovations have emerged out of London in recent years, where public officials— regardless of political persuasion—have worked since before the turn of the century to advance impact investing. Most prominent among these is Big Society Capital (BSC), a special-purpose "wholesaler" created in 2012 to invest in social investment intermediaries. BSC will grow to £600 million, including £400 million recovered from unclaimed bank deposits in the United Kingdom and £200 million from Britain's four largest retail banks, Barclays, HSBC, Lloyds Banking Group, and RBS. Sir Ronald Cohen was the chair of the Independent Commission on Unclaimed Assets, which recommended using money sitting untouched for more than fifteen years in dormant bank and building society accounts to fund the creation of the "social investment bank" that became BSC, and then became its founding chair.[13]

Another example in the United Kingdom is the Investment and Contract Readiness Fund (ICRF), a £10 million fund launched in 2012 to provide grant support enabling social ventures to secure new forms of investment and compete for public sector contracts. The fund's success has been made possible in part through the creation of an investor panel designed to review and approve applications for grant funding by applying investment criteria and perspectives to its decisions—a prime example of Collaborative Capitalism. As a 2013 World Economic Forum case study on the ICRF explains: "As investors, the panelists have a clear incentive to allocate grants only to the most promising of enterprises, by default ensuring that government funds are more efficiently deployed. Separately, the panelists have benefited significantly from exposure to the applications, gaining a unique insight into the pipeline of future investees in the UK social investment market, and from engagement with the expertise and perspectives of their peers."[14]

In the United States, the federal government has rarely played a foundational role in impact investing. The last time may have been in 1978, when Congress created the Neighborhood Reinvestment Corporation as a national loan-purchase resource for capitalizing local neighborhood housing services. Now known as NeighborWorks America, the organization is focused on providing grants, technical assistance, and training. For every $1 of appropriated federal funding, NeighborWorks leverages $34 in direct local investment.[15]

Although the direct role for government in the creation of NeighborWorks is unusual in the United States, the flavor of the organization's work is typical. Where government does engage in foundational Policy Symbiosis in the United States, it is almost always at the local level, leveraging deep, place-based institutional relationships that more closely resemble the networks that drive innovation in places like London. At a local level, targeted social outcomes are often clearer, as are the key stakeholders.

The community development organization Living Cities is prototypical of the more grassroots, private sector–oriented approach to impact investing in the United States—a partnership of twenty-two leading foundations and financial institutions, launched in 1991, dedicated to pooling a portion of their investments in low-income communities, with a focus on building institutional capacity in the housing and economic development sectors. Living Cities has catalyzed $1 billion of investment since inception, deployed primarily to help build housing, but also stores, schools, child-care options, and health care and job training centers, through two national CDFIs: LISC and Enterprise Community Partners.[16]

Living Cities considers government to be an equal partner nonetheless. The organization runs a program called the Project on Municipal Innovation, which educates public sector leaders on policy ideas that leverage collective action, including through a series of boot camps that bring key stakeholders together in particular places to address a critical issue facing their community.[17]

Living Cities is also part of a new wave of local impulse around impact investing in the United States, with government playing a collaborative role. The organization recently created an Integration Initiative in five cities—Baltimore, Cleveland, Detroit, Newark, and the Twin Cities (Minneapolis and St. Paul)—directing $85 million in grants, flexible debt, and commercial debt to revitalization initiatives connected to job creation for low-income individuals. The integration initiative includes the participation of policymakers as part of a "one table approach," based on the work of Ronald Heifitz, that seeks adaptive leadership for problems no single entity can solve alone and where legacy attitudes, priorities, and behaviors are part of the problem.[18]

Financial

MicroVest experienced a typically arduous, two-year period of capital raising for its first fund, which promised to provide equity and debt to microfinance institutions. In 2006, however, after the organization demonstrated the fund's viability by establishing an equity base of $15 million, the opportunity to test a new commercial approach to microfinance through MicroVest I was too good for government to resist. OPIC, the US government's DFI, jumped at the chance to invest $14 million in privately placed short-term notes and, together with other institutional investors, leveraged the fund to a total size of $48.5 million in September 2010.

Aavishkaar, in India, also welcomed a public sector investor late in the game after Vineet Rai, the firm's founder, came to realize that institutional capital was needed to achieve scale. Rai had raised about $1 million from eighty individuals and families from 2001 to 2005. The subsequent investment of the National Bank for Agriculture and Rural Development (NABARD), a financing entity connected to the Indian government, together with a number of philanthropic foundations, increased the fund's assets to $6 million by 2007.[19]

Fully eight of the twelve funds in our study received investment from government, either as an LP in the case of equity funds, as a lender on equal footing with private capital providers, or as the provider of "catalytic" grants, guarantees, or first-loss positions intended to de-risk the fund and attract the investment of others, as described in more detail in chapter 5.

Public Sector Investments in Eight Impact Investing Funds

- **Aavishkaar** raised the equivalent of more than $1.5 million from NABARD, India's national development bank.
- **ACCIÓN Texas Inc.** receives financial assistance from the US Department of the Treasury's CDFI Fund.
- **Bridges Ventures** was provided with a £20 million investment from the UK government, representing a one-to-one match for every pound raised for the £40 million Sustainable Growth Fund I.
- **Business Partners Limited** received half of its $24 million in initial capital from the South African government, matching the investments of a group of corporations.
- **Calvert Foundation** received a $999,000 grant from the US State Department for a diaspora initiative that uses Calvert Foundation's Community Investment Note to enable US diaspora members to invest in the development of their countries of origin or heritage and of US regions where their diaspora community is concentrated.
- **Deutsche Bank's Global Commercial Microfinance Consortium I** received a $1 million grant from the Department for International Development

(DFID) in the UK and a $15 million guarantee from the US Agency for International Development (USAID) in the United States.

- **MicroVest** sold more than $14 million in senior notes in MicroVest I to OPIC.
- **SEAF's SME Sichuan Investment Fund** raised more than $13.5 million in equity investments from four DFIs, namely DEG (Germany), Norfund (Norway), Swedfund (Sweden), and the IFC.

Government investments in the twelve funds arrived early in some cases and were more catalytic as a result, as was the case for Deutsche Bank, Bridges Ventures, SEAF, and BPL, when the public sector entity was directly involved in the fund's creation or seized on an opportunity to make innovation possible. For ACCIÓN Texas Inc., Aavishkaar, Calvert Foundation, and MicroVest, public support came later, following the fund's creation, when expanding and scaling the impact investing strategy were prime objectives.

The Power of Intermediaries

To be sure, coinvestment, as distinct from cocreation, is a common way for governments to engage in impact investing. By supporting intermediaries, governments are able to meet two imperatives: de-risking their direct involvement in the provision of social and environmental impacts by the private sector, and underwriting the essential infrastructure needed to build a market that thrives far beyond the governments' own engagement.

Investing in intermediaries—instead of directly in the enterprises to which the intermediaries ultimately deploy capital—ensures that the government is one step removed from the primary beneficiaries of public sector capital, and therefore protected from accusations of political interference.

The procurement of goods and services is generally shielded from similar accusations by stringent processes and a core focus on best value. And in the case of investments in impact investing intermediaries, similar conventions have emerged to ensure integrity and accountability, most notably through the creation of special-purpose institutions and programs that make these commitments in a prescribed and transparent fashion.

At the international level, these institutions include the previously described IFC, OPIC, and DFID; at the domestic level, they include Big Society Capital and other similar efforts, such as the US Small Business Investment Company program at the Small Business Administration (SBA), Australia's Social Enterprise Development and Investment Funds program, and Ghana's Venture Capital Trust Fund, all of which we describe in the next paragraphs. Many of these institutions have broader mandates related to economic development. However, what has united them in recent years has been a more intentional focus on creating measurable impacts.

In the United States, the SBA's Small Business Investment Company (SBIC) program, created in 1958, licenses and provides publicly guaranteed leverage to private investment funds for the purpose of capitalizing small businesses with up to five hundred employees or $21.5 million in revenues, depending on industry sector. The program currently oversees more than three hundred SBA-licensed funds with over $18 billion in capital—$9.4 billion from private investors and $8.8 billion from SBA leverage commitments.[20]

Although not explicitly an impact investing program per se, the SBIC program does have outcomes that are consistent with the practice, supporting intermediaries that are smaller (90 percent of SBICs have less than $60 million in private capital at licensing); relatively diverse (in 2012, 24 percent of SBIC applicants were women- or minority-managed); and investing outside of the more established US private equity markets in the West (California and Texas), Northeast, and Mid-Atlantic (around 45 percent of SBIC financings from 2008 to 2012 were in other areas). In an effort to more explicitly support impact investing, the SBA created a $1 billion carve-out for an SBIC "Impact Investment Initiative" in 2011, targeting underserved places and priority market sectors.[21]

Australia's Social Enterprise Development and Investment Funds (SEDIF) program was launched in 2010 out of the national government's Department of Education, Employment and Workplace Relations, and used a formal procurement process to support three funds with $20 million in grants, leveraging $20.6 million of private capital. The funds have two stated objectives: to improve access to finance and support for social enterprises to help them grow their business; and to catalyze the development of the broader impact investment market in Australia.[22]

In Ghana, the Venture Capital Trust Fund (VCTF) was created in 2004 to provide financial resources for the development and promotion of venture capital financing for SMEs in Ghana, and has invested $17 million in five funds. The five funds leveraged a total of more than $50 million for investment, adding the VCTF monies and private dollars. The VCTF was actively involved in developing the business plans and setting investment criteria for its initial investments, which provided a reference for subsequent applicants. In an effort to hone its understanding of and focus on impact investing, the VCTF received a $150,000 grant from the Rockefeller Foundation in 2012 to launch the Ghana Institute for Responsible Investment and comprehensively map the local market.[23]

The focus on intermediaries as a core element of impact investing infrastructure underpins almost all of the recent policy activity in the field internationally. The United Kingdom's Investment and Contract Readiness Fund (ICRF, mentioned earlier) is a prime example. The program is intended to directly build the capacity of social enterprises, but does this by requiring that the social enterprises channel most of their grant funding to twenty-eight intermediaries approved to supply advice to enterprises and apply jointly for ICRF funding.[24]

A New Era of Public Innovation

The role of governments in supporting impact investing should not be interpreted as static. On the contrary, the enthusiasm for public innovation and experimentation in impact investing is unprecedented. Consider the examples of two programs at the US government's aid agency, USAID: Development Innovation Ventures (DIV), which was recently scaled up in partnership with DFID in the United Kingdom, and the Development Credit Authority.

DIV is a quarterly grant competition for innovative private sector solutions to development. It provides more than $20 million annually, of which 59 percent has been at so-called Stage 1, or proof of concept, with an average investment of $119,000; 40 percent has been at Stage 2, or testing at scale, with an average investment of $700,000; and 1 percent at Stage 3, or widespread implementation, with an average investment of $5.5 million.

Most of the DIV funding (62 percent) has been provided to coalitions with more than three partners. Of these coalitions, 63 percent have contained at least one NGO, 40 percent include a social enterprise, 35 percent include an evaluator or academic, 26 percent include a for-profit firm (other than a social enterprise), and 17 percent include local government.

The power in the diversity of methods is clear—both in delivering social outcomes on the ground and in USAID's approach. The agency has received 3,727 requests for DIV funding since October 2010, from a pool of applicants of which 70 percent are new to USAID, laying the foundation for a whole new generation of relationships.[25]

The Development Credit Authority (DCA), which has provided guarantees to more than four hundred local banks since 1999, has made over $3 billion in private financing available to more than 139,000 entrepreneurs. However, of this amount, fully $1 billion was invested in 2012 and 2013 alone. As USAID administrator Rajiv Shah explained in late 2013: "It took us 11 years to open the first $2 billion under DCA, and only two years to reach the next billion. That reflects a fundamental difference in the way we're working."[26]

Regulatory

Government's role as a regulator is especially pronounced in markets characterized by failure or the presence of significant negative or positive externalities. These are the same markets in which impact investing thrives, expertly blending different types of concessionary and commercial capital, different investor preferences for financial and social value, and different types of knowledge and relationships, all in an effort to discover, sustain, or scale the markets where mainstream investors are underrepresented or altogether absent.

Working within, and to influence, the regulatory environment is therefore a key element in impact investing. Regulation does not create impact investing funds, but it does provide the critical conditions in which they may flourish. This is a more indirect form of Policy Symbiosis—one step removed from an entity-level foundational or investment relationship—but is "symbiotic" nonetheless, representing a multidimensional exchange of ideas and influence.

By way of example, as is true of many CDFIs, ACCIÓN Texas Inc. (ATI), the nonprofit microlender based in San Antonio, is in many ways a product more of regulation than of the direct investment of government. First, ATI receives the majority of its lending capital from local banks. This investment is driven by the Community Reinvestment Act (CRA), which requires banks to invest some of their assets in underserved communities. Second, ATI is certified as a CDFI by the CDFI Fund within the US Department of the Treasury, meaning that bank investments automatically qualify for CRA "credit" and that ATI can apply for grant funding from the CDFI Fund. Third, ATI has diversified its revenue by becoming an SBA "504 loan" servicer. ATI became an SBA Certified Development Company in 2008–2009 and, as such, an official approver of SBA 504 loans, which guarantee a portion of loans to small businesses, usually to purchase the buildings they occupy.[27] Although not a lender in this program (the typical structure is that a bank provides about 50 percent and has the first lien, the SBA guarantees 40 percent as a debenture, and the borrower puts up 10 percent), ATI services the loan for a price. It also receives a portion of the 1.5 percent fee paid by the borrower for the deal, and can receive compensation for packaging and processing.

ATI works hard to influence policy. CEO Janie Barrera serves as a local representative on the Federal Reserve Board's National Consumer Advisory Council. On a national level, in 2010, she was appointed to the President's Advisory Council on Financial Capability, contributing to the development of methods to improve financial literacy among the nation's poor and proposing new financial products and services that serve low-income communities.

What does all this regulatory symbiosis do for ATI? The most obvious answer is that it provides financial sustainability. Equally important, however, is the role of regulation in driving transparency, constituent alignment, and an outcomes orientation—all of the key tenets of Collaborative Capitalism. Regulations are designed to achieve measureable outcomes, by leveraging key stakeholders that are known, and clear flows of capital. The mission lock inherent in the work of ATI, supported by regulation, is hard to beat.

The power of regulation to influence the creation and operation of even the most commercially oriented approaches cannot be underestimated either. For example, Huntington Capital, the mezzanine debt fund located in San Diego, California, which counts some of the world's leading fiduciaries as LPs, has also been created with the benefit of public policy. Huntington's first fund was registered as an SBIC under the SBA program described earlier. As an SBIC, the fund had access to SBA leverage at a ratio of 2:1 to private investor capital. And although Huntington's second fund is not an SBIC, some of its institutional LPs have been motivated to invest by the CRA mandate and California state-level regulations that extend CRA-like requirements to insurance companies.

SJF Ventures, in Durham, North Carolina, is another fund to have benefited from the multiple positive effects of government-based fund certification programs, such as the CDFI initiative or the previously mentioned SBIC. SJF's first fund was a CDFI, and its third fund became the first national fund certified through the SBIC Impact Investment Initiative at the SBA. According to Dave Kirkpatrick, founder and managing director, the SBIC designation helped catalyze lead investments from Citi, Deutsche Bank, and State Street Bank, and helped build the momentum for the pension, endowment, family office, and wealth management investors who oversubscribed the fund. "Our final fund closing for SJF Ventures III was on $90 million, well above our $75 million target and triple the size of SJF Ventures II," Kirkpatrick notes.

Another key pillar of US impact investing heavily influenced by regulation is philanthropy. Among the impact investing tools at the disposal of philanthropic foundations in the United States (along with traditional grants and conventional endowment investments) are program-related investments (PRIs). PRIs are a category of below-market-rate charitable investments that count toward a foundation's annually mandated philanthropic spending, memorialized in the US tax code. The law was created in 1969 in response to the desire of foundations to make long-term, low-cost, and/or higher-risk investments in support of their mission. The capital returned from PRIs must be recycled into other charitable purposes, whether reinvested as a PRI or awarded as a grant.[28]

Advocacy Driven

The Indian Impact Investor Council (IIIC) was created in 2013 as a proactive response to the crisis in Indian microfinance in 2010 caused in part by a massive infusion of returns-seeking capital into the sector.[29] Among the IIIC's nine founding members are Aavishkaar and Elevar Equity, two of our case study subjects, along with Omidyar Network, Unilazer Ventures, and the family office of Ronnie Screwvala. The goal of the IIIC is to support government efforts to ensure that the impact investing field grows in a sustainable and appropriate manner—in part by setting the world's first binding guidelines for its members on everything from the sectors that qualify for impact investments, to the length of holding periods and measurement of returns.

Through the IIIC, Aavishkaar, Elevar, and their peers are practicing advocacy-driven Policy Symbiosis—which is essentially the flip side of regulation. Although all investors that are regulated by government engage in advocacy through their periodic interactions with public officials, some funds make it a point to influence policy directly at a market or field level by engaging with government entities more regularly. These firms realize public-private partnership to its fullest extent, recognizing that the success of impact investing initiatives depends, in large part, on the development of supportive policy infrastructure.

Janie Barrera, at ATI, is more involved at the national level than the typical fund CEO, for example, and her efforts are a beacon for others. Bridges Ventures plays a similar role in the United Kingdom and has been active in developing the public policy environment for social innovation more broadly, not least through the work of its founder, Sir Ronald Cohen, and his involvement with the Social Investment Task Force in the United Kingdom, the independent commission on unclaimed assets, Big Society Capital, and, most recently, the Social Impact Investment Taskforce, established by the G8.

Advocacy-driven Policy Symbiosis often takes place through direct engagement and interaction across sectors. However, it is also a core element of investment strategy in its own right when impact investors operate in low-income communities and market sectors where government is deeply involved.

W.K. Kellogg Foundation's (WKKF's) Mission Driven Investment program demonstrates a commitment to advocacy by way of its direct investments in later-growth-stage companies in health and education. The potential upside for WKKF is attractive, in part, because of the company's ability to "influence policy as a more established market player," explains Taylor Jordan, a cofounder of Imprint Capital and consultant to WKKF. WKKF's first direct and very strategic investment was in Acelero, one of the only for-profit companies managing and providing technical assistance to Head Start programs, which are part of the largest US government initiative supporting early education.

In a 2013 *Stanford Social Innovation Review* article, then WKKF CEO Sterling Speirn explained that after investing in Revolution Foods, a company that sells healthy school lunches, the foundation received "wholly new perspectives on issues of public policy, school and community food systems, and family and child behaviors that we can use to inform our grant-making and institutional efforts on the very same issues."[30]

The MacArthur Foundation: Program-Related, Policy-Driven Investment

The John D. and Catherine T. MacArthur Foundation is one of the largest providers of program-related investments (PRIs) in the United States, with a focus in the last decade on the development of affordable rental housing.

According to Debra Schwartz, MacArthur's director of program-related investment, the main goal of the $200 million–plus effort has been policy change, by building and coordinating a vast ecosystem of actors.

"The biggest issue with impact investing is how to embrace the market-creating role of government regulation, which will help unlock the motivation that investors have for social investments," says Schwartz. "The larger picture for investors includes understanding and working with government regulation and subsidies, rather than being dissuaded by or fearing them."

MacArthur's strategy includes facilitating a critical mass of transactions through PRIs—sufficient to provide evidence to policymakers—and supporting the development of market infrastructure through grants.

MacArthur's commitment to modeling an appropriate role for government has gone so far as to include in its Enhanced Tax Credit Fund a guarantee against the "appropriations risk" that the US Department of Housing and Urban Development will fail to fund the Section 8 rent subsidies that cover the difference between a building's operating cost and its tenants' capacity to pay.

The subsidy affects 1.5 million households, and, by providing a $20 million guarantee, MacArthur was able to catalyze $140 million in investments from one subordinate investor, Mass Mutual, and senior investors including JPMorgan Chase, MetLife, and United Bank, for the purpose of preserving eighteen Section 8 properties.

Opportunistic

All investors, including impact investors, succeed or fail on the strength of the performance of their investees. Providing every advantage to these investees is of the highest priority, including through the power and influence of public policy. In and of itself, this is not unique to impact investing. On the contrary, it is the very reason political advocacy and lobbying have grown so significantly.

Impact investors may have an advantage in working with government, however, because of their explicitly public objectives and cross-sector expertise—a form of Policy Symbiosis we call "opportunistic." Put another way, the government has a stronger interest in ensuring the success of companies delivering explicit social and environmental benefits, and is therefore likely to pay closer attention to their needs, whether for loans and other financing, land, permits, contracts, or any other supports.

This is a commercial proposition to be sure, and has been best articulated by Nancy Pfund, the founder and managing partner of DBL Investors, a successful impact investor in the United States with more than $225 million in assets under management, including for a significant number of institutional investors.

DBL Investors is a San Francisco–based venture capital firm focused on clean tech, information technology, health care, and sustainability-oriented products and services, with the goal of delivering tangible benefits to the community, including job creation in low-income neighborhoods and corporate engagement.

Writing in 2013 in the *Stanford Social Innovation Review (SSIR)*, Pfund recalls DBL's support for Tesla Motors, one of its investees:

> When we were looking for a site to build a manufacturing plant, DBL helped the company explore regions of the San Francisco Bay Area that might be suitable and where economic development incentives could help to level the playing field compared to other countries and states that had lower costs. This effort stemmed from aspects of our mission at that time, which included reducing the carbon footprint of transportation and creating high-quality jobs in Bay Area neighborhoods that needed them. Through a process that broke apart the conventional wisdom about whether California was an appropriate place to manufacture, the Tesla team's perspicacity helped it grab a plant (the former NUMMI plant in Fremont) that many thought was out of its reach, creating a strategic win for both the company and the community.[31]

The approach is entirely strategic. According to Pfund, DBL can "connect the dots a little sooner as to why a particular company idea might work" because it is "keyed into certain societal trends, problems, and policies that have been hard to solve and may even be getting worse."

Pfund concludes in the same *SSIR* article: "We believe that some aspects of double-bottom-line venture capital investing, such as working with broader constituencies, paying attention to place, and engaging in policy issues, will become mainstream."

In our group of twelve funds, SEAF's SME Sichuan Investment Fund, in China, stands out for how closely its managers have worked with local and regional governments, leveraging their relationships and knowledge of government processes and priorities to help portfolio companies obtain permits, including the seven approvals needed to make an investment and the six to exit.

Speaking at the SOCAP conference in 2013, SEAF executive vice president Mildred Callear explained that opportunistic Policy Symbiosis is a balancing act: even when government invests on a sustainable commercial basis, and funds are structured to restrict direct public sector involvement, plenty of opportunities remain for policymakers to have influence, as in Sichuan. This means that strong local relationships are essential.

IGNIA and MeXvi

IGNIA is a $100 million venture impact investing fund based in Monterrey, Mexico, that invests in companies that provide effective responses to the enormously underserved needs of low-income populations—both as consumers and as productive agents in value-added supply chains.

One of IGNIA's investments is MeXvi, a company that builds affordable houses on a customer's own land in rural and semiurban areas in Mexico and has improved the lives of more than twenty-five thousand individuals.

According to Álvaro Rodríguez Arregui, managing partner, IGNIA's investment in MeXvi provides a great example of the kind of proactive, on-the-ground work that fund managers need to do every day to help their investments succeed.

One of MeXvi's biggest challenges was to figure out how to get its customers financing for their home construction. MeXvi houses cost on average $7,000, much less than any informal alternative, yet customers could not access the necessary up-front cash. To overcome this hurdle, MeXvi worked with microfinance institutions (MFIs) to provide loans for people so that they could afford a MeXvi home.

MFIs were forthcoming with the idea, but, given their funding structure, only offered short-term, one-year loans. IGNIA therefore stepped in to make the case to government that moving people from slum housing to clean, affordable, efficient, and safe housing would require long-term MFI funding and support. It took more than eighteen months for the government to provide the appropriate help and allow MFIs to extend long-term loans—a task made more difficult because public loans to microfinance companies are not morgageable by land title.

Today, MeXvi has a successful partnership with fourteen MFIs to facilitate access to long-term credit for the payment of its homes. Thanks to IGNIA's advocacy and credibility, MFIs are part of a commercial ecosystem that has enabled the construction of fourteen hundred homes in rural and semiurban areas in states of Mexico in 2012 alone.

"When an entrepreneur goes to authorities and other players with the backing of a $100 million institutional investor, authorities are generally receptive. Opening these doors is where we spend a lot of our time and where our value-add shines through," explains Rodríguez Arregui.

According to Rodríguez Arregui, assisting portfolio companies is more than just providing ad hoc "technical assistance," from a distance. "Adding value to portfolio companies means being there day-to-day, twenty-four hours on call, putting your reputation on the line, providing advice when it is needed, and actively being a sounding board."

Note: This case study was originally published in Clark, C. Emerson, J., and Thornley, B. (2012, October). *A Market Emerges: The Six Dynamics of Impact Investing,* Pacific Community Ventures, Duke University, and ImpactAssets, http://www.pacificcommunity ventures.org/reports-and-publications/the-impact-investor-a-market-emerges-the-six-dynamics-of-impact-investing/.

The Policy Symbiosis Tool Kit

Speaking alongside Callear at the SOCAP conference in 2013, Vineet Rai, from Aavishkaar, reiterated the importance of taking a proactive approach to engaging with the public sector. According to Rai, on the face of it, impact investors are trying to make money in areas that are extremely sensitive and where government is a key provider of services—for example, in providing products to the poor, or basic resources like water.

"Many investors have a short history of impact investing and are excitable, with an eagerness to make high returns. The government doesn't see it that way. They want a lot of impact, and not a lot of money being made," Rai says.

As competition for the best deals pushes up valuations, Rai worries the story of impact investing will become more about profits than purpose, as was the case in microfinance in India in 2010, and wants to ensure that investors and entrepreneurs are positioned to explain to government that impact investing is much more complicated on the ground than it appears from a distance. "For example, our companies are not targeting the poorest of the poor, but low-income people with the desire to pay for access to services," he argues.

If there is a secret to Policy Symbiosis, it is reflected in Rai's example: to urgently and respectfully cultivate a deep partnership with government, and not to be reactionary when it is too late. The market is only now taking shape. This is the moment for impact investors to embrace the role of public policy in their work.

The Policy Symbiosis tool kit includes four steps:

1. **Acquire knowledge.** Know your market and the applicable policies.

2. **Build partnerships.** Share your experiences as a leading practitioner, and strengthen relationships with public officials and
other constituents that make impact investing possible.
3. **Be visionary.** Embrace public purpose as a strategic objective.
4. **Proceed with integrity.** Commit publicly to the highest ethical
standards.

Let's explore each of these in turn.

Acquire Knowledge

There are a multitude of policies related to the work of impact
investors. These policies do everything from mandating or incentivizing the supply of capital to impact investing, to "directing" that
capital to more impactful investments by setting standards or using
tax credits to make markets more attractive, to creating the
demand for impact investing (building the capacity and "invest-
ability" of enterprises) through early-stage R&D and other direct or
intermediated technical and financial assistance.

The framework shown in Figure 4.1, which was cocreated by
Ben while leading the research practice at Pacific Community
Ventures, provides an overview of the types of policies that interact
with impact investing. Add the government's role as a convener,
provider of data, and regulator more broadly, across the variety of
market sectors in which impact investors operate, and the picture
quickly gets complicated.

In Figure 4.1, "supply development" refers to policies that bring
more capital to the table; "directing capital" refers to efforts to
make particular established markets more attractive and impactful;
"demand development" refers to policies that create a pipeline of
opportunities for impact investors.

To understand the diversity of policies that affect impact
investing, consider a loan provided to a microenterprise by
ACCIÓN Texas Inc. (ATI) and a selection of federal policies
that act or have the potential to act on the three key parties to
the transaction: the investor, the intermediary (in this example,
ATI), and the investment recipient (see Figure 4.2). The Community Reinvestment Act and Program Related Investment tax law
unlock capital from banks and philanthropic foundations,

Figure 4.1   A Policy Framework for Impact Investing

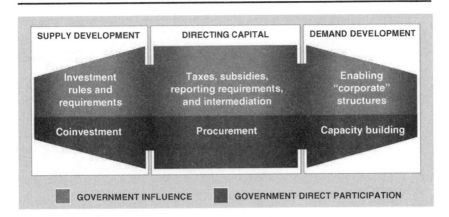

Source: Thornley, B., Wood, D., Grace, K., and Sullivant, S. (2011, January). *Impact Investing: A Framework for Policy Design and Analysis.* InSight at Pacific Community Ventures and the Initiative for Responsible Investment at Harvard University. http://www.pacificcommunityventures.org/reports-and-publications/impact investing-a-framework-for-policy-design-and-analysis/.

respectively, which is provided to ATI. Among the policies that ATI uses directly to achieve sustainability are the SBA 504 loan guarantee program and CDFI Fund. The enterprises in which ATI invests benefit from SBA's small business development centers, which provide basic information on creating and operating a small business, and the SBA's 8(a) business development program, which helps disadvantaged small businesses secure contracts with government.

To operate as effectively as possible in the market, impact investors should understand the full array of policies that influence the market and that might be harnessed to increase the probability of both social and financial success, not just those that act directly on their own organization.

This is not as easy as it seems—and there are very few impact investors as engaged with public policy as they ought to be, given its importance to both individual funds and the field as a whole. For example, the Community Reinvestment Act (CRA) drives billions in capital to low-income areas of the United States, including through SBICs. Investments in SBICs are automatically "CRA-qualified,"

Figure 4.2 Example of How Policy Has an Impact on a Fund and Investees

Investors (primarily banks, philanthropic foundations, and individuals)	ACCIÓN Texas Inc.	Microenterprises

Selection of Notable Policies		
Community Reinvestment Act: requires banks to invest in the low-income communities in which they have branches	*SBA 504 loan program:* government guarantees for asset-backed loans to SMEs	*SBA Small Business Development Centers*: 900 service delivery points providing a wide array of technical assistance to SMEs
Program-related investment tax laws: allow philanthropic foundations to make charitable investments that count toward their annual payout requirement of 5 percent	*CDFI Fund (US Department of the Treasury):* registers and provides subsidy to special-purpose institutions committed to operating predominately in low-income communities	*SBA 8(a) Business Development Program*: provides advantages in federal procurement to businesses owned by disadvantaged groups including ethnic minorities

meaning these investments fulfill a bank's regulatory obligation to support the underserved communities where they have branches. Yet in talking with SBICs, it is clear that very few have a view on the CRA more broadly, or are aware of the opportunities for supporting or strengthening the regulation.

There are numerous ways in which to become more knowledgeable about the role of government in the work you do as an impact investor. For starters, you should join sector and field-level trade groups, where influencing public policy tends to be a strategic priority (on behalf of members) and where information on the policy environment and its development is more readily available and targeted specifically to an investor's needs.

Independent research—including broadening your typical reading list—is also critical. A selection of organizations with a (sometimes nascent) focus partly on policy in impact investing follows. This list is intended to be representative and is certainly not exhaustive:

- Opportunity Finance Network (www.ofn.org) and Community Development Finance Association (www.cdfa.org.uk): the industry groups for CDFIs in the United States and the United Kingdom, respectively
- Council on Foundations (www.cof.org): membership organization of seventeen hundred grantmaking foundations and corporations in the United States
- European Venture Philanthropy Association (www.evpa.eu .com): membership organization of primarily European social investors and foundations
- Asia Community Ventures (www.asiacommunityventures.org): nonprofit organization focused on cross-sector collaboration in Hong Kong
- Impact Investing Australia (www.impactinvestingaustralia.com): nonprofit organization coordinating the Australian impact investing sector's engagement with the international Social Impact Investment Taskforce (created by the United Kingdom under the auspices of the G8) and building a platform for collective action in Australia more broadly
- Impact Investing Policy Collaborative (www.iipcollaborative .org): international network of researchers and public officials focused on the role of government in impact investing
- USSIF (www.ussif.org), UKSIF (www.uksif.org), and Eurosif (www.eurosif.org): membership associations for responsible and sustainable investment in the United States, United Kingdom, and Europe, respectively
- World Economic Forum (www.weforum.org): coconvenor, together with the IIPC, of the Global Learning Exchange on Social Impact Investing, created in partnership with the UK Cabinet Office with a strong focus on public policy in its work (WEF has also published on the subject of policy in impact investing).[32]

Whether you acquire information directly or from industry groups and networks like those listed, it should be verified and contextualized in consultation with peers, independent experts (for example, legal advisors), and core constituents, including investors and investees, who are themselves subject to the influence of policy.

Build Partnerships

Impact investors should strive to build authentic partnerships with public officials whenever possible, either directly or through platforms of engagement created by others. Only then will the "transaction costs" associated with developing, implementing, and iterating on smart public policy be mitigated.

Partnership demands an unusual level of openness on the part of government, which is why special-purpose institutions like DFIs, or Big Society Capital in the United Kingdom and the SBA in the United States, have been created to work directly with the private sector in markets where cooperation is essential.

This same heightened level of openness and engagement characterizes the approach of outstanding impact investing funds. You should therefore ask yourself a range of questions:

1. Are there industry convenings where policymakers are not present? If so, why not? As a field, we should be working diligently to attract representatives from the public sector to meetings, just as we do any other stakeholder. Every opportunity to educate policymakers on impact investing should be cultivated.
2. Is there more you could do to help policymakers? Public officials frequently hold hearings and solicit input on regulations, and are often looking for committed private sector leaders to join various advisory committees. Are you supporting these efforts with the same urgency you apply to growing portfolio companies, bringing all of the resources and networks at your disposal to bear?
3. Do your political leaders at the local, regional, or national level know what you do? Have they visited with any of your investees? It is important that those who directly represent you in government understand why and how to advocate on your behalf.
4. Have you identified areas of shared concern with public officials? Even if impact investing is not, in and of itself, something

a policymaker cares to understand or prioritize, there are surely interests you share—the development of the sectors you invest in or the impacts of your work on key constituencies (for example, your efforts to deliver high-quality health and education services to kids, in places with safe and affordable housing infrastructure). Are there high-priority policy programs already operating in key sectors locally that could be strengthened by adding an element of impact investing?

5. Are there any initiatives you could be pursuing jointly with public officials? Could research be jointly commissioned, for example, or could you help facilitate hearings or other events focused on key issues of practice and concern? Could you create a "residency" or "exchange" program that allows individuals to be seconded in either direction? There will always be opportunities to partner creatively and appropriately in impact investing, so long as you are mindful of the need for public officials and institutions to operate with the utmost integrity.

The emergence of a more authentic form of partnership should also flow naturally from a deeper sharing of knowledge. Partnerships make it possible to have an easier form of give and take, and to clarify the needs, priorities, and limitations of both parties. It is important for impact investors to share their insights as leading practitioners with public officials, who are eager to understand what does and does not work as they develop new markets and policies enabling product innovation. Data and insights from the front lines are essential. For public officials, the opportunity to put themselves in the shoes of investors and to test ideas as part of a continuous cycle of learning is invaluable.

To some extent, knowledge sharing happens automatically, when investors interact directly with the public sector by applying to be part of a government program or fulfilling mandated reporting requirements. However, there are many opportunities for investors to provide information more intentionally. The following practices in knowledge sharing are indicative:

- Blogging regularly on experiences and key learnings
- Maintaining an active presence on social media, by disseminating your own experiences and "curating" third-party content

- Partnering with established thought leaders or convenors on events, research, and other forms of field-level engagement
- Publishing white papers and reports, and undertaking deeper research
- Contributing data and insights as part of a larger peer group (for example, an industry association)
- Participating on conference panels and at other in-person events
- Participating in "advocacy days" together with peers, visiting with legislators and public officials
- Providing formal feedback on particular policy initiatives (through well-considered comments; letters of support; testimonials; or in direct, private conversation with public officials)

As this list indicates you can cultivate informal relationships with public officials in numerous ways, from participating in conferences to being part of an active industry group. You can cultivate more formal relationships, where insights are actively solicited by policymakers, directly or through the facilitation of a trusted intermediary.

It also helps to be mindful of the different types of information that public officials require. Career officials tend to have sector or market-level interests. They need details about where and why there are inefficiencies in the system and about the clear, addressable barriers on which they should focus. Elected officials are committed to bolstering the economic vitality of the communities they represent and will be eager to understand the broader benefits of impact investing in these places.

Be Visionary

Impact investors seek to explicitly generate social and environmental impacts and are embracing this "public" purpose, positioning their small and innovative contribution within the bigger picture of social change that many policymakers have in mind.

As Elevar Equity notes on the home page of its website, "Every community and person has intrinsic economic and social value. Accordingly, our entire investment focus is to capitalize entrepreneurs who create global systems access for disconnected communities." According to its site, Calvert Foundation "enables people to invest for social good." And ATI is "helping the most vulnerable people in our society who are striving for a better life." In other words, Elevar, Calvert Foundation, and ATI are unequivocally stating their intention to serve a broader public purpose. This is a vision and message that speaks directly to policymakers and distinguishes the three organizations as contributors of social value to be reckoned with and leveraged by public officials.

Vision may seem a question of semantics. However, it is primarily strategic. Being visionary means having a robust investment thesis of change, discussed in chapter 3, and articulating that ITC more clearly than many investors might be accustomed to. In mainstream investment markets, organizational vision tends to be more narrowly construed, emphasizing value creation and the centrality of clients as guiding principles.

To the extent that Policy Symbiosis remains and continues to grow as an essential best practice in Collaborative Capitalism, you should embrace the ideals of and manage to your public purpose, ensuring that it is confidently communicated to public officials.

Proceed with Integrity

The final step in the Policy Symbiosis tool kit is translating a vision into a public commitment. Broader notions of accountability and sustainability are implicit in impact investing and should be reflected in a firm's commitment to operating ethically, including through such mechanisms as industry and sector codes of conduct and voluntary principles.

Reflecting on Deutsche Bank's ongoing commitment to impact investing, initiated with the Global Commercial Microfinance Consortium, former managing director Asad Mahmood emphasizes the ethical dimension: "Ethical behavior is crucial, no matter what form it takes, whether it is good customer service, appropriate pricing, or after-sale service. It simply means setting and maintaining high standards. It means addressing the needs of the customer."[33]

Deutsche Bank has been a leading participant in the drafting of microfinance client protection principles—just one example of the work that has already been undertaken at the sector and field levels to establish performance standards, as the following examples illustrate:

GIIN's definition of impact investing. In 2013, GIIN reaffirmed that the core characteristics of impact investing include intentionality, investment with return expectations across a range of asset classes, and impact measurement. As discussed earlier, it also put a stake in the ground on what it means to track and report impact rigorously.[34]

Smart Campaign. In 2008, Smart Campaign brought together hundreds of key stakeholders in microfinance to endorse six core Client Protection Principles and commitments to implementing specific improvements in products, practices, and policies. The principles address such issues as the appropriateness of a product for clients, overindebtedness, transparency, responsible pricing, fair and respectful treatment of clients, privacy of client data, and complaint resolution.[35]

UN Principles for Responsible Investment (UN PRI). With more than eleven hundred signatories representing almost $35 trillion in assets under management, UN PRI has emerged since 2006 as a "license to do business" in many countries, utilized by investors and intermediaries to publicly demonstrate their commitment to responsible investment and incorporation of environmental, social, and governance (ESG) issues into their investment decision making and ownership practices. The six principles focus on ESG integration, active ownership, encouraging reporting on ESG issues by investees, advocacy for the principles in their own right, collaboration on the principles and related best practices, and reporting on the implementation of the principles.[36]

Deutsche Bank's Mahmood rightly argues that proceeding with integrity is good business. Yet this was not always the case. The three examples listed here are all relatively recent. Impact investing is only now emerging; and in any case, there will always be opportunities to approach all elements of impact investing more ethically. That effort, in and of itself, has the potential to engage and enthuse policymakers.

Unilever: The Corporate Perspective on Public Principles

Many of the world's largest multinationals have played a public role for decades and provide a useful guide to Policy Symbiosis. Among this group, Unilever's explicit statement on public policy and advocacy, displayed prominently on the company's website, sets the standard. The following is a sample of the statement's core elements:

- We need to actively engage with governments and regulators to create an environment that can help us achieve the commitments set out in the Unilever Sustainable Living Plan. The private sector, governments, and NGOs can achieve a lot more if they work together in partnerships.
- The Unilever Sustainable Living Plan sets out our vision for a future in which people can improve their quality of life without increasing their environmental footprint.
- Many of the impacts of our operations fall outside of our direct control, so we need to engage governments to create an environment that is supportive to meeting the big sustainability challenges the world faces.
- Our Code of Business Principles guides all aspects of our conduct internally and with external parties. It commits us to behave with honesty, integrity, and openness, and with respect for the human rights and interests of our employees and other stakeholders and to obey the laws of the countries in which we operate.
- We believe that Unilever should play an active role in shaping legislation and regulations that enhance positive social and environmental outcomes.
- We encourage our companies to engage with local governments and other organizations to help inform public policy. This is done both directly and through bodies such as trade associations. We take part in multi-stakeholder debates and when relevant respond to public consultations. We also engage with organizations that are critical of our actions and seek to understand and address their concerns.

The Five London Principles

We conclude this chapter by turning the tables and offering you a window into the way policymakers are thinking about impact investing and the opportunity it presents. By understanding the perspective of public officials, investors will be better positioned to engage across sectors.

The most compelling illustration of the approach of policy-makers is the Impact Investing Policy Collaborative (IIPC) London Principles (http://iipcollaborative.org/london-principles/), which were developed in 2013 through a process of deliberation that included researchers and public officials from more than fifteen countries. The principles are intended to help governments understand how public policy intersects with impact investing, and offer guidance on the characteristics of the policies that have been most effective. The London Principles offer a number of important takeaways for investors that reinforce many of the ideas in this and prior chapters:

- Policymakers are generally looking for very specific impacts through their actions. This reinforces the need for investors to clearly articulate the social outcomes of their investments with some precision.
- Public officials are focused on inclusive market engagement as they develop and implement policy. Investors that bring multiple perspectives to the table—and relationships with a full range of constituencies, not least the ultimate beneficiaries of their investments in portfolio companies—will be best positioned.
- Policymakers have a holistic, market-level interest. Investors should therefore be mindful of precisely where government interventions are required and where they are not. The best strategy may be to advocate for other parts of the market that are more in need, or at the very least for a highly coordinated policy response.
- Governments are working in their own right to develop a powerful, evidence-based case for impact investing as a tool for delivering social value. Investors should be mindful of this need and contribute excellent data to that effort and the full support of a high-profile cast of business and financial sector leaders.

Clarity of Purpose

Clarity of purpose, on the part of government, reinforces strategy and policies that are integrated into existing policy and market structures, target specific social objectives, and clearly define the role for impact investing in achieving those objectives. Clarity of purpose allows governments to avoid the inefficient use or misallocation of resources, insufficient policy support that impedes achievement of outcomes, and disjointed policy regimes.

Governments should

- Clearly identify the social objective(s) that the impact investing strategy or policy is meant to target.
- Clearly identify why the impact investing strategy or policy might be an appropriate tool to meet those objectives, and how impact investing complements broader policy systems.
- Define realistic expectations for the results that the impact investing strategy or policy might achieve and the time it might take to achieve them.

Stakeholder Engagement

Stakeholder engagement brings discipline and legitimacy to policy design. By institutionalizing dialogue and feedback, with relevant stakeholders, governments can bring important additional resources to support impact investing strategies and policies. Effective stakeholder engagement ensures that all actors are included, manages expectations, and avoids the development of policies that are unfit for purpose.

Governments should

- Identify, engage, and collaborate with key stakeholders, from concept to implementation to revision of strategies and policies.
- Support shared ownership of policy and a dynamic process of policy development and review.
- Guard against misaligned incentives or unequal power structures that work against effective impact investing strategy and policies.

Market Stewardship

Market stewardship ensures a holistic vision for impact investing strategies and policies. It focuses on a balanced development of investor interest, investment opportunities, and mechanisms to deliver intended social outcomes. Effective market stewardship sets appropriate levels of regulation and mitigates unnecessary management of market activity.

Governments should

- Identify the appropriate use of market interventions, including at which point they should be made, for how long, and by which agencies and institutions.
- Develop markets holistically, balancing capital supply, investment readiness, and support for enabling intermediary infrastructure.
- Support reliable and responsive policy, mindful of stakeholder priorities, incentives, and limitations.

Institutional Capacity

Institutional capacity allows for the effective use of resources, adds value to existing policies, and creates the potential for developing innovative strategies and tools that address key social problems. Institutional capacity establishes reliable and resilient markets, and avoids sending mixed signals to investors and civil society on the potential for intended policies to deliver on their promises.

Governments should

- Determine cross-sector resources within government currently available, or necessary to be developed, for successful strategy development and policy implementation.
- Develop public sector leadership to implement policies where needed and provide stability over time.
- Measure and evaluate the impact of policies against stated objectives, and act efficiently to refine or scale accordingly.

Universal Transparency

Universal transparency mandates that stated objectives are clear and that progress toward their achievement is openly measured and reported to relevant stakeholders and the public at large. Effective universal transparency enables leadership in public innovation, protects against the risk of real or perceived bias, realistically manages expectations, and empowers citizen participation.

Governments should

- Report rigorously on performance and develop a culture of transparency that includes all impact investing actors.
- Commit to a continuous process of shared learning, including through an open dialogue on successes and failures.
- Foster engagement and fidelity to stated social objectives.

Our research firmly establishes the cross-sector nature of impact investing and the importance of engaging fully with government.

These are certainly difficult relationships to cultivate. Among all the actors in impact investing, the conversation between investors and public officials may be the most difficult. Public officials, by definition, care most about impact, and they often know the least about the tools of finance and are suspicious of investment intermediaries as a result.

According to Mildred Callear, from SEAF, which remains committed to being extensively engaged in policy, SMEs sometimes succeed in emerging markets because they operate *below* the radar. In one instance, in Georgia, SEAF's work to ensure that all its portfolio companies maintained the highest standards of regulatory compliance actually led to each and every one of them being chosen to undergo tax audits: a counterintuitive outcome.

In other words, Policy Symbiosis is an element of impact investing that may require the hardest work, but also offers tremendous rewards, as the twelve funds in our study demonstrate more broadly. To be sure, without Policy Symbiosis, success in impact investing will be that much more elusive at the fund level, and that much more difficult to replicate and scale at the field level.

Replication and scale are two key themes in chapter 5 as well, which examines the concrete ways in which investors are leveraging the capital provided by diverse actors to catalyze massive impact. To the perspective of policymakers, chapter 5 adds an approach that draws on the work of two odd bedfellows: philanthropy and structured finance.

5

The New Deal

Q: What's the benefit of investing alongside the leading foundations in the field?

A: Program-Related Investments can be complicated and labor-intensive to source, structure and manage. Investors new to PRIs may find it useful to leverage the experience of the pioneers of the PRI field. By participating in the Living Cities [Catalyst] fund, investors who care about the future of America's low-income urban neighborhoods can:

1. Leverage the experience of the leading foundations in the community development field
2. Build a diversified portfolio of investments quickly, efficiently and cost-effectively
3. Lower transaction costs through economies of scale
4. Reduce risk
5. Access a broader pipeline of potential investments
6. Avoid the need to underwrite and monitor individual investments
7. Maximize the impact of their investment dollars.

—Excerpt from Living Cities' Catalyst Fund
Frequently Asked Questions

The Terrain for the New Deal

One of the common questions practitioners are asked when they say they are involved in impact investing is, "How does it differ, really, from regular investing?" And indeed, impact investing has much to draw from the basic practices of finance.

At the same time, it is clear investing for outcomes may require different strategies, policies, and intentions, as our other chapters make clear. But the question of exactly *how* you do deals, and do them differently, has remained largely opaque to outsiders. And when practices are identified, there is a great deal of uncertainty about which ones are simply variations and which might actually lead to high performance and thus be worth emulating.

Although we realize in some ways, effective impact investing is simply sound investment practice augmented with consideration of social and environmental aspects, in other ways, impact investing is an evolving and different animal from traditional investment practice and deserves closer scrutiny.

When we delved into the twelve funds, we looked closely at what it takes, strategically and tactically, to succeed in impact investing. And what we quickly realized was that investing for most of these primarily private equity and loan funds, both for their limited partner (LP) investors and their general partner (GP) managers, was a very collaborative exercise.

Some of this has to do with the perception of risk. If you are making a new kind of investment or an investment in a strategy that is new, it is often prudent to make that investment alongside others whose capital can de facto lower your risk. But part of it also has to do with the variety of investment objectives among different parties.

For traditional, nonimpact funds, the process of syndicating a deal or bringing a group of investors together to make an investment in similar terms at the same time can be quite complicated. But in that case, the objectives of the parties have been boiled down in most cases to a simpler, single goal: What are the terms that will maximize financial return and also support the success of the entrepreneurial team?

For impact investors, nearly every party has a set of more complicated and diverse objectives that blend financial and strategic goals. And as indicated by the earlier quotation from Living Cities, these objectives may be quite varied: wanting to learn; to diversify risk; to pay less for each deal; to access more deals than you could otherwise; to encourage other parties to come in with more money than you can; to piggyback on other people's work, such as their due diligence or their investment monitoring; to show that profits can be made or markets may be formed; and to build relationships with other stakeholders that can help maximize the impact the investments create.

We found the practice of intentional collaboration in deal making among different parties with various objectives so pervasive that we gave it a name: Catalytic Capital. To us, it really is a new way of doing business, and with it, the impact investing field becomes the terrain for what we call "the New Deal." Catalytic Capital as a widespread practice also serves to unleash impact investing as an instrument for generating broader social value. It permits many smaller players to come together to make deals happen at greater levels of capitalization than they might otherwise, and often requires them to work hard to find ways and design terms for their varying interests to align.

Let us reiterate this relatively intuitive concept: catalytic investments are those that trigger the future flow of capital to a desired company, asset class, sector, or geography. In some sense, all investments with more than one investor involve some sort of catalytic effect. This can occur as investors enter into a single, syndicated round in which they cooperate to simultaneously deploy capital. Or it may occur over time, as new actors invest in subsequent rounds, benefiting from earlier-stage efforts. Investing is a group sport, and growing successful companies through financial markets has always depended on multiple catalytic interactions.

In the field of impact investing, catalytic investments encourage the flow of capital for distinctive strategic reasons, beyond the pursuit of financial return alone. We have always known impact investors provide capital for strategic as well as financial reasons; however, we did not expect this explicit rationale to have been so prevalent among our outstanding funds. As it happens, every one of the twelve has *benefited from* or *deployed* Catalytic Capital.

For funds benefiting from Catalytic Capital, we see different attributes in the behavior of their LPs. Those LP motivations, perceptions of risk, ability to reach out to engage other kinds of institutions, and willingness to engage on terms that sometimes do not maximize their own returns exemplify the catalytic nature of their intentions. Other LPs realize that if they are large, reputable, or sophisticated, or bring a strong credibility from their field of interest, they may improve the fund's credibility and visibility to other investors.

An example of this is Elevar Equity's first fund, whose cornerstone investor was Omidyar Network, an established LP investor in microfinance debt funds at the time, which wanted to put its weight behind the first microfinance equity fund by making a program-related investment. According to Eliza Erikson, investment team director at Omidyar, the investment was made because they wanted to support one of the more seasoned, robust teams in the industry as well as support their relatively new investment thesis. "We were impressed with their focus on the earlier-stage side, and their ability to cocreate businesses. And at the time, the field of microfinance was facing limitations arising from its primarily nonprofit base. We also wanted to show that you could do microfinance from a for-profit equity fund investing in for-profit microfinance enterprises." Omidyar's catalytic investment in Elevar Equity is discussed in more detail later in this chapter.

For funds that deploy Catalytic Capital, we see fund managers considering their own direct investment as a way to engage and influence other investors and stakeholders in the deals.

RSF Social Finance, for example, has become adept at using an integrated approach in its lending, tapping philanthropic capital to both reduce risk and increase community engagement, making more borrowers eligible for RSF financing. RSF's "integrated capital" approach also resurfaces throughout this chapter, providing several innovative examples of how to leverage Catalytic Capital.

The work of the Mexican fund IGNIA to engage the community it invests in, described in chapter 4, could also be thought of as catalytic. IGNIA's interest is not just in supporting its own portfolio companies but in creating new markets or industries that can be ignited by the successful venture. In doing so, it builds financial and strategic support so that as the venture matures over time and creates competition, there can be more institutional support as well as more efficiencies. According to Álvaro Rodríguez Arregui, managing partner, "Ultimately, this can culminate in a better value proposition for the end consumer. By identifying and working to engage other stakeholders up front, from suppliers and regulators to partners, we work to catalyze new industries in a bottom of the pyramid market with long-term impact potential."

Our research provides insight into how Catalytic Capital is emerging as a common practice and how it has been instrumental in the growth of impact investing through four distinct purposes, presented later in this chapter. Understanding the contours of these purposes can assist investors in seeing the true intentions and needs of investment partners, and help them structure deals more effectively based on those needs. In fact, the problem of reconciling the different purposes of Catalytic Capital across a variety of investment players is not a new one. It is a structuring exercise that financial institutions have grappled with for decades. What is new is the need for a deeper understanding of Catalytic Capital and its application to the strategic and mission objectives of different types of investors. These transactions often require more time and energy, and benefit from the help of a negotiating intermediary. Financial innovation in structuring capital to catalyze multiple sets of investors for impact is, quite simply, at the heart of impact investing.

Myths of Catalytic Capital

As impact investing has evolved, so too have a variety of beliefs regarding what impact investing is and—more specifically—what role capital plays in impact investing practice. As is true of any "myth," there are aspects of these beliefs that are partially grounded in truth. Yet, over time those "truths" become overwhelmed by misunderstanding and, eventually, untruths. We think it important to pause in our discussion to call out four of what we feel are the most common myths. These four misconceptions in the marketplace about Catalytic Capital are as follows.

Myth 1: Catalytic Capital Is Concessionary or Subsidy-Based

There is a misbelief that Catalytic Capital is only used by investors willing to accept below-market-rate returns. Although there are examples of investors using Catalytic Capital with the intention of achieving a lower than market-rate return alongside their catalytic purpose (for example, through grants or tools like foundation PRIs, the investment mechanism discussed earlier that is specifically designed to encourage mission-aligned investments that target below-market returns), there are investors that use private debt and equity to achieve market-rate returns alongside their catalytic purpose. For example, in MicroVest's first fund, some of the low-income financial institutions (LIFIs) in their portfolio received investments from other international microfinance investment vehicles precisely because these funds trusted MicroVest's intensive, financial due diligence.

Myth 2: Catalytic Capital Will Distort Markets

Although Catalytic Capital may have the potential to negatively distort individual company behavior (for example, by encouraging unnecessary risk taking) or market behavior (for example, by preventing a commercial market from developing naturally), we found at the fund level, Catalytic Capital has been transformative, unlocking billions of dollars of noncatalytic investments into impact funds and enterprises. This is consistent with the experience of many mainstream investment markets. The US CDFI Fund and SBA programs, for example, each have Catalytic Capital components specifically targeted to provide leverage to funds and other intermediary asset managers. It appears catalyzing intermediaries may be a strong market-making strategy, rather than a market-distorting one.

Myth 3: Providers of Catalytic Capital Are Always Philanthropic or Governmental Organizations

There are many examples of philanthropic and governmental organizations that use Catalytic Capital. But our research revealed private sector players are starting to engage with catalytic purposes as well, finding ways to blend their strategic objectives around community, sustainability, or other impacts, with layers of capital that encourage others to participate. We think this is a positive development, and several of the fund managers we researched agree. Deutsche Bank, for example, announced the launch of the Essential Capital Fund in fall 2012, which intends to provide "first loss" loans to social enterprises and impact investors, in order to catalyze the participation of capital providers that are socially motivated and risk-averse. "There are many investors that have pent-up demand and are waiting for the right opportunities to deploy capital into impact investing," notes RJ Lumba, senior relationship manager at Deutsche Bank. "What is preventing them from doing this is the unavailability of another party who takes the first step to provide risk capital. Our thought was that we could be that provider."

Myth 4: Philanthropic and Government Organizations *Only* Provide Concessionary and Subsidized Catalytic Capital

Many people misperceive that to be an outcomes-oriented investor you must be a below-market-rate investor. This is simply not always the case. One can be an outcomes investor aiming to catalyze markets that target market-rate returns. The US government's OPIC invested in MicroVest only once its first fund had raised a significant volume of initial capital, providing a senior loan at a competitive rate, but with catalytic purposes nonetheless— namely, the goal of scaling MicroVest's commercial approach to microfinance.

The Omidyar Network's classification of three categories of actors in impact investing—market innovators, market scalers, and market infrastructure, described in chapter 2—is an effort to better discern those that may require concessionary capital and those that do not, recognizing at the same time that each type of actor has a critical role to play in catalyzing new markets.

Catalytic Capital is needed at each stage, but will come with a different set of risk-and-return profiles and different motivations for different investors, including for government and philanthropy. Relatedly, in *Priming the Pump,* Omidyar Network discusses its own approach to the use of subsidies:

> It's extremely important to note that subsidy is not the only way to kick-start for-profit sector development, even for lower-income consumers. At Omidyar Network, our focus on developing deep sector and geographic expertise frequently leads us to price risk differently than generalist or geographically remote investors. A high percentage of our investments are in businesses that we believe—against conventional wisdom—have the potential to generate strong financial returns. Such willingness to question more

conservative perceptions of risk is a major way that impact investors can accelerate the growth of new industry sectors. And in many cases, this approach can give impact investors a competitive advantage in finding promising profitable new business models that don't necessarily require subsidy.[1]

Four Purposes of Catalytic Capital

Catalytic Capital occurs in many forms: through grants, letters of credit, guarantees or first-loss capital, collateralization, subordinated loans, insurance, reserve accounts, concessionary or cornerstone debt, and equity investments. Following are the four distinct purposes to which these tools are put to use:

Sustaining. Some segments of impact investing require ongoing grants or concessionary investments, particularly where market failure is endemic.

Seeding. Making one of the first investments in a fund is often essential to initial operations, and can help develop a track record necessary for attracting other capital.

Risk-reducing. Several financial instruments as well as tiered fund structures can reduce financial risk for investors in both funds and companies.

Signaling. If an LP is particularly large, reputable, or sophisticated, investing in a fund can improve the recipient's perceived credibility and visibility to other investors.

Sustaining

Community development venture capital (CDVC) funds have been operating in the United States for more than twenty years, with approximately $2 billion in capital under management. CDVC funds provide private equity and long-term loans to underserved markets, seeking market-rate financial returns as well as social impacts. Some of those funds that self-identify as CDVC funds have been registered with the US Department of the Treasury's CDFI Fund. Others were created as part of a special SBA program initiated in 2002 and since terminated, the New Markets Venture Capital fund program. Still others have been created as SBICs more broadly, with support from the SBA. Over two-thirds of CDVC funding can be considered "sustaining capital," coming from subsidized sources like banks, foundations, and the public sector.

It is interesting to compare CDVC funds to "minority-owned" or "minority-focused" private equity funds that have invested predominantly in companies owned by people of color, drawing on the research of Julia Sass Rubin at Rutgers University.

Minority-focused funds were created in 1969 with the introduction of the federal Minority Enterprise Small Business Investment Company (MESBIC) program, later renamed the Specialized Small Business Investment Company (SSBIC) program, again under the auspices of the SBA.

Through the MESBIC program, Congress intended to catalyze new equity and long-term debt investment in minority-owned small businesses. Yet despite the program's termination in 1996, dozens of minority-focused funds have been created since. In other words, the public support provided through the MESBIC and SSBIC programs enabled minority-focused funds to develop a robust and self-sustaining industry. The industry's trade association, the National Association of Investment Companies, includes forty-eight full or affiliate members managing over $10 billion in assets.[2]

In contrast to CDVC funds, the portion of sustaining capital required by minority-focused funds is quite low—just 10 percent of capital from banks and a much smaller proportion from foundations and governments. Instead, most of the current funding for minority-focused funds comes from unsubsidized sources, such as pension funds seeking competitive, market-rate returns.[3]

The parallel development of these two US markets demonstrates the different roles that sustaining capital can play, providing either an *ongoing* or *transforming* subsidy. In the first instance, exemplified by the CDVC program, it is clear that some segments of the impact investing market will require Catalytic Capital over the long term in the form of ongoing grants or concessionary investments. These funds often work at the margins of investment markets, where even commercial players struggle to achieve profitability, and market failures are deeply entrenched. The fund's investments may target places where the types of infrastructure needed to ensure the success of the private equity model—markets of certain scale or potential, business skills, networks, and so on—

are simply not present. In such instances of market failure, concessionary capital can provide ongoing operating funding if its constituents decide that the social impact supersedes the need for a "pure" market. Such market failure can exist for many different groups—disconnected and dispersed populations (for example, in rural areas) or low-income populations, to name just two. Low-income people and places, in particular, are the focus of much of the CDVC and CDFI sectors in the United States.

ACCIÓN Texas Inc. (ATI) is one example of a fund working in the CDFI sector, requiring ongoing sustaining capital. ATI works across eight states in the Delta region of the United States, and receives half of its $14 million operating budget from grants—a fraction that is shrinking due to the organization's internal push toward self-sustainability, but will likely never reach zero. ATI targets very small enterprises, and the service it offers—loans averaging $15,000—is much more costly to provide than can be recouped through borrowing margins, especially given the cap on interest rates under US state usury laws. The organization proactively works to identify other ways to generate profits, but will not increase the rates on its loans. ATI brings in additional capital by servicing loan portfolios for some of its investors, and by selling the use of its own internally developed microloan management software. But its loan program will always be anchored in the underserved niche of the market, a segment that will never be truly profitable so long as interest rates remain capped.

In its second role, sustaining capital can also provide *transforming* subsidy that breaks down barriers to market growth and scale. In these cases, certain markets may appear doomed to fail, when actually innovation, experimentation, and renewed leadership and networks may prove otherwise. "Minority-focused" funds were historically overlooked by the "primarily white and male venture capital industry," for example.[4] Yet once their businesses were given opportunities to thrive and their viability was demonstrated, new connections to networks and capital were created that allowed the industry to become more competitive in traditional markets. Microfinance is another prime example of such a market. After thirty years of subsidy, experimentation, and other dedicated forms of Catalytic Capital, microfinance now has a commercial core.

This distinction between *ongoing* and *transforming* subsidy is echoed in research on enterprises seeking intentionally to create social and environmental outcomes ("impact enterprises"), which found a positive correlation between growth and impacts for minority-serving businesses, but a negative correlation for those serving low-income people generally. In a 2013 study of for-profit impact enterprises in the United States, CASE at Duke University found that tangible commitment at the enterprise level to impact, as expressed through specific, verifiable practices, was strongly correlated with overall business growth factors, including revenue growth, profit growth, number of capital raises, and growth in number of employees. This trend was statistically valid across all industry segments (all industries were clustered into seven industry segments), company ages, and geographies.

But when different kinds of mission impacts were isolated, the correlations changed. According to the historical data collected, all the industry segments showed a positive correlation, on average, between high growth and high impact. However, regardless of industry, companies in the United States working to serve under-served populations, including low-income populations in the United States and internationally, had been less successful at achieving high growth, on average. The significant exceptions to this were the niches of impact entrepreneurs targeting minorities and disabled populations, which were the only segments serving underserved populations that showed a positive correlation between impact and growth.[5] The data reinforces the suggestion that some markets are prone to market failure, while others can become purely commercial—thanks in part to the efforts of Catalytic Capital providers like minority-focused funds, or governments and philanthropy.

The different roles of sustaining capital are also seen in the case of Business Partners Limited (BPL). BPL was created in the 1980s to provide suitable institutional financing for small and medium-size enterprises (SMEs) in South Africa. In addition to the matching investments made by the South African government, BPL accessed public grant funding between 1981 and 1996, which enabled the firm to work in higher-risk sectors and to target start-up companies. The separate public grants program targeted what were thought to be "risky" transactions and supported troubled companies by providing lower-cost capital. By 1993, however, as BPL rethought its structure, this grants program was retired, and BPL introduced equity and quasi-equity investment vehicles.

As demonstrated by both BPL and ATI, the use of sustaining capital by the funds varies greatly depending on the conditions of the market they aim to target—and echoes the distinction we make in chapter 2 between funds considered "first responders" and those that are "early-stage innovators." The use of sustaining capital also depended on the investment philosophy and approach of the fund's founders to some extent. For example, the investment philosophy of the founder of Aavishkaar, Vineet Rai, *rejected* sustaining capital. During his first round of fundraising, Rai turned down a $500,000 grant offer from a development finance institution. "This was the toughest decision I've taken in my lifetime," Rai reflected, as accepting the grant would have doubled Aavishkaar's fund size and allowed the team to live more comfortably. But Rai rejected the offer, convinced that the grant would destroy his business by distorting the market for seed-stage investment in India and undermining his objective to grow early-stage, impact-driven businesses in a financially sustainable manner.

"I wanted to be an entrepreneur myself and prove to other entrepreneurs that they could succeed without grants. By surviving and struggling, I was on an equal moral footing while asking the entrepreneurs to take low salaries as well. Entrepreneurs took $5,000 to $10,000 annual salaries, seeing I was doing the same thing," Rai explains. As of October 2013, Aavishkaar still has never accepted any grant or subsidy to cover the costs of its core business activities. Put another way, Rai discovered that he was able to use innovation rather than subsidy, placing Aavishkaar in the early-stage innovator category.

In contrast, sustaining capital is *foundational* to the investment approach of those first responders, like ATI, that target markets with deep market failures, even as these funds are equally financially disciplined. ATI's mission is to serve "unbankable" populations—and, indeed, as many of them as possible—but CEO and president Janie Barrera is adamant that the organization focus just as rigorously on increasing its own financial independence through product innovation and diversification.

The stories of BPL's, Aavishkaar's, and ATI's evolution and calibration of their investment programs within the larger eco-system of capital providers and capital recipients demonstrate the many considerations an impact investing fund must take into account when utilizing sustaining capital. Depending on the market a fund aims to target and the investment approach of the fund's leadership, there are countless ways that sustaining capital may be leveraged to attain the desired combination of financial returns and social impact.

Seeding

Another role for Catalytic Capital is that of the first investor, often called an anchor or seed investor. And in some cases, that seeding function can be carried out collaboratively. For example, Small Enterprise Assistance Funds (SEAF) was launched in 1989 as an experimental project of CARE, a large international humanitarian organization, for the purpose initially of assisting Eastern European countries in making the often rocky transition from communism to capitalism after the fall of the Berlin Wall. Governments throughout the region were privatizing state-owned enterprises and laying off thousands of government workers, leading to high unemployment and economic crises.[6] SEAF believed that the growth of private SMEs was critical to creating desperately needed jobs and stimulating local economic growth; and, after successfully launching several funds throughout Eastern Europe through the 1990s, the fund developed a strong case for its uniquely SME-focused approach to economic development. By the end of the 1990s, SEAF had positioned itself as the leading SME investor in Europe, generating a strong (above 25 percent) gross internal rate of return (IRR) as well as creating jobs and improving income levels for thousands of people.

SEAF's funds were often seeded by a single investor with a particular social and economic need in mind and, in early 2000, the International Finance Corporation (IFC), which had previously invested in a SEAF fund in Macedonia, inquired whether the Sichuan Province of West China might be of interest. As discussed earlier, Sichuan was highly underdeveloped and, acutely aware of this growing inequity, the central Chinese government had spurred

IFC's outreach to SEAF, the preeminent SME equity investor in formerly socialist countries seeking to transition from state-run to market-driven economies.

IFC anchored the creation of SEAF's Sichuan SME Investment Fund, drawing in New York Life Insurance, one of the largest life insurers in world, which had received an especially enticing "carrot" from the Chinese government. New York Life was in the process of obtaining a license to offer insurance in China, and its corporate counsel was informed by government officials that if New York Life were to kick-start an SME fund in Sichuan, where unemployment was a bigger problem than a lack of insurance, Beijing would look on New York Life favorably.

To be sure, New York Life and the IFC viewed SEAF as more than just a highly attractive potential partner. Their selection of SEAF was out of necessity. "This was so remote and out of the way that nobody else would do it," recalls Bert van der Vaart, SEAF's founder and executive chairman.

Although SEAF's story in China is quite unusual, it also reflects a trend observed across all twelve funds: *alignment of seed and follow-on investors around a shared objective is key.* In SEAF's case, the alignment of several influential investors around the common goal of improving economic activity in rural China quickly catalyzed the creation of their fund.

Every fund has at least one seed investor; in the field of impact investing, however, the role can be even more important, as it often helps lessen the widespread perception of risk in these currently underfunded markets. Although alignment with seed investor interests is also critical for traditional financial funds, impact investing funds face unique opportunities and challenges when it comes to alignment. For example, in the twelve funds studied, seed investors were often motivated to invest based on a shared social goal or a shared interest in a local geography.

In our group of twelve funds, seed investors were most often foundations, government agencies, or multilateral organizations that stepped in because they wanted to proactively create a fund aligned with their objectives. It is rare for a commercial investor to provide seed capital in the impact investing funds we studied, although policy can be instrumental in creating "carrots"—or financial incentives—for commercial players to step into this role. As seen in the case of SEAF, the Chinese government played a key role in motivating the institutional capital of New York Life. And the public sector undergirded the creation of Huntington Capital's second fund, which targeted a local geography of interest. Among the larger investors in HC II were Union Bank of California, motivated by the CRA, and a number of California-licensed insurance companies (through the intermediaries Impact Community Capital and Macquarie Funds Management), driven by the California Organized Investment Network (COIN), a California Department of Insurance program modeled after the CRA that requires insurers to invest in underserved communities on a voluntary but closely monitored basis.

In contrast, Aavishkaar's seed capital did not come from institutional investors, and therefore the fundraising process looked quite different. The first notable fundraising accomplishment for Vineet Rai was in 2001, when he was introduced to several alumni of the Indian Institute of Management in Ahmedabad.

According to Rai, these alumni "wanted to play a role in shaping the future of India." As a first step, several of these individuals agreed to foot the $500 bill for Rai to fly to Singapore, where he pitched his business plan to a large group of influential nonresident Indians. Remarkably, Rai convinced half a dozen people to contribute $5,000 to $10,000 to Aavishkaar on the spot.

Rai maintains close relationships with many of these seed investors; as of 2013, several of them sit on Aavishkaar's investment committee and management and advisory boards. Some, including Anantha Nageswaran, Pravin Gandhi, Sameer Wagle, and Arun Diaz, went on to fundraise on Rai's behalf. In Aavishkaar's case, this shared objective to "shape the future of India" provided the critical alignment—around both a shared social goal and a shared geography—needed to attain seeding capital.

From the point of view of the fund manager, another essential element in the practice of seeding is the alignment among investors regarding ultimate objectives, which can allow for access to more capital and more stakeholders committed to a fund's success for strategic and not just financial reasons.

There is another outcome, however, that we noticed in our research. If investors change their minds along the way and decide their priorities must shift, fund managers can become caught

up in some very difficult governance conversations. In our confi-
dential interviews outside of the twelve funds we profiled, there were
several examples of funds with investors who had changed their
objectives over the term of the partnership (often lasting five to
ten years or more, and sometimes with different people involved).
The conversations at the level of the fund investment committee
became more difficult as the managers struggled to find ways to
meet needs that differed significantly from those expressed at the
outset and that had not been captured in any of the official fund
documents. Anecdotally, they affirmed the most important need
was for a fund to agree on strategy with a seed investor and on the
kind of blended value the investor was seeking. Overall, it was more
common for funds affiliated with philanthropic foundations and
government to evolve their strategies over time. The outcomes-
based interests of these investors can change frequently as they learn
about the markets they are trying to shape, creating difficulties for
the intermediaries they have supported. Institutional investors like
banks, who are often motivated by regulatory carrots that change
more slowly, may be less likely to change strategies over time.

Risk-Reducing

RSF Social Finance stands out among financial institutions for its
integration of investing, lending, and support for philanthropic
giving by individuals under a single nonprofit, public charity
umbrella. These service offerings help the fund take advantage
of the different ways to layer and leverage different kinds of
Catalytic Capital.

At RSF, "integrated capital" refers to the creative stacking of
capital sources to finance impact investments. The practice relies
on some combination of debt, equity, and philanthropic sources to
meet capital needs during critical phases of an organization's life
cycle. RSF thus takes beneficial advantage of the strategic interests
of different organizations, leverages their resources, and spreads
risk to more closely match investor expectations. The synergies
between funders make the loan possible, converting an "unbankable" investment into an attractive impact opportunity.

In 1984, RSF's inaugural loan to Pine Hill Waldorf School in
Wilton, New Hampshire, used funds sourced from fifty families in

the Wilton community, which had a vested interest in seeing the school rebuilt. Today, the concept of engaging the community remains at the core of the RSF mission, and RSF has become adept at using community risk-reducing capital in its lending. Working closely with potential borrowers, RSF has encouraged its stakeholders or outside philanthropic partners to create first-loss layers at the individual borrower level. This approach can both reduce financial risk and create important local constituent buy-in for the growth the capital is intended to support. Risk-reducing Catalytic Capital can take on many forms, such as grants, guarantees, and concessionary investments, and has opened up more opportunities for outside donors to integrate into the RSF model, thereby increasing awareness of RSF and its mission. In addition, RSF plays an important role in the emerging ecosystem for social enterprise, by showing banks and other market-rate lenders that these borrowers are creditworthy.

In other cases, the lending program relies on pledges of support from the community to make it possible to underwrite a particular loan. These pledges consist of legally binding commitments to make charitable donations, which may be drawn on in repayment of all or a portion of the loan and provide security for repayment of the loan. However, the amount and type of security required for each loan are at the sole discretion of the fund. In some cases, the fund may make unsecured or undersecured loans based on strong financial performance or other factors.

Ted Levinson, RSF's senior director of lending, explains that the balance between catalytic interventions and benchmark investment criteria is subjective but important. "We walk away from a deal if we think we won't get paid back. If we think the project is going to be successful but there's a modest gap between RSF's comfort level and the amount being requested, then we find philanthropy to make the loan happen. We need 98 percent confidence that we'll get paid back to make a loan. If we're only 90 percent confident, then we look for philanthropic capital to bridge the gap and get to a yes."

At the same time, RSF is learning to apply different kinds of Catalytic Capital to offset different kinds of risks. According to Levinson, "Sometimes RSF has a borrower right up its alley from a mission standpoint, and has strong confidence that it will be paid back, but doesn't see how it could recover the money if it's mistaken. A lot of borrowers don't have a good answer to that second question." For example, Hana Health, a health clinic operating on government-owned land, needed money to build a commercial kitchen. RSF couldn't get a deed on the building because it was on government land. Although RSF was confident Hana Health would pay back the loan—cash flow was strong, and the project was good—there was no enforcement mechanism. Most of the time, RSF uses a foundation guarantee to strengthen the collateral position. In other cases, when a nonprofit borrower has good collateral but weak cash flow, RSF tries to find grants to lower the loan amount.

As exemplified by RSF, Catalytic Capital can play a variety of roles in reducing risk. At its core, an important role of Catalytic Capital is to reconcile and respect differing perceptions of risk in the marketplace. Often investors have asymmetrical knowledge about impact investing markets and thus differing perceptions of risk. Catalytic Capital can encourage the flow of capital to these opportunities by improving their risk-and-return profiles, thus incentivizing others to invest. There is a market-making factor here as well: over time, the perception of risk can be reduced. An investor who earns back a return on an investment she thought was risky may be more willing to make another.

RSF's use of integrated capital is just one approach to risk reduction. GIIN's 2013 *Issue Brief on First-Loss Capital* describes in detail some additional structures used by risk-reducing first-loss capital investors, both in the roles of provider of first-loss capital and of the recipient of first-loss capital. It defines first-loss investments as grants, equity, and subordinated debt that are both catalytic and purpose driven, meaning these investments enable other capital to be committed and also seek to achieve specific social and/or environmental goals.[7] "From Grants to Groundbreaking: Unlocking Impact Investments," a white paper produced by ImpactAssets about how philanthropy and investment can collaborate, also explores how the previously referenced nonprofit intermediary, Living Cities, structures capital to leverage a host of other investment capital to bring impact deals to market.[8]

Nearly all risk-reducing capital requires tiered fund structures to recognize different levels of risk and return for investors. There is an art to creating financial structures that layer investors, and there are some players in the marketplace and in our study who do it extremely well. As Debra Schwartz of the MacArthur Foundation, who has spent the last decade layering capital in multimillion-dollar funds supporting affordable housing and community development, explains, "It is a creative exercise, not one-size-fits-all. High-impact layered capital that works for a range of investors will be made, not found. Roll up your sleeves!"

The Bay Area Transit-Oriented Affordable Housing Fund (TOAH) is one case where investors truly "rolled up their sleeves" to create a customized solution. The fund—now with $50 million to deploy—was set up to address the need for equitable transit-oriented development. It provides capital not only for both market-rate and low- to moderate-income housing but also for the development of child-care centers, charter schools, and health care facilities—all located conveniently near transit hubs. Toward this goal of equitable development, the public sector has provided $10 million of subsidy (essentially through a grant). These funds take the most risk, thereby decreasing the overall risk of the transaction for each of the other participants in the fund, including institutional investors, foundations, and CDFIs. In effect, this funding serves as the fund's foundation—without the subsidy, CDFIs would not lend; without the CDFIs, philanthropic investors would not lend; and without philanthropic investors, the senior noteholders would not lend.

As is true of other forms of Catalytic Capital, these types of layered structures are not unique to impact investing, yet given the new spectrum of "unknowns," impact investing funds typically approach these activities with fresh perspectives and creativity. Structured finance is not new; what *is* new is the skill of figuring out how to manage a diverse set of strategic investments in one deal. In order to develop these new approaches, there is a need for more active deal structuring in the current impact investing market ecosystem. For example, as Laurie J. Spengler, CEO of Enclude, an impact investing advisory firm, recently observed: "What we see is a real dearth of professional intermediation in deal structuring, deal negotiation, and deal execution. And when you take half a step back and you think about mainstream finance, advisors are in abundant supply for small companies, large companies, and financial institutions. We should have the same expectation as our work becomes more professional, and our industry professionalizes."[9]

Enclude is an expert at this type of intermediation between a diverse range of stakeholders, leveraging another best practice, Multilingual Leadership (discussed in chapter 6). In one example, Enclude helped Ecobank, a large financial services provider in Africa, improve the products it offered to small businesses. By meeting with local entrepreneurs to understand their needs, while simultaneously understanding the challenges and opportunities at Ecobank, Enclude was able to refine the bank's 250 varied financial products targeting SMEs into five strategic and more effective offerings. Spengler explains: "Both sides of the equation have to have additional skills and capacity, and a willingness to come together. When it works it's fantastic. But if we're only affecting the banks, it won't work. And if we're only touching the entrepreneur, it won't work either. . . . The supply and the demand side have to be attended to."[10]

One final innovative example, demonstrating the myriad of possible deal structures, can be found in the United Kingdom's new Social Outcomes Fund. The Social Outcomes Fund is a £20 million fund managed by the UK Cabinet Office aiming to catalyze the use of social impact bonds (SIBs) by providing "top-up" funds to the specific government departments, local authorities, and other commissioning bodies working to develop a SIB in their jurisdiction.[11]

SIBs have been highlighted as a new product to fund social enterprise and an alternative approach to the government's provision of social services. They are partnerships in which private investors provide capital to nonprofit social service providers in order to achieve desired objectives. The government agrees to make "performance payments" to investors that are dependent on the realization of specific, previously agreed-on social outcomes. Through this partnership model, SIBs provide cost savings to the government and present enormous opportunities for impact investors and social entrepreneurs.

A primary obstacle to the growth of SIBs has been that social problems often span various government silos, making it difficult to determine who will provide the performance payments and at what amount. The UK Cabinet Office describes these challenges and their strategy to overcome them: "It can be challenging for a single [public] commissioner to implement an early, preventative intervention programme where benefits fall across the system when budgets are tight and evidence is limited. The Social Outcomes Fund enables commissioners to provide these services by providing a top up to their outcomes payments recognizing wider savings to the public sector."[12]

The "top-up" capital is intended to incentivize the development of new SIB projects and to gather new data and insight into the SIB development process for future deals. The Cabinet Office explains: "By paying for outcomes the fund will enable innovation. It will also generate new evidence about what kinds of intervention work and how the outcomes of projects can be effectively measured. An important aim of the fund is to collect an evidence base on the existing barriers to the growth of SIBs. Reporting and assessment of performance data is therefore a condition of funding, and will generate evidence on the effectiveness of the project and mitigate barriers in the future. This data will also form an evidence base of benefits that accrue across government departments to incentivize cross-government working."

The importance of risk-reducing capital in impact investing markets cannot be overstated, particularly considering that many roles and responsibilities are yet to be created, providing huge opportunities for new innovation and partnerships, contingent on high levels of transparency, clear communication, and Multilingual Leadership.

Signaling

The last type of Catalytic Capital signals to other investors that an investment is legitimate. Seed investments may signal the market as well, but any investor can join the deal at any time to have a signaling effect. If an investor is particularly large, reputable, or sophisticated, investing in a fund can improve the recipient's perceived credibility and visibility to other investors—a practice as common in commercial investing as it is in impact investing.

Signaling is particularly important in impact investing, however, because these markets are idiosyncratic, and investors must understand not only the financial profiles of funds and companies but also the social issues and theories of change being deployed. This adds many new layers to the due diligence process, which signaling can help expedite.

Elevar Equity has benefited from the signaling of its seed investor, Omidyar Network (ON), and has used this in turn to benefit its investees. ON not only signaled that the fund was legitimate but also introduced Elevar to numerous other investors. When making an investment in a company, Elevar now tries to partner as often as possible with reputable coinvestors. Coinvestors in the fund's portfolio companies include both impact investors (such as the Michael and Susan Dell Foundation and ACCIÓN International) and commercial investors (such as Sequoia Capital, Silicon Valley Bank India Capital Partners, Helion Venture Partners, WestBridge Capital, and Wolfensohn Capital Partners). Elevar works to scale its investments very rapidly after the first twenty-four months of investing, and has used signaling extensively to project the quality of its investments to potential investors in the market and ease the way for the large capital raises it will need to follow its own.

Huntington Capital also benefited from an early signaling investor, Bank of America Merrill Lynch (BAML), with which its objectives of providing access to finance for underserved SMEs, creating quality jobs in low-income communities, and increasing workforce and entrepreneurial diversity were well aligned. BAML went out of its way to introduce Huntington Capital to other institutional investors, including Hamilton Lane, which was deploying capital on behalf of CalPERS, the largest pension fund in the United States.

Signaling, however, is not a strategy limited to LP investors. Funds can also play a signaling role for their investees, as does the W.K. Kellogg Foundation's (WKKF's) Mission Driven Investments (MDI) for the enterprises in which it invests, in the education, health, food, and community development sectors.

In 2007, WKKF's board of trustees endorsed a strategy of proactively aligning some of its financial investments with programmatic objectives. A key element of the strategy was making direct investments in impactful enterprises, a practice virtually unheard of in endowment and even "mission-related" investing circles. Tom Reis, who led the MDI team at the time, argues that going direct unearthed a tremendous, untapped source of investments.

"There's all this entrepreneurial talent out there that traditional investors are overlooking. I continue to believe that we barely scratched the surface. If you are really into both financial and impact returns, then you need to find these people and fund them. These entrepreneurs are highly credible."

The strategy has paid off for WKKF—delivering excellent financial and social returns (two realized exits out of six total direct investments delivering IRRs of 46 and 65 percent, and 53,300 vulnerable kids supported)—and for its investees. WKKF signals that its investees are delivering significant impacts—having cleared WKKF's stringent diligence process related to mission alignment—and, as a large and well-connected foundation, is an important strategic partner more broadly.

MicroVest, one of the first US-based asset managers to invest in low-income financial institutions (LIFIs, which are similar to microfinance institutions, or MFIs) in emerging markets, is another good example of a fund providing signaling capital for its investees. LIFIs have been boosted by having an international investor with a strong reputation in the field, providing them with what has affectionately become known as the "MicroVest Effect."

Doug Young, managing director for investments at MicroVest, explains that it is quite common for two or three of MicroVest's competitors to approach LIFIs once the LIFIs have received financing from MicroVest. This is primarily due to MicroVest's reputation for performing particularly in-depth due diligence. Young offers the example of Kompanion in Kyrgyzstan, Constanta in Georgia, and Confianza in Peru as a few successful LIFIs that received their first international financing from MicroVest and subsequent funding from other international investors.

MicroVest plays a signaling role not only for its investees but also for the broader microfinance sector. The performance of MicroVest I influenced investors' subsequent participation in impact investing and microfinance. "MicroVest informed our broad strategy for investing in microfinance, especially with regard to the right level of financial product evolution and the right level of financial return expectations," explains Charly Kleissner, cofounder of the KL Felicitas Foundation and an investor in MicroVest. "MicroVest also informed our strategy on the PRI [program-related investment] side, because it was our first PRI and is a great example of an investment type that continues to be in our portfolio. These are debt notes with a 2 to 4 percent return."

Similarly, Parnassus Investments, an investment management company with $9.2 billion of assets under management, and the Clara Fund have increased their appetite for investing in LIFIs as a direct result of their experience with MicroVest I. "MicroVest's first fund created the desire for us to get more exposure to the asset class," explains Marc Mahon, CFO of Parnassus, citing the firm's increased investment in MicroVest from $250,000 to $10 million as of October 15, 2013. Clara Fund's financial advisor initially advised Lorene Arey, the foundation's president, not to invest in MicroVest, but has since changed his tune. "Today, my portfolio manager has actually recommended MicroVest to three of his other clients who were pushing for impact investing opportunities," says Arey.

Deutsche Bank's Comprehensive Use of Catalytic Capital

Deutsche Bank's Global Commercial Microfinance Consortium I demonstrates how all four forms of Catalytic Capital—sustaining, seeding, risk-reducing, and signaling—can successfully be deployed in one fund.

Sustaining. When beginning the fundraising process, Asad Mahmood, then managing director, had a clear idea of the financial structure needed to attract mainstream investors and, as a first port of call in raising the necessary funds, approached some of the major development finance institutions and aid agencies, including the International Finance Corporation, US Agency for International Development (USAID), and the UK Department for International Development (DFID). USAID agreed to provide a guarantee of $10 million, or 25 percent of the value of an anticipated $40 million in senior notes. DFID provided a grant of $1.5 million. That grant layer also served to be risk-reducing for the fund, but the fact that it came first was essential in the creation of the fund. The other fund layers, which included several for commercial companies and investors, were made possible by DFID's initial support.

In addition, throughout the development process, the consortium received subsidy through services provided internally at Deutsche Bank (such as HR, credit control, and legal). The largest subsidy that the consortium received was not internal, but was instead from one of its service providers: White and Case, the consortium's external legal counsel, offered a 66 percent discount on its services, which amounted to significant savings over the life of the fund—equivalent to over 15 percent of the total management fees collected.

Seeding. Even before Mahmood began external fundraising, the first task was to convince senior executives within Deutsche Bank to provide introductions to key potential supporters, especially to several of the bank's departments. This resulted in much of the internal, sustaining support and technical assistance noted earlier, but also resulted in Deutsche Bank's making a $1 million investment in Class B shares through the Deutsche Bank Americas Foundation. Gary Hattem, the foundation's president and chairman of the consortium board, reflects on the foundation's decision to provide seed funding for the consortium: "The consortium represented an important milestone in Deutsche Bank's commitment to aligning similarly motivated investor capital toward the goal of helping the microfinance sector not only grow but reach maturity as a responsible and client-focused industry."

Risk-reducing. The layered structure of the fund, which Figure 5.1 illustrates both at the point it was first created as a $50 million investment and then

Figure 5.1 The Capital Stacks in Deutsche Bank's Global Commercial Microfinance Consortium I

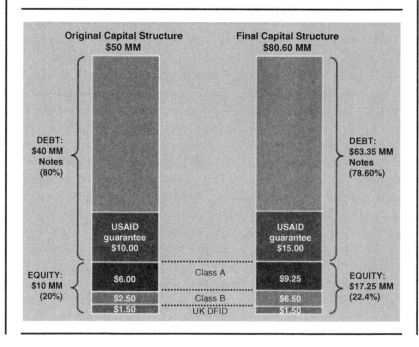

when it finally closed and was oversubscribed at $80.6 million, allowed the consortium to accommodate the needs of a wide variety of investors. The USAID guarantee made the consortium more attractive to commercial investors because it not only reduced investment risks but also allowed Deutsche Bank to offer noteholders an increased estimated risk-adjusted return. As described earlier, if noteholders' entire $63.35 million were at risk, Deutsche Bank estimated noteholder return at a 6.6 percent IRR based on estimated pricing of LIBOR + 1.25 percent. As only $48.35 million of noteholders' capital was actually at risk because of the USAID guarantee, however, Deutsche Bank offered noteholders an estimated 16 percent risk-adjusted IRR.

The fund's subsequent performance revealed the power of layered products to respond to the diverse needs and priorities of LPs. Even as several MFIs were unable to meet their obligations to the consortium as scheduled—due to the Great Recession's impact on MFI delinquency rates, a few cases of fraud, and regional microfinance crises—all but the most risk-tolerant investors received their promised financial return: LIBOR plus 1.25 percent for senior noteholders representing $60 million of the capital, and a 7 percent net IRR for Class A equity investors representing $9.7 million. Only Class B equity investors, with $6.5 million, have underperformed, receiving a 3.5 percent IRR against a goal of 12 percent. However, because of the transparency that a structured fund allows, this group is generally pleased with their return, as they were investing with a primarily philanthropic, market-building goal in mind.

Signaling. As a significant institution in its own right, Deutsche Bank, with its reputation, relationships, and financial capabilities, signaled to other institutions that a pioneering new approach to microfinance was possible, ultimately resulting in investments in senior notes from over a dozen others.

Institutions were eager to benefit from the knowledge of social markets they would gain through exposure to the consortium. Some have gone on to build dedicated units, such as the Co-Operative Bank, which has subsequently created a microfinance specialist team within its social banking division that launched a £25 million microfinance loan fund; and Storebrand Life Insurance of Norway, which in 2008 was instrumental in launching and funding the Norwegian Microfinance Initiative, a public-private partnership that manages $100 million through three microfinance investment vehicles.

The Catalytic Capital Tool Kit

The underlying concepts of Catalytic Capital discussed in this chapter translate into a set of practical steps investors can take, across the life cycle of your investments, to ascertain and act on the strategic goals of your partners, including LPs, coinvestors, enterprise managers, and even the ultimate beneficiaries of the business.

More broadly, those who want to leverage Catalytic Capital will need to take the time to understand, in an engaged way that builds trust between parties, the real strategic interests of stakeholders and the alignment of these interests with your own. A critical success factor will be the manager's ability to combine two high-order skills: first, knowing how to structure multiparty transactions in ways that are consistent with the fund's capital requirements and goals; and second, engaging those parties in conversations and then negotiations that end in a win-win structure that honors asymmetric goals and allows each party to emerge with their strategic, impact, and financial goals met in the right order of priority.

At its essence, the practice of using Catalytic Capital is a multi-stakeholder exercise. We recommend the following steps as funds consider catalytic purposes in their investment activity:

1. **Know how.** Learn the tools of structured finance and multi-party transactions.
2. **Know who and why.** Understand the motivations of different types of investors and the way they use their capital to achieve various ends.
3. **Think expansively.** Revisit strategic objectives and approaches and understand whether you could be playing a more catalytic role.
4. **Invest strategically.** Focus your efforts on an approach aligned with the organization's mission.
5. **Review collectively.** Track your catalytic impact individually, but also by examining the deal and sector holistically, assessing the way your impact has influenced and coordinated with others.

Let's explore each of these in turn.

Know How

Catalytic investors will benefit from being aware of, or even fluent in, the tools of the trade in terms of options that can be built into fund and deal structures. If your team does not have this knowledge, you can seek it out; you can study other transactions; talk to lawyers, accountants, and financiers; or start doing deals in the space and learn what some of the variations and norms are within their investment area of focus. Some of you will want to partner with third parties who have this knowledge, specifically in the impact space. Imprint Capital and Enclude, for example, are two firms that specialize in multiparty transaction structures and negotiations, but there are others that have expertise in different industries, impact areas, and geographies. If you want to learn these techniques yourself, you will need to combine both acquiring skills for structured finance, and listening and learning to norms of the moment. Successful fund managers have a broad range of tools to help them identify the right structures to apply to each party, as Deutsche Bank did in the case of the Global Commercial Microfinance Consortium I.

Know Who and Why

Fund managers will want to take some time to identify potential types of investors both as capital providers and as cofunders. To do this, they should read and do research broadly to go outside their comfort zone and think about what other kinds of companies, funds, or asset owners may actually have an interest in the outcomes that they care about. Sometimes these may not be obvious, and they may cross sectors. Think about private sector partners, including large companies that might have distribution networks on the ground that would benefit from an impact partnership of some type. Could you create relationships with other stakeholders who also care about your impacts, which could be government partners, international NGOs, and so on? Deutsche Bank, for example, discovered that the institutional noteholders in its consortium were primarily attracted for strategic reasons, which required that Deutsche Bank engage directly with the CEO rather than the CSR division or investment division, both of which lacked a full enough understanding to get on board.

The first step is to cast a wide net and make lists of different types of potential partners based on geographic, impact, industry, and stage interests. Imagine a sample investment in the portfolio. You may wish to do an informal "ecosystem analysis" for that company, scoping out its peers, its competitors, including parties that will be displaced if the company succeeds (or not), the company's suppliers, intermediaries, organizations that might displace the company if it does *not* succeed, and key government officials and agencies, NGOs, and philanthropic funders active in the market or with an interest in the social outcome targeted.[13] All of those relationships are valid possibilities for finding alignment with outcome-oriented stakeholders.

The next step is to ascertain the real motivations of those stakeholders. Do they share your profile of risk, return, and impact, or are there asymmetries to take advantage of? In order to know them, you will need to attend industry conferences in that area, make new connections, ask a lot of questions, and try to figure out ways to build collaborative relationships with new parties. It is not an accident that several of our profiled funds got started from nonprofit organizations—they were collections of individuals acting in the public interest who saw the need for targeted solutions, and recognized capital as a means to the end. Sitting on boards of other organizations can be another good strategy for meeting people in different parts of your ecosystem. They provide a safe space for field-level conversations about desired outcomes in the area in which you are working.

A word to the wise: try to find the right anchor/seed investors for your own fund. Realize that a large portion of your LPs will have strategic, and not just financial, reasons for investing. Without clear alignment, investors may lose faith if markets or performance temporarily falters.

Finally, work to identify and create peer groups of structural innovators in your field. Deep experience in structuring products and blending catalytic and commercial capital is at the crux of impact investing. This core skillset—including a deep understanding of a variety of financial tools, capital providers, and product uses—should be identified, nurtured, and proliferated through an intentional process of network and knowledge development.

Think Expansively

Here, you will need to put the spotlight back on yourself. Consider the following searching questions:

- What exactly are you trying to achieve?
- What is in your comfort zone and what is not?
- What kind of catalytic role do you want to play, and which kinds are not acceptable to you?
- Are you going to be an actor who structures relationships for a set of diverse parties, or do you prefer to let someone else do that and to step in when the opportunity seems to match your own interests?
- Do you want to sustain, seed, reduce risk, signal, or combine some or all of these purposes? Do you want to apply this to just some investments or to all? When are those purposes not appropriate for you?
- What kind of leverage is most needed by the stakeholders you identified in step 2, and can you offer it?
- What are the implications of these choices on specific deals or on the fund as a whole?
- What can you learn from your investees or other partners about what has been tried before? What would really help your investees succeed in a new way (for example, coinvesting with a supplier so as to cement the relationship and eventually lower costs)?
- How can you take advantage of other experts outside of your networks to help build a knowledge base of best practices that your fund can use going forward?

By responding to these questions, you will emerge with a clearer sense of the kind of fund you want to create and the contours of your own fund's "build or buy" strategy. You'll want to "build" your own expertise around a few functions that you do yourself and become recognized for, and "buy" or partner on other aspects. And by thinking about these choices up front, you are more likely to identify useful partners to help you succeed, and to possibly identify ways you can work with others to help them succeed as well.

Invest Strategically

This is where you move from the broad exploration of options to specific practices. You should emerge from this phase with a clear set of strategic priorities for how you most want to catalyze investments. These priorities can become a road map for a set of investments you make over time. And, as you make new investments, you can revisit your analysis and see what needs to be adjusted or revised.

On the investment side, work with stakeholders to see if your priorities match theirs. Hone your ideas through interaction; don't assume that one size fits all or that your plan in the abstract will work when it's time to get detailed with various stakeholders. Examples of methods of engagement include the following:

- *Meetings and networking.* Participate actively in third-party events, strategically ensuring that you are at the table, or in the same room, with the right people at the right time. Are there boards or topical networks that you can join? Host a roundtable alongside an existing conference where you know relevant stakeholders will be, or organize a proprietary gathering bringing people together specifically for this purpose.
- *Research.* Design or participate in a research process that necessitates outreach to stakeholders, either independently or in partnership with others. For example, if you were investing in health care and had a particular knack for financial innovations, you might lead or participate in a project or convening, scoping the opportunity for new, structured funds in this area and exposing you to others with similar interests (investors, funders, health care providers, beneficiaries, and governments) in a neutral setting, such as a conference, educational institution, or industry interest group.
- *Communication.* Share your opinions, through blogs, the press, and other means, and actively solicit responses from readers.

Leave time for negotiating intensively among parties if you want to create multiple layers in a financial instrument. Don't fix the terms too early, but don't let everyone pass the buck until you have no real commitments either. And don't forget that you can be a catalyst in your own right. Think about others alongside whom you want to invest and the strategic value of having them in the deal. Is there a role for your capital in anchoring the delivery of nonfinancial value in different deals or in making a contribution with other investors?

Review Collectively

Now that you are acting as a catalytic investor, you have a responsibility to figure out whether your fund or deal investment actually fulfilled that objective.

You'll want to identify best practices in tracking performance, especially around the outcomes you've selected and the catalytic approach you chose. For example, if you were a seed investor in a deal, how much capital was leveraged afterwards? If you were a sustaining investor, how well did your sustaining strategy work for the fund or enterprise—has it met the recipient's own sustainability goals? Don't be afraid to work directly with constituents, including investees, coinvestors, and actors in other parts of the market, to conduct this oversight well. Seek advice and support from third-party experts around best practices in your field. Work to identify opportunities to share results and findings publicly so that other managers can learn from your work.

In addition, catalytic investors who aim toward market development as their goal have an additional task: to create a market-level theories of change and tools for understanding how their efforts have affected the approach of other actors. Many government and nonprofit funders have spent years honing these strategies, and impact fund managers can learn from them. For an out-of-the-box resource, consider reviewing the way that policy advocates—with very diffuse influences—are trying to track their impacts. A good overview was provided in 2007 by Organizational Research Services on behalf of the Annie E. Casey Foundation, emphasizing the importance of clarity and specificity in setting high-level strategies and outcomes.[14]

■ ■ ■

Many transactions in the impact investing space, from social impact bonds to layered capital structures, require the complex combination of skills we have highlighted here. And usually the parties best able to build complex transactions can speak across organizations and sectors with fluency, in order to reach agreement and manage relationships going forward—which leads us to what we call Multilingual Leadership.

In chapter 6, we discuss the specifics of developing Multilingual Leadership as a skillset, and complete our journey through the four key, distinguishing practices of impact investing.

6

Multilingual Leadership

*The leadership task ahead . . . is daunting but exciting. That
is why impact investing is becoming the life's work of so many
experienced and emerging leaders.*

—Katherine Fulton and Carolien De Bruin,
Monitor Institute

MULTILINGUAL LEADERSHIP, THE ABILITY TO "SPEAK" AND OPERATE across
market sectors and silos, reveals itself in a variety of ways:

• At MicroVest, it is in the singular commitment to investing
with a commercial approach to microfinance, built on distinctly
social sector origins and governance structures. As discussed earlier, an attentiveness to social outcomes is the "ballast" in Micro-
Vest's ship, even as management is provided with the freedom and
incentives to apply the utmost financial discipline (i.e., the commercial "sail") to its work, and to scale the business with confidence. Gil Crawford, MicroVest's CEO, personifies the balance.
Crawford was trained at Chase Manhattan Bank after working for
the Red Cross and the US State Department; founded Seed Capital
Development Fund, a US-based nonprofit that created financial
instruments and attracted funds to capitalize microfinance institutions; and worked for the Latin American financial markets division
at the International Finance Corporation (IFC). Crawford thus has
had deep experience in the public, private, and nonprofit sectors,
and in international development.
• At ACCIÓN Texas (ATI), it is in the background of
Janie Barrera, now president and CEO. Barrera grew up working

in her family's restaurant—both in front of and behind the counter—which gave her a solid grounding in small business management. As a former sister with the Sisters of Charity of the Incarnate Word, she developed deep experience in the social sector—at both programmatic and administrative levels. And prior to serving as founding president of ATI, she worked as the head of marketing for the US Air Force's Morale, Welfare, Recreation and Services Agency and had completed an MBA that helped her connect the dots among management, capital, and investing.

• At Aavishkaar, it is in the fund's activities in multiple, dynamic markets like agriculture, health, water and sanitation, and education, working with a wide range of stakeholders whose interests affect not only how the market works but also how companies within it evolve. An ability to work with these different actors, all with their own interests and motivations, is key to the fund's success and explains an aptitude for creating innovations like the Indian Impact Investor Council (discussed in earlier chapters), an India-focused industry membership group.

Many mainstream fund managers would rightly argue that all funds have diverse stakeholders, including among their investors; but at a general level, the central interest of GPs in traditionally managed funds is to effectively maximize financial return to LPs. Although Aavishkaar and other impact investors share that interest as well, the diverse perspectives of investors extend to the nature of impact, as well as to a variety of opinions on how that goal should be pursued.

New Skillsets for New Leaders

In some ways, Multilingual Leadership may be the most obvious topic addressed in this book. The importance to successful impact investing of leaders' and teams' being able to draw on multiple perspectives and skill types would seem self-evident. That said, we were deeply impressed in the course of our research to find just how critical professional experiences cutting across various silos were to the success of the funds we analyzed—both at the individual leader and team levels. In some ways this was simply sound interdisciplinary thinking—but in others it was much more. Multilingual Leadership speaks to the need for individual leaders and their teams to become fully fluent in moving smoothly from one context and set of actors to another. Multilingual Leadership has been central to the success of some of the outstanding funds in impact investing.

At its core, impact investing is an inherently interdisciplinary field, requiring board members, entrepreneurs, fund managers, and advisors to draw on diverse skills, perspectives, and insights in order to effectively manage capital for optimized impact. The goal of impact investing is to address social and environmental problems through the application of the tools of finance. This requires impact investing professionals to have an understanding of how finance works, but perhaps more important, a deep knowledge of the issue area—such as microfinance, renewable energy, community finance, or sustainable agriculture—within which they seek to operate.

Beyond financial expertise, impact investing frequently requires collaboration with many different types of stakeholders—financial institutions, civil society and community groups, foundations and nonprofits, and government agencies—all on a simultaneous basis. And being an effective leader demands more than the ability to be able to talk with folks from various stakeholder groups—she needs to truly understand their core perspective and how they view the world. This is not something developed in an academic way, from reading and discussion, but rather over time, as leaders play through and actually work in diverse areas of interest.

Understanding how to be an effective actor in private capital markets is not, on its own, enough to be an effective impact investor either. As chapter 4 explained, many impact investment funds are intricately linked with government. They were formed in partnership with government, took investment from government agencies, or actively advocate for policies that will allow them or their portfolio companies to do better work. Understanding—and respecting—the role of the public sector in creating an effective enabling environment within which impact investing can flourish is a key aspect of being able to best position private capital both to make the best use of this public support and to take its appropriate place in the "capital stack," enabling deals to come to market that might otherwise have not been successfully closed or executed.

Chapter 5 highlighted the nomenclature of philanthropy and ideas of "catalytic impact" and moving the needle on an issue, or a fund or enterprise in this case. In this chapter, we explore how these approaches come together in the staff, structures, and strategies that characterize our twelve exceptional funds.

Each of the leaders of the funds exhibited excellent Multilingual Leadership, and the teams they built also manifest this same set of broad perspectives.

Multilingual Leadership in the Research

Our world is largely a bifurcated one that asks us to choose from the start what we will do. Go into business? The arts? Development finance? Human services? Generally speaking, the career paths we're offered force us to choose between either doing good or doing well—and if we stay on one side or the other, we can pursue a career of significant social value generation or wealth creation—but seldom both at the same time. When we step out of the silo—moving from either traditional business or nonprofits into impact investing—there is an immediate challenge:

How do you think and talk and act in this Alice in Wonderland world of investing for both social value creation and the generation of financial returns to investors?

The newcomer is confronted with terms (SIBs, IRIS, impact) that are new, and practices (capital stacking, impact performance assessment, and more) that for many—including some of those already operating within the impact investing community!—can remain befuddling for months if not years. What, then, does leadership in this "space in between" look like? How do leaders emerge, and how are they trained? More specifically, what are the exact skills and practices they must develop if they are to be not only successful but effective in their efforts to lead organizations into the great, muddy middle and ultimately beyond the divide?

Leadership manifests itself in various ways in the world. It should be no surprise that this is also true when discussing the diverse application of Multilingual Leadership within the most successful impact investing funds. As we explored the twelve funds in our sample group, we found Multilingual Leadership was present throughout the organizations and in different ways within individual leaders of each fund.

Some individuals were aided by having come up through the ranks in different fields and through different types of organizations; at the organizational level, some funds were created as intentional collaborations between actors operating in different sectors, and this led such funds to be founded as fundamentally interdisciplinary institutions. Other organizations recognized the need to build out multidisciplinary capabilities from the outset in order to succeed as a firm, and therefore formulated explicit strategies to acquire talent and exposure to work in the sectors where expertise was lacking.

We also witnessed how Multilingual Leadership can aid fund managers at different stages of the fund's life:

• In creating a new fund, cross-sector experience allowed founders to see opportunities more traditional players did not.

With limited knowledge of investing or entrepreneurship prior to founding Aavishkaar, Vineet Rai described himself as an unlikely candidate to launch a fund. However, his nontraditional background with a paper conglomerate and government-sponsored incubator was key to Aavishkaar's existence: most Indian venture capitalists in 2000 had experience in Silicon Valley, and had concluded that the Silicon Valley venture capital organizational structure was too expensive to operate in rural India.

According to Rai, other would-be early-stage investors in rural India were trying to replicate the Silicon Valley model, making the same investment sizes and using the same mathematics to invest in India. Their minimum fund size was near $20 million, and they wanted to invest only in Bangalore and Mumbai. Aavishkaar, in contrast, raised a roughly $12 million fund focused on India's enormous rural population, estimated at around seven hundred million people. To make the model work, Rai chose to start people with low salaries, "with the idea of making a difference," and share the fund's profits with them in a "socialist" manner, in order to motivate his team and continue to attract talent. In the minds of Aavishkaar's would-be competitors, what Aavishkaar tried to do was impossible. Yet it has flourished—generating financial returns with significant impact.

• In attracting capital, many successful impact funds received investments from public, private, and nonprofit investors. The ability to speak the language of these different types of organizations is crucial to raising impact capital.

Crawford's experience at MicroVest gave him a unique perspective on the importance of a more explicitly commercial approach to microfinance, but also allowed him to effectively communicate with nonprofit and foundation stakeholders.

Investors uniformly cited their interactions with Crawford, and his deep knowledge of microfinance from multiple perspectives, as a reason for investing with MicroVest. "Gil struck me as a very solid business professional who was running an investment firm as if it were [operating in] the commercial space," says Lorene Arey, president of the Clara Fund and an investor in MicroVest's first fund. She went on to discuss how the combination of Crawford's traditional investing and microfinance experience, along with his passion for international development, was critical to her investment decision. "While the business model was commercially structured, Gil also was very excited about what MicroVest was doing in terms of benefiting the BoP and underserved sectors of the economy. It wasn't pure business—it was business with a heart."

• Having experience in both the private and social sectors enabled fund leaders to define and track both financial and impact performance in a meaningful way.

Calvert Foundation is already—and increasingly—linking its performance and reporting to the more discrete values and impact preferences of its thousands of investors, a process made possible by its deep connections to, and experience in, retail investing and the social sector. In its Women Investing in Women Initiative (WIN-WIN), for example, investors can invest in a portfolio of organizations in which the majority of clients served (50 percent or more) are women; the organization has a mandate to serve women in its mission or has a specific program targeting women, and/or the majority of the organization's products or services offered have been shown to especially benefit women. Accountability on the back end with input from multisector groups and perspectives allows Calvert Foundation to push out new kinds of investment initiatives to more investors.

Multilingual Leadership as Cross-Disciplinary and Collaborative

In reflecting on the reality that successful impact investing funds require leaders who are able to "speak across the divide," we are also aware that such leadership is not limited to the impact investing arena. In fact, many of today's social, economic, and environmental challenges must be addressed with strategies that are inherently interdisciplinary. We are not the first to comment on this. Others have addressed the need for cross-sector solutions to today's problems, and in this chapter, we seek to build on their observations with our own experience.

In *The Solution Revolution: How Business, Government and Social Enterprises Are Teaming Up to Solve Society's Toughest Problems*, William Eggers and Paul Macmillan identify the types of organizations that are leading innovative solutions to social problems.[1] They point to

- Philanthropists using commercial strategies to develop afford-able products that provide basic services for the poor
- Corporations that contribute the time of their employees and their core competencies to address social problems related to their lines of business
- Social entrepreneurs who create businesses that explicitly create social value in addition to financial value
- Volunteer groups that are increasingly empowered by the Internet to crowdfund and contribute skills-based volunteering to support solutions to community problems

In describing this ecosystem of social innovators, Eggers and Macmillan particularly point out the value of conveners—those leaders who can bring together decision makers from across sectors to partner on new social and business endeavors. Indeed, a core characteristic of leaders across the funds we reviewed was the ability to convene decision makers from just these types of organizations, in order to seek guidance, partner on projects, or make investments.

New efforts to focus on such cross-sector collaborations are not only more frequent but taking hold at unprecedented scale within governments, nonprofits, and corporations. For example, in April

2014, former secretary of state Hillary Clinton and USAID administrator Raj Shah announced USAID's Global Development Lab, "a new entity within USAID that brings together a diverse set of partners to discover, test, and scale breakthrough solutions to achieve what human progress has only now made possible—the end of extreme poverty by 2030."[2]

"But we can't do it alone," Clinton and Shah proclaimed, naming more than twenty-two Cornerstone Partners, ranging from higher education institutions to corporations, that have committed to share knowledge, solve problems, and scale solutions to hundreds of millions of people. This effort builds on more than twenty years of public-private partnerships USAID has undertaken; it includes an explicit goal of building alliances with private sector investors over shared interests in the outcomes USAID seeks to achieve (see the box "Multilingual Leadership in Action"). Similarly, the United Kingdom leveraged its presidency of the G8 in 2013 to create the Global Learning Exchange on Social Impact Investing (GLE), coconvened by the World Economic Forum and the Impact Investing Policy Collaborative. The stated purpose of the GLE is to create a platform that facilitates interaction and knowledge sharing among impact investing actors from different sectors and geographies.

Multilingual Leadership in Action: USAID Global Development Lab

Since 2001, USAID, a global leader in building public-private partnerships for development, has formed more than sixteen hundred public-private partnerships with over thirty-five hundred distinct partner organizations, including a wide variety of private sector actors, leveraging more than $19 billion in public and private funds toward increasing the sustainable impact of its development assistance programs. Through its Development Credit Authority, USAID has mobilized $3 billion in local capital for more than 130,000 borrowers since 1999. Building on this legacy, USAID established the Global Development Lab (the Lab) in early 2014 to lead its efforts in applying science, technology, innovation, and partnerships to solve global development challenges and improve its development impact. The Lab will enable USAID to bring together a diverse set of partners—entrepreneurs and world-class experts from corporations, NGOs, universities, science and research institutions, and its missions around the world—to discover, incubate, and scale breakthrough development innovations, in such sectors as water, health, food security and nutrition, energy, and climate change, that can reach hundreds of millions of people. (For examples, see Smith, G., Kalil, T., [2014, April 4], "U.S. Global Development Lab Launches to Develop and Scale Solutions to Global Challenges," USAID, http://blog.usaid.gov/2014/04/u-s-global-development-lab-launches-to-develop-and-scale-solutions-to-global-challenges/.)

Leading across such diverse groups of stakeholders is by no means an easy task. Other authors have also commented on the specialized skillsets needed to create successful partnerships between diverse organizations. David Archer and Alex Cameron survey a number of successful leaders of cross-sector partnerships in *Collaborative Leadership: How to Succeed in an Interconnected World*. They find a number of shared charactcristics that have helped leaders in the United Kingdom create partnerships across organizations. To paraphrase some of their key observations:[3]

- Leaders of collaborations must be able to communicate a clear, persuasive vision to stakeholders across multiple organizations. When coordinating across organizations, it is important to present a vision that is concise enough for all participants to understand, but one that can also be adapted to the slightly different goals and motivations of each stakeholder.
- When confronted with problems in relationships, these leaders don't concern themselves with assigning blame and seeking punishment, but instead address problems in a transparent way, maintaining a focus on creating long-term value from the partnership.
- Collaborative leaders build trust across organizations by consistently delivering on promises, developing a deep understanding of the goals and motivations of partners, and building strong personal relationships.
- Because the development of multi-stakeholder partnerships can be complex and can require large amounts of time, it is important for leaders to have patience in developing relationships.

Partnerships that are both innovative and highly valuable don't often develop quickly.

- Leaders of successful cross-organization collaborations tend to be good at sharing credit for accomplishments with all the teams and individuals involved in the relationship. By actively sharing credit and elevating the contributions of others, leaders can encourage individuals across organizations to take ownership of the shared mission.

- Collaborative leaders are able to identify and address hard problems that arise within collaborative relationships. These leaders are able to build relationships in which all participants feel comfortable addressing uncomfortable problems in an open and cooperative way, before such challenges grow out of control.

Whereas many books have been written about the skills needed to lead *within* organizations, the characteristics listed here are unique in that they relate to the skills needed to successfully lead *across* organizations. Leading across organizations is in many ways a more complex and challenging task; when leaders cannot rely on their authority to create change, they must be able to persuade, build coalitions, create strong personal relationships, and develop a deep understanding of the motivations of their partners in order to achieve true collaboration.

In his book on social entrepreneurship *How to Change the World: Social Entrepreneurs and the Power of New Ideas,* David Bornstein reflects on the qualities of successful leaders of social ventures. He concludes that a fundamental quality shared by such leaders is a willingness to cross disciplinary boundaries. Bornstein observes, "Independence from established structures not only helps social entrepreneurs wrest free of prevailing assumptions, it gives them latitude to combine resources in new ways. Indeed, one of the primary functions of the social entrepreneur is to serve as a kind of social alchemist: to create new social compounds; to gather together people's ideas, experiences, skills, and resources in configurations that society is not naturally aligned to produce."[4]

It seems clear that Multilingual Leadership is an essential part of social innovation, and also of impact investing. We turn now to examples of successful Multilingual Leadership in impact investing and discuss strategies practitioners may use to build multilingual skills for themselves and within their organizations.

Defining Multilingual Leadership for Impact Investing

Although there is strong commonality in the characteristics of Multilingual Leadership and cross-disciplinary and collaborative leadership, the qualities of leadership present within the impact investing funds in our sample hinged on an ability to communicate complex ideas to audiences (both internal and external) that were more fully based within one silo or another. The multilingual leader distinguished herself by being able to express concepts and practices across silos, and in an equally compelling manner, to audiences from finance, community development, nonprofit management, and the public sector.

The seeds of Multilingual Leadership have been sown over recent decades as specific individuals have moved from silo to silo over the course of their career. We call this "career zigzagging," and we saw it in all the fund leaders we studied. The multilingual leader is one who may have started her career within a traditional financial institution, moved on to the World Bank, and then joined a regional impact investing fund. Or worked within a charity, building a deep understanding of a population's needs, followed by time in investment banking, before building his own fund strategy and operation. The training of such individuals came "on the job" and, for many of those in our research, predated formal graduate education and training opportunities presently available to those pursuing careers in impact investing. Such individuals drew on a range of resources, both from within the organizations in which they found themselves and from outside sources of knowledge and skill development.

A frequently asked question is, What are the core skills of the impact investor? Is it being comfortable with the world of finance, spreadsheets, valuations, and term-sheets, onto which a layer of multisector familiarity can be added? Or is it better to have deep knowledge of an impact area and then add on the tools of finance? The answer from our research was that it's both. The path can go one way or the other, but the important thing is that the leader individually and the team as a whole have a flexible fluency and can each represent any sector's perspective convincingly and confidently. The currency in the field today is almost always "finance is key" in terms of the knockout skills you must possess to be a top fund manager, but when you look at the backgrounds of our leaders, those skills simply are not always part of their foundation.

Another key question, outside the serendipity of a multisiloed, zigzag career, is whether and how people can proactively prepare for this kind of multilingual fluency. Very few higher education institutions aiming to prepare impact investing leaders at the graduate school level have understood this need for new kinds of blended cross-sector experiences, although we expect others to follow as Multilingual Leadership becomes more widely understood. For career changers, the training outside of finance is mostly experiential, as there are few formalized opportunities to learn how to apply impact thinking and practices in the financial realm. Many experienced investors turning to impact investing find themselves attending conferences, reading reports, and learning the lingo for much longer than expected. This need to become "grounded in impact" may also be a real gating factor for the growth of impact investing to date; there is a human capital development component that takes a lot of time, and the pipeline of leaders who truly excel at all of these skills may take a while, perhaps even five to ten years, to emerge, as today's MBAs start to create zigzag paths for themselves more explicitly. Everyone may be able to be a change-maker, but a top-performing impact investing fund manager is, for today at least, a rare breed who depends on specialized skills and qualities of mind and experience.

So what are the most important skills for multilingual leaders? These leaders may best be thought of as possessing the qualities we discuss in the following sections.

Able to Think Critically

First and foremost, multilingual leaders must possess a mind that is both curious and critical. Why are certain answers to current problems the norm? How could they be approached differently? What are the underlying forces keeping systems in place as opposed to moving forward? These and other questions are front and center for those looking to put new parts together in the creation of new solutions to traditionally intransigent challenges.

This analytical ability can apply to deal structuring, analyzing the ecosystem of a new innovation in another country, or creative ways to structure engagement with partners. Multilingual fund managers think critically at all levels and then build their analysis back up to simple and compelling visions.

Able to Focus on Ends Rather Than Means

Multilingual leaders do not confine themselves to the tool kit with which they begin their journey. They stay focused on where they ultimately want to go and are intrigued by any option (within reason!) that may help them attain their goal. The fact that a given tool or framework comes from business or the nonprofit sector or government matters less to them than the relevance of that framework in offering a potential solution to a given problem.

Able to See the Forest—and the Trees

Multilingual leaders are capable of understanding the specific issues of the challenge immediately before them, but at the same time are able to place that challenge within the larger context in which they operate. Sometimes referred to as "systems thinkers," they are capable of keeping their eye on the ultimate outcomes sought while questioning the levers of the status quo solutions. They are able to think about the big picture while simultaneously addressing the complexity of the specific resources, teams, and actors needed to address a particular challenge today.

Nonideological

Multilingual leaders operate within conceptual and practical frameworks in order to execute their work—but they are not confined to those understandings of what is and what could be. In fact, they may begin with a set of intellectual tools (let's say, an approach to viewing the world through the lens of economics or business), yet when they find that those frameworks are not up to a given task (addressing poverty on a sustainable basis), these leaders will shed the traditional framework of business for that of social entrepreneurship or, in this case, for impact investing as a new and better way to understand the world and their place within it.

Entrepreneurial

Multilingual leaders are entrepreneurs willing to build and create new organizations and execute innovative strategies to apply investing practice in pursuit of financial returns with social and environmental impacts. They are not limited by organizational structure or form or by lack of resources, and, in fact, are willing to create new structures and vehicles to drive toward their ultimate goal.

Financially Savvy

At the end of the day, impact investors are investors, and they must bring or build a knowledge base about the tools of finance they are being paid to exploit for social and financial return.

Capable of Exceptionally Strong Communication

Our successful impact investors have all created new financial relationships among stakeholders who may not know they have common interests. They have worked to listen carefully to the needs of their stakeholders and have decided how to structure responses to them that can be operationalized. They persuade people constantly; build trusted relationships with entrepreneurs, partners, governments, and others; and exude integrity and humility.

Willing to Take Risks

At their core, multilingual leaders have been professional risk takers willing to step out of the traditional definition of their career. They may have begun as a financier or activist—and may well carry that identity into their evolving role over the course of a career—but they are willing to step out of their traditional professional development track, to take the risk of moving into an unfamiliar area of work and pursue their vision of impact.

Taken together, these core attributes of multilingual leaders combine to make for a transformational executive capable of empowering staff to follow their lead and garnering the confidence of investors looking to the future of finance.

The Multilingual Leader: From Individual to Team to Firm

Aspects of multilingual leadership may be observed at various levels, from individual to team to firm. Understanding how these aspects are manifest at each level may be of critical importance for those building successful impact organizations.

The Individual

All businesses are personality driven to some extent. We designate individuals to take ultimate responsibility for the enterprises they serve and, in return, provide them with the flexibility to allocate resources and make most other key decisions accordingly. Whether we like it or not, individual leaders become the "face" of an organization and, through their actions, often make the difference between success and failure. Impact investing is no different. In fact, in some ways the field may be more personality driven than other sectors of the investment market for the simple reason that these leaders are mission driven, and the definition of the mission they strive to accomplish is of their own creation. In order to pursue that mission, they cannot be limited to a traditional understanding of what finance is or how best to advance social impact. Rather, they embody many of the characteristics outlined in the previous section in order to attain their goal of mobilizing capital for community and individual change.

An Individual Profile: Janie Barrera of ACCIÓN Texas Inc.

Janie Barrera's experience with small business, the social sector, and business school, highlighted in the introduction to this chapter, equipped her to scale up ACCIÓN Texas Inc. (ATI) by collaborating with many types of partners.

With so rich an interdisciplinary background, Barrera puts Multilingual Leadership into action as a matter of course. For example, when she was ready to grow ATI from its founding office to cover regions all over Texas, she consulted with local banking leaders to decide on an organizational structure based on a bank branch model. As she worked to open new offices across Texas, she did so in partnership with city governments, local community leaders, and federal agencies like the Department of Housing and Urban Development. Collaborating with all these organizations required her to understand their goals and how they worked, build trusting relationships, and identify specific ways they could partner to meet both of their objectives.

Barrera is also uniquely qualified to solicit the half of ATI's funding that comes from foundation and government grants. She works as the public face of ATI to investors and donors, and her fluency in multiple sectors enables her to tell the organization's story effectively to different audiences. Barrera is also dedicated to influencing public policy in the United States in support of greater financial inclusion for all—a task that requires a social sector sensibility in addition to an understanding of policy. She has served on President Obama's Advisory Council on Financial Capability, the Federal Reserve Board's National Consumer Advisory Council, and the board of directors for the San Antonio branch of the Dallas Federal Reserve.

The Multilingual Team

The multilingual team operates with many of the characteristics of the individual multilingual leader, but is assembled from a variety of individuals who may complement each other's specific skills and in the process create a unified force for executing impact investing at its best. In some cases, this is a case of "right actors, right opportunity," wherein a team simply gels as a result of having accidentally hit on the right recipe for creating a powerful, cross-silo set of qualities. In other cases, CEOs or boards have intentionally sought out certain characteristics they felt would best serve the fund's purpose and help it attain its promise.

A Team Profile: Elevar Equity

The team at Elevar Equity is a case in point. Three of the founders came from the nonprofit Unitus, and shared for several years the experience of lending to nonprofit microfinance institutions and watching them hit walls beyond which they could not scale. Each also had complementary backgrounds, one as an economist and financial analyst, another as a lawyer, and a third as a venture capitalist. Johanna Posada, the economist, Chris Brookfield, the venture capitalist, and Sandeep Farias, the lawyer, started to wonder whether it was the right time for an equity fund model that could more appropriately invest in the new for-profit microfinance institutions emerging in India and Latin America, or whether they could help convince the most high performing ones to do so. Maya Chorengel, who had come out of a straight investment banking and private equity career at James D. Wolfensohn Incorporated and Warburg Pincus, had recently started to zigzag herself, having started to focus on BoP markets at the Dignity Fund, a microfinance-focused private debt fund, when she added her expertise to the team. Together, they were extremely well rounded—deep legal knowledge, nearly ten years' combined experience with how finance products can be distributed in low-infrastructure environments and with the limits and uses of debt, and know-how in building equity products. Their comfort with philanthropy was immediately rewarded when the firm's first investment came in the form of a program-related investment (PRI) from the Omidyar Network (ON), that philanthropic organization's first PRI in an equity fund. Elevar articulated the catalytic effect of commercializing scalable models, first making the case to ON and then emphasizing the inherent financial attractiveness of that proposition to mainstream investors, who filled out the remainder of the first fund.

The Institution

In the same way individuals may seek out the skills and experience to become a multilingual leader, and boards may assemble a "crack" team of professionals who manifest multilingual characteristics, organizations may, over time, come to embody many of the attributes of what could be called a multilingual organizational culture. Such institutions are open to integrating ideas and practices from other sectors. They view themselves as thriving on diversity of leadership and staff, as promoting innovative thinking and risk taking, and as not being limited to a narrow strategy in pursuit of their mission. They have a culture that on the one hand is working to maintain a high level of professionalism and skill, while on the other is not limiting itself to being "a business" or "a nonprofit." Instead, it is an organizational culture willing to reinvent itself, add new vehicles, and promote a future vision, as opposed to merely defending its institutional past.

An Institutional Profile: Calvert Foundation

Calvert Foundation is in many ways a poster child of the multilingual institution. Calvert Foundation was founded in 1988 as a 501(c)(3) when Calvert Investments, a mutual fund family, found strong interest among its clients to invest directly in underserved communities. As the offshoot of a mutual fund company, it inherited—and still retains—a strong corporate culture and practices around risk diversification and product marketing at scale. Today, Calvert Foundation works to "empower investors to empower communities" and has more than $220 million invested in roughly one hundred and forty nonprofits and social enterprises working in approximately eighty countries. Its portfolio partners are a diversified mix of high-impact organizations working in affordable housing development, microfinance, women's empowerment, fair trade and sustainable agriculture, small business development, and critical community services, and Calvert Foundation itself is a registered community development financial institution (CDFI). Calvert Foundation's staff blends an aptitude for risk and debt management—through a very disciplined deal diligence and management process at a scale few other institutions in the space can match—with a culture of financial innovation. Calvert Foundation's history is a litany of firsts, as the institution accomplished the following:

- Created the Community Investment Note—the first impact investment available to every day investors online and in their brokerage accounts. The Note has been offered online since 2007 for as little as $20, and now is available on its own platform, at vested.org.
- Developed relationships with hundreds of brokerage firms and financial advisors to allow them to offer the Note to their clients
- Created the only impact investment of its kind that enables everyday investors to invest in women's empowerment, called WIN-WIN

- Developed industry-leading practices for reducing impact investment risk
- Contributed to the "Gateways for Impact" research, demonstrating $650 billion in market potential for sustainable and impact investments
- Incubated the first suite of Donor-Advised Fund products to incorporate impact investing, which became ImpactAssets

When CEO Jennifer Pryce talks about the team at Calvert Foundation, she talks about the huge advantage it gives them to be a blended-culture, multilingual organization. They can talk community development and policy as a CDFI; they can talk electronic trading as a brokerage offering; and, increasingly, they can leverage their nonprofit status and relationships to be an R&D arm for other philanthropic-outcome "buyers" looking to build products that can scale and can attract noninstitutional, retail investors.

Building a Multilingual Team: Acquiring Multilingual Capacity

Multilingual Leadership is ultimately a strategic imperative and posture. Where it is inherently a part of a firm's DNA, it must be nurtured. Where it is lacking, it must be cultivated.

In some cases, that means adding financial discipline, as was the case for Aavishkaar. Founder Vineet Rai had a vision of supporting rural businesses in India with venture capital, but had no substantial financial background himself. To be successful in realizing his vision, he created a multilingual team that would bolster the financial skills and legitimacy of Aavishkaar. Rai hired staff with backgrounds in private equity and investment banking, which required him to be creative in offering them a greater portion of the fund's profit.

In other cases, cultivating Multilingual Leadership means very intentionally developing the capacity for impact, as was true for Huntington Capital, thousands of miles away in San Diego, California.

Huntington was founded as a mezzanine debt and equity fund created to invest in underserved SMEs. After Huntington successfully deployed its first fund, the firm realized that it could sharpen its focus on outcomes and, through the provision of needed capital to promising entrepreneurs in lower-income areas, develop an intentional impact strategy. By being explicit with regard to its impact strategy, and leveraging supportive regulation, the firm could raise capital from a larger group of investors and more knowingly contribute to its surrounding community in a way that was important to both the fund's partners and its principals.

With a more explicit commitment to social impact written into the fund's investment strategy, Huntington's leaders needed to deliberately increase its capacity to both understand and create impact, and spent months developing an integrated system of impact measurement to use in its investment review and management process. It began collecting data about the extent of companies' operations in low- and moderate-income areas, businesses owned and operated by minorities and females, and the income characteristics of its employees. These metrics helped Huntington create a firm-level definition of impact investing based on supporting businesses that were underserved by traditional investors, located in low-income areas, and owned by women and minorities.

Huntington committed to investing at least 60 percent of its capital in impact-oriented deals. This helped attract investment from the Golden State Investment Fund, a private equity fund created by CalPERS to invest in areas of California traditionally underserved by private equity. For its next fund, Huntington Capital will continue dialing up its impact practices by making use of the GIIRS rating system to track its impact.

■   ■   ■

The lessons learned from these and other impact fund experiences are quite clear:

First, impact investors seeking to maximize the value of Multilingual Leadership to their firm must *recognize the type of multilingual expertise and relationships that will best enable them to reach their goals.*

Second, as investors educate themselves and build their teams, they should do this in a way that *strategically incorporates the interdisciplinary background of founding team members and of new hires, and contributes to the continued learning processes of the company,* as well as those of potential partners.

The Multilingual Leadership Tool Kit

To assist organizations in becoming capable of Multilingual Leadership in impact investing—with the ability to operate across sectors—we have developed a tool that highlights three stages of effort:

1. **Learn.** Frame your goals and work through the distinct lenses of the business/finance, nonprofit/philanthropic, and public sectors.
2. **Adapt.** Clarify your role by identifying core strengths and opportunities to add value.
3. **Act.** Operationalize cross-sector approaches and play a truly multilingual role in the market.

The first two stages are concerned with gaining multilingual "perspective"—that is, understanding the approaches and languages of different sectors. The third focuses on operationalizing Multilingual Leadership. Let's explore each of these in turn.

Learn

The "language" and strategies of impact investing are multifaceted, of course—more like a cacophony. However, knowing that the three core sectors in impact investing (business/finance, nonprofit/philanthropic, and public) each see the world differently and approach the same problems from varied perspectives, you should be able to frame your goals and work through these distinct lenses.

We have explored these perspectives in this and prior chapters. Table 6.1 is intended to offer some broad (and admittedly simplistic) linguistic rules of thumb. Interestingly, we found that partners in impact investing deals often trade roles—a testament to their collaborative credentials—with nonprofits talking about cost and benefit and their private sector partners talking about outcomes. This is a great sign of Multilingual Leadership in action!

Table 6.1   Sector Concepts and Quotations

Sector	Priority	Key Concepts	Example
Public	Improving the quality of life for all citizens	• Market systems, failures, and externalities • Public goods • Efficacy and scale	Ben McAdams, mayor of Salt Lake County, commenting on a new United Way of Salt Lake results-based financing initiative for low-income preschool students: "In other states where rigorous standards and a high-quality curriculum have been used to offer preschool to economically-disadvantaged children, the return on investment has been 7 to 1—that is a \$7 benefit to the local budget—money not needed for special education, crime or public assistance as well as higher wages for consumer spending—for each dollar invested. It's the right thing to do for children, and the fiscally responsible course for taxpayers."[5]
Business and finance	Maximizing risk-adjusted returns	• Risk mitigation and return on equity • Efficiency • Supply and demand • Price and willingness to pay	Andrew Kuper, founder and president of Leapfrog Investments, featured in the *Financial Mail* (South Africa) discussing his firm's second fund:

| Nonprofit and philanthropy | Doing good in the world | • Theories of change
• Catalytic investment and innovation
• Articulation of demonstrated outcomes | "Kuper says there is little point in selling to people earning less than $1.25/day. The sweet spot is from $1/25 to $10/day. He says Leapfrog is not the kind of private equity fund that sacks half the workforce and then gears up the balance sheet. "We are there to help with operations. Among the partners there is expertise in product design, distribution and regulation."[6]

Molly Baldwin, founder and executive director of Roca, the nonprofit delivering services under the largest pay-for-success financing in the United States, aimed at reducing youth recidivism in Massachusetts:

"The Massachusetts Pay for Success Initiative is about changing the odds. It's about confronting the stubborn trends of incarceration and poverty among justice-system-involved young men, and standing in solidarity to say to these young men, 'We will not leave you behind, you deserve more than jail or prison, and we will give you our time and support to help you make a better future for yourself and your community.'"[7] |

Leading news sources and blogs in the space provide a ready resource for familiarizing yourself with the language of the different sectors. Look out for articles written by representatives from different silos—and those working hard to bridge the divide, such as the GLE, an initiative of the UK Cabinet Office, the Impact Investing Policy Collaborative, and the World Economic Forum. For more web, blog, and conference resources, see the resource guide at the end of this book.

There is no substitute for learning on the job, of course—so long as workplaces create conditions that accommodate both formal and informal training and mentorship. Ensuring that organizations in impact investing embrace cross-sector learning ought to be of the highest priority.

Adapt

Once an organization understands the market—and the different perspectives of multiple actors—it is important to find the right place to call home. This is a strategic imperative—understanding how different sectors approach your fund's issue and clarifying where you fit into it. There are a handful of steps to consider as you work to identify core strengths and opportunities for alignment:

Step 1: Test your Investment Thesis of Change (ITC) against the following core, cross-sector elements:

a. Does it address a market failure or weakness?
b. Is it consistent with other (noninvestment) approaches to addressing the social outcome at hand?
c. Is it catalytic, with the power to change market systems and bring new actors to the table?

Step 2: Identify the key government, philanthropic, and financial stakeholders that are active in your focus area. Figure out whether and how their interests align or conflict with each other. How do they discuss and organize their work?

Step 3: Write out a series of draft one-page overviews of your work that address the full range of audiences (that is, investors, nonprofit partners, policymakers, and beneficiaries). How much does the way you tackle the issue naturally overlap with the anticipated approach of others? By understanding where the link is intuitive and where it is not, you will gain a clearer understanding of either your own lack of knowledge on how others might approach the issue, or your own place in the market relative to others.

Step 4: "Find your voice" by workshopping ideas and language internally and with key external, cross-sector stakeholders. Although it may pay to have a few ways to describe what you do (depending on the audience), you should ultimately settle on a more unified approach and vision that confidently states your *core* contribution to the market (essentially through your ITC), even while you adapt the way you understand and present that core activity "relative" to actors from the other sectors. Speak out and explore openly how multilingual concepts are best applied to your work. Begin to develop and express opinions about how the higher-level themes of impact investing can add value to the goals of your investments.

Act

Acting on Multilingual Leadership—and not just speaking—involves elements that are both internal, in order to operationalize multilingual approaches, and external, in order to play a truly multilingual role in the market.

Consider the following ways to ensure that your execution lives up to your rhetoric:

1. Recruit multilingual leaders to your team. Incorporate multilingual leaders into your organization by hiring staff with relevant interdisciplinary expertise.
2. Invite multilingual leaders you admire to join a board or advisory group.
3. Provide your current employees with a continuing education allowance that they can use to pursue classes that relate to your impact area.
4. Continue to raise the bar on performance measurement. Identify impact metrics that point to the outcomes that are created by your organization's work, look for practical low-cost ways to incorporate these metrics into your existing accounting systems, and, where possible, make sure to collect, organize,

and frame metrics in a way that diverse audiences (government, private sector, social sector) can appreciate.

5. Begin to advocate for policy that enables progress in your area of impact investing.

6. Volunteer with or donate to organizations that address your area of impact. These groups may be future strategic partners.

7. Engage in pro bono work that applies your core skills to the impact areas in question, but that approaches those areas from a new angle (with which you are unfamiliar).

8. Look "across the silo" from you to see what actors are present with whom you might engage. For example, if you're involved in community development finance, identify a branded impact fund in an emerging market that is executing a strategy similar to yours, and explore partnerships and learning opportunities; if you're a mainstream private equity investor or manager, identify a community venture capital fund to learn about and possibly partner with.

9. Identify conferences and other learning opportunities focused on similar social outcomes, but for actors you would not ordinarily consider peers, from other sectors or silos.

10. Read the *Nonprofit Quarterly, Stanford Social Innovation Review, Harvard Business Review,* and other mainstream business periodicals; convene discussion groups within your firm to explore the themes, issues, and ideas presented in these publications that "crosscut" to your own firm's work and strategy.

11. If you have a background in social sciences, get a business degree; if you have a business degree, get a social work degree; and if you're considering business school, pick institutions that will allow you to take courses in various other schools at the university (to explore environmental sustainability, government and public policy, education, and so on).

Beyond Impact Investing

Multilingual Leadership is the last of our four key practices in impact investing—and by extension Collaborative Capitalism. Impact investors need to be especially multilingual, but given the markets they operate in and partners with which they work, all of business and finance is increasingly demanding a similar set of skills. In a time of increased transparency—by design, or forced on private sector actors by activists and advocates—businesses and financial institutions have no option but to engage with and respond actively to multiple stakeholders, including those that speak a different "language."

Having explored the four essential elements of leadership and strategy needed to maximize your prospects of personal and professional success in a new era of Collaborative Capitalism, we ask the question: What now?

In our next, final chapter, we speculate on some major market developments that are likely to accompany the rise of impact investing. We should all be on the lookout for these trends. They will indicate that the more complete integration of Collaborative Capitalism is under way and is having a profoundly transformational influence.

PART THREE

LOOKING AHEAD: TRENDS AND CHALLENGES

7

The Writing on the Wall

It is urgent that the governments throughout the world commit
themselves to developing an international framework capable of
providing a market of high impact investments, and thus to
combating an economy which excludes and discards.
—His Holiness Pope Francis, Rome, June 16, 2014

MANY REPORTS AND OBSERVERS HAVE PREDICTED THE RISE OF IMPACT
investing in coming years. Research by J.P.Morgan and the Rockefeller Foundation speculated that impact investing will become
"one of the most powerful changes in the asset management
industry in the years to come" and estimated that as much as
$1 trillion of capital could be put into impact investments by 2020.[1]
As previously mentioned, the World Economic Forum has found a
large majority of US-based institutional investors expect to begin
allocating capital for impact.[2]

We believe these developments are coming and have achieved
a degree of momentum that is unstoppable at this time in the
evolution of practice in economics and investment. Yet we must
acknowledge there are those who are skeptical about whether
impact investing is anything new or will stand the test of time. And
there are others who remain uncertain in regard to many of the
fundamentals of impact investing. Stepping back to observe what is
often a tumult of discussion and confusion regarding this question
of what, exactly, impact investing is, one is reminded of the old
story of the blind men and the elephant. Each man reaches out to
touch a different part of the elephant, and each believes that in

touching his part, he knows the measure of the whole. In discussions of impact investing, there are numerous newcomers to the conversation holding an ear or a trunk. These newcomers ask many questions:

- Is impact investing a new form of philanthropy?
- Is it screened funds and investment strategies?
- When is impact investing best able to create impact?
- Can you really make money while having impact, or are the two antithetical?

What makes for much of this uncertainty is that each newcomer to the discussion enters through the silo from which she came and thus reaches out to hold the part of the elephant immediately in front of her. Some arrive from the nonprofit, academic, and philanthropic communities, others from traditional finance and investing. We hear people refer to a "blurring" of the boundaries between business and nonprofits and government—yet it is a blur only if we remain standing in one silo attempting to make sense of other silos spinning by. If we step more fully out of a silo and look at the whole—at the spectrum and not the individual color, at the portfolio and not the individual investment tool—we are better able to understand the whole as the sum of its parts, in the process seeing that capital is simply a continuum, and value creation a blend of economic, social, and environmental components.[3]

Many of those within impact and traditional investing arenas are reaching a common understanding that traditional frameworks of finance and economics do not prepare us for the complexities of making money in a world of pandemics, climate change, and supply chains structured on an unsustainable basis; meanwhile, traditional understandings of philanthropy, of the role of the public sector as solely responsible for advancing public good, and of the nonprofit sector as the purveyors of social "change" are inadequate ways to think about how best to overcome the challenges of today's world. Those who do not see the larger whole that constitutes the coming together of these various parts have a hard time finding solid ground on which to stand as these various elements move by them, and they seek to understand what impact investing "is."

Given this cloud of confusion, it is no wonder many (both new and old) who come to this discussion are left scratching their heads or making specious statements and claims regarding what impact investing is or is not. As we now turn from these past developments to exploring a number of future trends that portend the continued evolution of impact investing, it is important to ensure that you, our dear reader, are standing on more solid ground!

At the core of impact investing is the reality that all capital creates impact and the belief that it should be managed to optimize positive social and environmental outcomes. All capital has the potential to create financial performance and, in allocating capital across a portfolio of asset classes and investment strategies, investors should seek to optimize financial performance as appropriate for any given asset class while simultaneously managing that investment to optimize social and environmental returns. Within this understanding, effective capital management is not a set of trade-offs between doing well or doing good, but rather a set of decisions with regard to how each individual investment strategy or asset class may integrate the pursuit of financial return *with* the generation of impact—and how asset owners may combine a variety of individual investment strategies within an overall "Total Portfolio Management" approach to ensure that *all* their capital is being managed for effective financial and impact outcomes.[4]

Within this framework, philanthropy is just one more type of investment capital to be managed, and market-rate investment vehicles simply one more tool for investors to advance social and environmental value creation. There are a host of approaches investors may draw on across the entirety of their portfolio and within virtually every asset class. Some categories have long track records (screened funds), whereas others are still emerging (sustainable hedge funds), but the truth is across each asset class, we are witnessing growing innovation and adoption of investing strategies that pursue a more integrated approach to value creation.

The approach is a recognition that capital is whole in the aggregate and the pursuit of "impact" cannot, in the long term, be disaggregated from its economic elements. This was the key consideration of the concept of blended value introduced in 2000 and the central insight of research published in 2003 as *The Blended Value Map* (which may be found at www.blendedvalue.org).

With this understanding in mind, our challenge and opportunity is to "dial up" the aspects and elements of impact investing that advance Collaborative Capitalism, with the promise of redirecting the forces of capital flows from a singular focus on financial performance to financial performance infused with consideration of optimizing sustainable, consistent, and considered social and environmental value creation.

In chapter 1, which introduced Collaborative Capitalism, we make the claim that this trend is in motion, and, as the mainstream adopts the most promising practices of the fringe, impact investing will become an accepted practice for a growing pool of investors. The questions now become *How do we look forward and divine the future growth of this practice?* and *What are the trends and events we should look for to tell us that in fact the train has arrived at the station and that it is time to settle the new frontier?*

Although some of these "Top Ten" global impact trends are currently under way, others are only just emerging from the swirls of a dynamic market:

1. From outputs to outcomes to integrated performance
2. The investor's right to know
3. The globalization of financial impact innovation
4. Innovation in impact education
5. Postpartisan public leadership
6. The twenty-first-century fiduciary
7. The promise of philanthropic rebirth
8. The great thaw
9. Corporate alignment
10. Going all in: the family office as foundation, investor, and advocate

As we explore each of these in turn, we will also offer leading indicators that impact investors may use to gauge the progress of the trend as it develops. Impact investors looking to gain an edge in their own investment practices should reflect on how, for whatever strategy or approach they are executing, these developments might be integrated into their own investment approach and practices.

Trend One: From Outputs to Outcomes to Integrated Performance

Over the past two decades, we have witnessed a fundamental shift in how metrics and performance measurement tools are developed, tracked, and applied. Traditionally, we as a society have focused on outputs—focused on the question of how many people were served by a nonprofit strategy or how many customers bought a given product. As we reflect on the current state of reporting and metrics, we must first acknowledge that what we "know" about metrics has itself evolved over recent years. The metrics we use to assess financial and business performance have changed over the decades, just as the nature of business itself has changed. In addition, with the creation of institutional responses like the US Environmental Protection Agency in 1970, environmental metrics entered the equation, with companies being asked to report on their use of natural capital and their environmental impacts— carbon footprints, pollution reporting, sustainable business practices. More recently, we are asking firms to report on stakeholder and community engagement. In sum, the way we think about the component parts of the reporting process for both for-profit and nonprofit firms has changed significantly over past decades.

This evolution is reflected in the fact that Bloomberg terminals now offer analysts information on the environmental, social, and governance (ESG) aspects of publicly traded companies. The Global Reporting Initiative asks companies to commit to reporting on a variety of social and environmental factors and is dialing up its reporting requirements for signatory firms. With the creation of groups such as the Sustainability Accounting Standards Board and the International Social Return on Investment Network, there are now professional associations setting standards, creating common practices, and offering certification for those working to document the extrafinancial performance of both companies and capital.

Within the impact investing community itself, we have seen the development of the IRIS typology—in essence, a directory of indicators—which are the metrics used by many funds and entrepreneurs to track the impact of their operations. This suite of metrics is being used both by companies to assess their performance and by investors looking to understand the relative impact of their capital. Created through aggregating a host of indicators used by development finance organizations and others active in using capital to create community-level change, IRIS is built on both the experience of the past and the ideas of the present in order to offer a coherent and relevant set of metrics focused on understanding how capital as an input creates the output of social and environmental performance. And the IRIS metrics are themselves the foundation on which the Global Impact Investing Rating System (GIIRS), an impact reporting standard, is based.

But that is not all. Of perhaps greatest interest is how our understanding of these reporting parts as a whole have also evolved. In its time, John Elkington's introduction of the concepts and practices of triple-bottom-line accounting moved the ball far down the field of performance monitoring, but now the focus has shifted from the parts—the three bottom lines of people, profit, and planet—to the whole, to an integrated approach to reporting on corporate and portfolio performance. Robert Eccles and Michael Krzus's book *One Report* is a great overview of this framework, built on a simple idea: value is whole, and the performance of companies should also be viewed, tracked, and assessed on a holistic basis. Bifurcating our reporting between financial and nonfinancial aspects of performance allows us neither to see the total performance we're creating nor to manage for the overall impact we seek to achieve.

This integrated reporting approach both allows us to assess the full sustainability of companies and (from an asset owners' perspective) lays the foundation for a total portfolio reporting (TPR) framework to assess how *all* capital—from philanthropic to near market and market rate—generates the variety of returns and impact we seek. HIP Investor, the UN-PRI, and a host of other actors are creating the new tools of TPR and will continue to develop them over the coming years. The actual application of integrated reporting will differ based on the type of asset owner (pension fund, family office, independent foundation, and so on), but the opportunity to assess how the entirety of one's capital base is being managed for financial returns with environmental and social impact will be a significant driver for many asset owners for years to come.

Leading Trend Indicators

- Watch for more companies to move from sustainability and CSR reporting toward the adoption of integrated or "one report" approaches bringing financial and impact aspects of performance into a single public report. When pension funds and private investors require such reporting as a condition of receiving investment, the trend will be part of mainstream practice.
- Growing numbers of entrepreneurs will want to move from using impact metrics as a reporting requirement to generating information to inform internal managerial and capital investing practices of their own firm. Who pays for the creation of these reporting and management information systems (MISs) will continue to be an issue, but in the same way investors and entrepreneurs would never seek to manage a venture in the absence of sound financial and other MISs, they will want information systems capable of tracking financial and impact performance together.
- Asset owners will require advisors and investees to report to them on the basis not simply of financial returns but also of integrated impact. They will want to see how their investments are advancing not only the fund manager or entrepreneur's personal vision but the larger interests of stakeholder and community groups as well.

Trend Two: The Investor's Right to Know

The metrics evolution has taken place against a backdrop of another evolution in perspective, having to do with the investor's "right to know." In general terms, virtually all the reporting and other practices of mainstream investing have been based on the idea that investors have a right to understand all the potential risks and dangers of investing. That said, in truth many investors have not fully understood the myriad aspects of the specific investments in which they have been involved. In part, this has been a function of the complexity of modern investing—but as was seen in the period leading up to the financial crisis of 2008, it has also been a function of investment opportunities being misrepresented to potential investors or a result of the "black box" investing strategies of some firms that make it impossible for investors to discern specific holdings of a fund manager.

This recent experience of asset owners finding themselves invested in vehicles they did not fully comprehend has been complemented in the impact investing arena by a trend of investors' demanding to know more about the particulars of the investment strategies, firms, and funds into which their capital has been allocated. "Know what you own" has long been a mantra of sustainable and responsible investing, and this practice of mandating greater transparency has now become a fundamental part of many investment approaches, impact investing included. The investment association Ceres has been a leader in engaging corporations in dialogue with investors to explore a host of issues with regard to environmental and social impacts of publicly traded companies. Carbon Tracker is initiating analysis of publicly traded firms in order to analyze potential liabilities of "stranded assets" and how corporate valuations will be altered as a result of our living on an increasingly carbon-constrained planet. And a number of initiatives have focused on transparency and disclosure practices within the microfinance industry.

This requirement for greater transparency comes right at the top, with investors wanting disclosure of what were formally thought to be "off-balance-sheet" risks having to do with environmental practices, supply chain management, production processes, and so on. This interest in understanding the full context within which an investment takes place will play out at both the institutional and individual investor levels as a core part of the standard due diligence process.

One example of efforts to increase the transparency of environmental risks at the level of the institutional investor is the Ceres Investor Network on Climate Risk (INCR). INCR is a group of one hundred institutional investors representing more than *$11 trillion* in assets that works with portfolio companies to increase reporting on climate risks. INCR members encourage their portfolio companies to improve disclosure regarding their efforts to reduce emissions and adapt to the effects of climate change so that investors may better understand companies' exposure to risks related to carbon regulation and the effects of a changing climate.

For portfolio companies falling short of INCR's climate risk reporting expectations, the network supports shareholder resolutions that press management to address these risks.[5] Recently, a shareholder resolution proposed by INCR members led ExxonMobil to commit to reporting on the levels of greenhouse gas emissions caused by its operations. The oil and gas giant also approved plans to publish reports explaining how it weighs the risks of climate change regulation, which has the potential to significantly increase costs for the corporation.[6] This level of attention to climate risk by one of the world's largest oil and gas companies—together with other major petroleum firms—would likely never have developed without leadership from investors seeking to gain a broader sense of environmental risks.

The Carbon Tracker initiative also works to improve the transparency of risks associated with carbon emissions in equity markets. Carbon Tracker addresses the problem that the valuation of many oil and gas companies depends in part on the value of fossil fuel reserves, a great portion of which cannot be burned without pushing climate change beyond 2 °C of average warming, the level that the Intergovernmental Panel on Climate Change has determined as the global limit for managing climate change. Carbon Tracker calls for companies owning fossil fuel reserves to consider carbon emissions restrictions against the revenues expected from their reserves, and it asks that regulators require companies to report such information so that investors are better able to identify assets in the fossil fuel industry that are at risk of underperformance.[7] Investors understand that responses to climate change will require fundamental changes in the oil and gas industry, and they are actively asking for information that will enable them to differentiate between companies at risk of suffering from the change and those that are prepared for it.

In addition to tracking climate change risk, institutional investors increasingly view broader practices of tracking on environmental and social performance as a standard part of their due diligence process. A 2012 survey of seventeen of the largest global private equity firms found that private equity LPs are increasingly asking fund managers to report on their ESG strategies and performance. LP investors see ESG activities as an important part of managing risks and creating investments that have long-term value. Due to this demand for ESG consideration, 94 percent of private equity fund managers surveyed said that their attention to ESG issues will increase over the following five years.[8] Reflecting this trend, leading private equity firm KKR has been publishing ESG reports for investors and the public since 2010. Interestingly, its most recent ESG report framed sustainability initiatives as "best practices for operational excellence" that will enable companies to be "better positioned in the future as diminishing resources, changing consumer demands, and increased regulation are expected to pose greater challenges."[9]

These and other examples demonstrate mainstream investors are fast recognizing the importance of tracking environmental and social issues that have significant bearing on the operations of companies and their ability to perform financially. As the world and its economies have become increasingly globalized and interdependent, investors are realizing that businesses cannot be separated from the environmental and social contexts in which they operate. Companies need to actively manage and improve their relationships with the communities and environments that host them in order to create real value, or else they risk negative consequences for themselves as well as society as a whole.

Fortunately, tracking ESG issues is not all about avoiding risk. It is also about identifying new investment opportunities. As society must adapt to climate change, increasing resource scarcity, and growing populations, and as consumers increasingly base their economic choices on the social reputation of companies, there will be great business opportunities for companies that can navigate these changes successfully. Investors are asking for the data that will help them assess which companies those will be.

Leading Trend Indicators

- Presently, private accredited investors rely on independent financial advisors to engage in deep due diligence and to "open the curtain" on investment opportunities and their underlying holdings. As impact investing continues to grow to include more mainstream investors without the ability to hire personal advisors, watch for funds to become more transparent in discussing specific holdings as well as disclosing a variety of off-balance-sheet risks of interest to all investors, large and small.

- In the past, many asset owners worked with fund managers who executed technical investing strategies (which draw on esoteric algorithms and "big data" to project future market moves and arbitrage opportunities). In the future, growing numbers of impact investors will allocate a greater percentage of their assets toward fundamental and direct investing. Such strategies will focus on building value from the bottom up as opposed to attempting to play the market or use deep analytics to predict future investment opportunities.

Trend Three: The Globalization of Financial Impact Innovation

If there ever was a time when "innovations" moved from the developed North to the developing South, that time has surely long since passed—especially when it comes to financial innovations. Microfinance was pioneered by BRAC in Bangladesh in 1972 (two years prior to the founding of Grameen Bank, which is often credited with the innovation of microfinance) and, just over a decade later, had spurred the creation of microfinance groups in the United States. The first two IPOs of microfinance organizations first took place in Mexico and India, gaining the attention of numerous investors and increasing the momentum of capital flows into microfinance investment vehicles around the globe.

Innovations move "sideways" as well: the concept of social return on investment (SROI) was pioneered by REDF in the United States as the first formalized methodology to monetize the economic value of social impact, transferred east to the New Economics Foundation in London, which added a stakeholder component to the model, and then promoted throughout the United Kingdom, laying the foundation for the introduction of pay-for-performance contracting, which then evolved into the social impact bonds (SIBs) developed by Social Finance UK. SIBs have now returned in force to the United States and are being widely celebrated as a financial innovation to raise needed impact investment capital to help address a variety of issues in more than ten countries.[10] Social innovation funds (SIFs) are another example of the globalization of innovation strategies.

First introduced in the United Kingdom, the idea of creating national funds to finance and scale new impact strategies has now spread to Ghana, the European Union, the United States, Colombia, Hong Kong, Peru, and Australia.

What is driving this process of financial innovation and engineering is that reliable, investible models of impact investing and development finance are highly transferable—what is pioneered in one region is taken to scale in another—as investors seek out new and credible investment instruments capable of taking both impact and capital to market. This will only continue to evolve as investor appetite for sound investment vehicles maintains its rise and expansion.

Leading Trend Indicators

- SIFs will continue to gain traction around the world. Watch for private investor opportunities to coinvest in broad strategies seeded by such funds as well as opportunities to directly invest in specific opportunities "endorsed" by SIFs.
- As these initiatives grow, investors and entrepreneurs will also "connect the dots" with other funding innovations, such as crowdfunding platforms and secondary markets—both of which have the potential to leap boundaries and borders to capture new opportunities and investment ideas in emerging markets around the world.
- At the same time, moving models to new places allows for local adaptation and refinement as well as the engagement of local stakeholders, which will be essential for true Collaborative Capitalism to take root. Look for local investors and other stakeholders, including beneficiaries, to have a strong role in creating and operating the new models, products, funds, and platforms in the future.

Trend Four: Innovation in Impact Education

As we have noted elsewhere in this book, there was a time when students chose between several simple alternative routes for their education: the humanities and arts, the sciences, public policy, or business. Today students in business select courses in public management, government, and social innovation. Social workers learn structured finance and development finance. And everyone wants to be creative! In recent years, the Social Enterprise Club of Harvard Business School has been the most in-demand club on campus, and Net Impact attracts thousands of students to its gatherings across the United States. The Aspen Institute's Business and Society Program continues to convene leading CEOs and academics to explore the future of business education in a changing society and world. And it is no surprise that cross-silo education is not simply for twenty-somethings: at virtually every level of adult education, offerings are being made that cut across disciplines and previously segregated teaching modules.[11]

Leading Trend Indicators

- Although significant momentum has been building over past years, it is not at all clear that the academic community will embrace and advance this trend. Educational institutions are hard to move and influence. A leading trend indicator to watch in this regard is whether or not undergraduate and graduate schools take these new curricula and embed them into mainstream academic structures and degree programs. In this context, change is generational, and until the "old guard" retires at institutions across the country, educational innovations and the creation of social enterprise and impact investing curricula will continue to move in fits and starts. Watch for those fits, and work to advance the starts!
- Watch for the introduction of new, peer-reviewed (not simply general academic or field-focused) academic and professional journals exploring various aspects of Collaborative Capitalism, new finance, and impact investing, as a sign that these innovations have truly taken root within academia.

Trend Five: Postpartisan Public Leadership

Although the preeminence of market-based and free enterprise approaches to our world's problems is taken by some as a given, the interesting secret within impact investing is that a majority of the highest-performing impact funds reviewed in our research were in one way or another the product of deep public-private partnership. What is clear is that the battle for supremacy of private markets over public support is now concluded; actors from a variety of perspectives are setting a place for a shared meal of new ideas and effective solutions to our common challenges—ideas and solutions that are not owned by the "left" or the "right."

This experience of collaborative engagement has helped us see the strengths and weaknesses of private sector and public sector actors—in a way enabling us to understand how each plays a critical role in enabling markets to function and enterprise to take place. Whether it is in the form of joint ventures or pay-for-performance contracts or governments' creating the tax and regulatory environment within which innovation may thrive, the critical role of both in advancing solutions for the future is clear. Yes, there will be continued disagreements about how to best apply carrots and sticks, yet overall the beneficial roles played by public and private actors in advancing impact investing to this point illustrate the critical importance of each.

As the concept and practices of impact investing continue their migration into the mainstream, we will see a growing number of CEOs and politicians continue to pick up the banner and wave it high. Moving beyond the topic of breakouts at Davos in 2001 to national gatherings at the White House and 10 Downing Street in 2010 and afterward, impact investing is gaining significant traction in capital cities everywhere for the simple reason that it promises to leverage private capital for public good.

Considering the state of US politics in particular, it is hard to believe we may be on the verge of a postpartisanship period, but the reality is that impact investing embraces a nonpartisan agenda. Conservatives like its market and free enterprise fundamentals, while progressives are drawn to the idea of being able to direct private capital to advancing solutions connecting capital with community.

Leading Trend Indicators

- Watch for impact investing to become part of the nomenclature in Washington and on the global political stage. In 2014, the G7 will be entertaining initiatives that seek to advance impact investing both within and between nations across the world. As these initiatives are embraced and advanced across the aisles that currently divide many nations' capitals, they will portend further expansion and opportunities for impact investors.

- If they are simply given lip service, the forces advancing impact investing will decrease and remain fragmented. Watch to see how impact investing is perceived by "old actors" and whether it is slotted into historic divides or used to build a bridge across the aisles of party allegiance.

Trend Six: New Perspectives on the Twenty-First-Century Fiduciary

There was a time when the definition of fiduciary responsibility hinged on a constricted view of the role of the fiduciary as managing for financial returns alone. As issues such as global climate change, the need for educational reform, and the ravage of pandemics continue to have a negative impact on the ability of firms to execute their business models, a growing number of fiduciaries now recognize that *not* taking environmental and social factors into account when structuring an investment approach may be a violation of their fiduciary duties. Especially for investors focused on producing consistent returns over the long term, ESG considerations are particularly important.[12]

Our economic systems are growing ever more interconnected and interdependent. It is increasingly difficult to separate the performance of a company from the performance of the social and ecological systems that support it. Fiduciaries are beginning to acknowledge this; and, as a few large investors have put robust ESG measurement systems in place, we will see increasing numbers of institutions break with the herd mentality that has thus far controlled our understanding of fiduciary responsibility. Although interpretations of fiduciary responsibility have tended to gather around what mainstream players consider reasonable prudence, the good news is that once a herd starts to change direction, the whole group follows relatively quickly.

Our understanding of fiduciary responsibility is based not simply on regulation but on institutional culture and practice. That leading institutions are not waiting for regulators to give them explicit instruction to shift the terms of fiduciary duty is consistent with history; as we noted in chapter 1, there was a time when trustees managing assets in the State of New York were obligated to invest solely in bonds issued by the State of New York—and that practice was overturned as a result of fiduciaries claiming a higher obligation to diversify their portfolios and more effectively manage risk and opportunity.[13] Indeed, today we see ESG considerations increasingly taking hold among European fiduciaries as they continue to lead the way in this area.[14] And major accounting firms report that institutional investors are coming to view financial and extra-financial performance as "two sides of the same coin," with credit rating agencies more frequently inquiring about corporations' sustainability practices.[15]

Today's fiduciaries are being defined not only by a new understanding of the need to consider off-balance-sheet environmental and social risks but also by a shift in trustee demographics, which will continue to ripple through the boardrooms of endowments, foundations, and pension funds. As a new generation of stewards takes over from the existing generation, new perspectives, concerns, and understandings of investment discipline will continue to evolve. A recent survey of more than five thousand Millennials across eighteen countries found that the next generation of professionals considers the main priority of business to be "improving society"[16]—it is this generation that over the next forty years is due to inherit an estimated $41 trillion from the baby boomer generation.[17] This is not to say that in the coming decades the conservative practices of mainstream finance will disappear—but rather that those practices will be augmented with new experiences and skills of a younger generation of trustees seeking to manage off-balance-sheet risks with a desire to capture the investment opportunities such risks may offer.

As these asset owners and fiduciaries voice their interest in new investment products and vehicles with an impact edge, Wall Street will (as always) hear the siren call of financial opportunity and create new offerings to meet that demand—and, in fact, this process is already under way. The challenge, of course, will be to separate out the "impact-washed" financial products from those offering deep impact together with sustainable financial returns. Regardless, the new fiduciaries will make their presence felt in tomorrow's boardrooms, foundation offices, and capital markets.

Leading Trend Indicator

- Watch for the continued evolution of family office pension fund trustees' understanding of their responsibilities as fiduciaries. If such investors continue their move toward integrating environmental and social factors into their investment strategies, the fiduciaries of other large institutions like universities and foundations will follow their lead, opening up an array of new investment and coinvestment opportunities for those seeking and managing impact capital investment.

Trend Seven: The Promise of Philanthropic Rebirth

One might imagine that the most natural advocate for innovations in social sector and community economics would be the foundation community. These institutions are created to advance public good and are financed through tax breaks provided to donors and supported by taxpayers, large and small. It would therefore seem perfectly reasonable for us to assume that all foundation assets would be managed in a financially prudent manner to advance social and environmental value creation.

Although it is often challenging to make a single statement or observation with regard to foundations (as the old saying goes, "When you see one foundation, you've seen one foundation!"), in point of fact, private and family foundations (regardless of their particular political bent) continue to be bastions of traditional charitable thinking: manage capital assets to make more money in order to give more money to charitable causes. As a result, the vast majority of foundations actually manage only their grant making in pursuit of mission (less than 5 percent of their annual net income—or whatever remains after paying administrative salaries, expenses, and travel). What this means is that nearly 100 percent of their institutional mission is being driven by less than 5 percent of their assets, while 95 percent of their assets are managed—at best— in a manner neutral to that mission, even as significant amounts of their investment capital are invested in companies that may possibly be contributing to the creation of the very social and environmental problems the foundation was created to address—not exactly a compelling capital investment strategy!

Over recent years, a number of initiatives have sought to present philanthropy with ideas and strategies for using more than their 5 percent payout to drive impact. For example, Mission Investors Exchange and Harvard University's Initiative for Responsible Investment, as well as various regional efforts, all represent attempts to advance alternative practices of philanthropy that offer a promise of moving from charitable giving to impact investing.

That said, the foundation community has been a place of promise and possibilities deferred rather than attained, with even many of those institutions enthusiastically providing grant support to impact investing being less inclined to put their endowment dollars to work.

Why, then, would we opt to include the *promise* of philanthropy as a trend that impact investors should watch? We offer philanthropy for two reasons.

First, although dwarfed by mainstream capital markets, foundations in the United States still control more than $850 billion in assets—all initially targeted for the advancement of societal good, however defined. It is clear that a small but growing number of foundation trustees and staff are realizing we cannot grant our way out of the profound challenges before us and are looking for more tools to apply in their efforts—tools such as program-related investments, mission-related investing, and, across the whole, Total Portfolio Management. If structured for impact, foundation assets could be used to create substantial, positive community- and state-level impacts in a time of ever-decreasing public funding and investment. Although relatively small potatoes, foundations are potatoes that could be whipped up into quite a dish!

Second, although many foundation executives aspire to be viewed as innovative and visionary, in reality many foundations move along common trend lines within a shared understanding of what it means to be effective and responsible philanthropists. When it comes to investing assets, most foundation investment committees follow the lead of traditional advisors and the practices of their often equally well-endowed institutional siblings, such as pension funds. Therefore, as the dam begins to break, it has the potential to break *big* and with a flood of capital following in the path of courses initially cut by pension funds and family offices. Indeed, foundations are worth keeping an eye on, for when they do step up and into the impact investing arena, something will clearly have changed!

Leading Trend Indicator

- Impact investors should watch for shifts in the investment practices of family offices, pension funds, and mainstream investment banking groups promoting impact investing. As these sources of capital move—executing both impact and sustainable responsible investment strategies—growing numbers of foundation fiduciaries will follow their lead and, once the path has been cleared, play a significant and ultimately innovative role in the expansion of impact investing.

Trend Eight: The Great Thaw

With the introduction of the term, concepts, and practices of impact investing, many of those already engaged in using capital to advance social and environmental value creation responded with a great shrug—if not an outright smirk. Although the idea of impact investing resonated, these professionals had built their careers and spent their lives operating within spheres of practice they had helped conceive, shape, and build. Needless to say, their response to this new way of framing their previous work was not always welcoming!

And why should it be?

Those executing strategies within traditional responsible investing and community development finance had done great work and have, in fact, created significant impact in the world—to our collective benefit. Some felt that by promoting a new vision of a broader tent, impact investing was both denying the force of their own specific efforts and asking them to forgo the identities they'd spent lifetimes sculpting. Although the critiques offered by leaders of these established subsectors of responsible investment practice include many good observations, the tone tends to be more defensive than insightful or engaging of new ideas and perspectives.[18] Perhaps, more important, whereas these other approaches to mobilizing capital had been around for decades, impact investing as both a concept and strategy was felt to be untested, hubristic and dismissive of the efforts of others.

The irony, of course, is that impact investing *is* sustainable and responsible investing, just as community development finance is impactful and offers impact investors vehicles through which to attain their goals. Furthermore, virtually all those carrying the banner of "impact" manage their assets through sustainable, responsible, and community development funds as well as various impact-branded vehicles. The twist, however, is that when many of the "new kids" appeared on the block, what engaged them was not the particulars of sustainable, responsible, or community development investing, but rather what those approaches represented as part of a broad and wide community of practice that included those themes, but also a host of others, like microfinance, sustainable ranchland investing, and integrated ESG. What the new kids wanted was to play sports and not debate whether soccer was better than football or basketball.

There is certainly legitimacy in recognizing the importance of particular and unique impact investing strategies, but if we focus on the parts, we will miss the potential power of the whole. And ultimately, a growing number of investors are focusing more on the end goal of impact and change than on the particulars of identifying with any single tribe—whether impact investing, responsible investing, or community investing. It is for this reason that such concepts as Total Portfolio Management (wherein all capital, from philanthropy to near market to market rate, is managed on a sustainable, high-impact basis) or such groups as the 100% Impact Network (wherein members—whether family offices or foundations—are engaged in a peer-based learning initiative to share promising practices) are now gaining ground. These are big-tent actors interested in being a part of and learning from *all* of the capital innovation efforts under way around the world—not simply a single brand, strategy, or practice of investing.

In the past, we have identified ourselves by the silos we kept. We were businesspeople or social workers or government civil servants or artists. Today, we are increasingly known for the innovations we advance—we are social entrepreneurs, impact investors, and venture philanthropists. Our coauthor, Jed, together with others, has long argued that actors from one silo needed to understand what was happening within other silos—but that our common focus should be on the *crosscuts* between those silos and on our collaborative efforts to maximize total blended value for both company (whether for-profit or nonprofit) and community. More specifically, the previously referenced *Blended Value Map* identified a number of crosscuts between silos: capital, metrics, leadership, organization, and public policy. The most important priority should be for actors within silos to focus on solving for crosscutting issues that affect the potential success of each silo, rather than working simply to build individual silos in isolation from the larger vision and set of common practices.

Over the coming years, we will be known less by our specific address (on Wall Street or Main Street) than by our neighborhood or theme—we create impact through funds, whether within the thematic areas of real asset ranch and farmland investing or the complex, interrelated parts of a new transit-oriented development fund. Over the coming years, we will sing similar hymns out of shared songbooks as we look to leverage a variety of resources for multiple returns. We will work across the silos while maintaining respect for the particular role we each play and the contributions we make. There will be a great thaw as we move out of the friction of stasis and toward the flow of all capital structured for optimized impact with multiple returns.

Leading Trend Indicator

- Watch for a growing number of associations and organizations to advance their particular perspective, yet engage in "cross-silo" conferences and produce articles, reports, and analysis focused to a greater degree on the whole than on promotion of the parts. As you see more of these activities, it will be an indicator that the thaw has taken hold!

Trend Nine: Corporate Alignment

At its core, Collaborative Capitalism requires two things to function: capital and corporations. In this regard, there are two issues to consider in corporate alignment. First is the nature of the corporate form itself: How will it evolve to become a more effective vehicle for creating positive, integrated impact? Second, within these corporate structures, how will we best be able to effect change and develop corporate practices that advance sustainability and positive impact?

In the future, we will see continued evolution in our thinking with regard to what constitutes the appropriate corporate form to serve as the vessel of our impact resources. In the past, we thought in terms of for-profit or nonprofit—depending on whether we sought to do well or do good. In today's context, we are agnostic with regard to both corporate form and capital structure. We think in terms of which corporate form will most effectively advance the execution of our business model and what types of capital— philanthropic to market rate—will best fuel its growth.

As this shift continues, we will see growing numbers of mission-driven for-profit ventures and nonprofits with compelling business opportunities. We will read of corporate mission statements and for-profit theories of change. We will see the C-suite extended to include positions such as chief impact officer and chief integrated reporting officer. These leaders will be housed not simply within for-profit or nonprofit corporations but within B Corps, cooperatives, Community Interest Companies in the United Kingdom or Employee Stock Ownership Plans. Just as form follows function, corporate entities will continue an evolution as they are reshaped to maintain relevance to new markets, new opportunities, and new understanding of the value we seek to create. There will, in a word, be corporate alignment of investor interest and market opportunity as we build the new vehicles of an impact economy.

In addition to advancing new ways of understanding corporate forms, the overall approach to advancing change within the corporate community itself will also continue to evolve. In the early years of the social entrepreneurship movement, the focus was largely on creating new ventures as alternatives to existing corporate structures; mainstream companies were viewed as the opposition, not necessarily the target of our efforts.

Over time that strategy has changed. Yes, many social entrepreneurs still seek to launch their own ventures, and we celebrate those actors, yet many have also come to understand that we must also proactively engage traditional corporate practice if we are to effect change in the mainstream. For example, Gary Hirshberg, the cofounder of yogurt company Stonyfield Farm, began his work to support local dairy farmers through a nonprofit organic farming school and then decided it would be more effective to create a for-profit firm. More than twenty years later, that firm, which had become the world's leading organic yogurt company, was acquired by the global firm Dannon, which kept Hirshberg on, first as CEO and then as chair, to help the parent company learn about managing organic brands globally. The premise is that if change can be effected from the inside, we may ultimately be able to have an impact on millions of consumers and influence the practices of multimillion-dollar companies.

Leading Trend Indicators

- As this trend continues to evolve, watch for whether the acquisition of smaller companies by larger firms results in the smaller company actually being able to influence the acquiring firm. Look for shifts in sourcing and supply chain management, the introduction of more sustainable business practices, and other changes in corporate practice.
- There will likely be pushback from traditional companies and their advisors and attorneys. With the introduction of new corporate forms, there will be greater opportunities for creating vehicles to effectively advance impact, but there will also be resistance from institutions and actors invested in maintaining the existing structures as the dominant corporate forms.

Trend Ten: Going All In: The Family Office as Foundation, Investor, and Advocate

We are used to talking about funds and investment houses, foundations and development agencies, but the mainstream conversation about impact investing has not focused as much on the role of the family office. Family offices are created to manage the assets of high- and ultra-high-net-worth individuals—those with investible assets in excess of $100 million. Usually these offices are managed with white glove discretion, for the sole interest of any given family. What has been interesting to watch over the past decade has been the emerging role of the family office as impact vehicle.

Family offices may be structured in any number of ways, but at their core they have investment vehicles in the form of trusts and often also maintain family foundations as related charitable vehicles. The role of the family office has been important to the past and future evolution of impact investing in at least two ways.

First, as accredited investors, they have functioned as a significant part of the private sector capital to complement impact investing of both private and public development finance entities. They buy microfinance debt and invest in impact investment funds executing a range of strategies, including wetlands mitigation banking, affordable housing, small business development, solar installation, and alternative energy development. Acting as LPs and anchor investors in new impact strategies, many family offices have provided much of the bridge capital linking public sector initiatives with private sector capital markets.

A second role family offices have more recently come to play is what could be called "all-in" impact investors: investors managing their *total* net worth—100 percent as opposed to simply 5 or 10 percent for charitable giving—as impact investors. By demonstrating how a Total Portfolio Management approach may be executed and developing total portfolio reporting practices, these family offices show how asset owners may invest capital across a continuum of strategies and instruments—philanthropic capital to near-market-rate and market-rate capital—all managed on an integrated basis with regard to an appropriate level of financial return for any given asset class *together* with the intentional management of impact returns.

These family offices might best be thought of as "capital incubators" in that they may be operated at the discretion of principal investors who (while fulfilling a variety of fiduciary obligations depending on the nature of the trusts and other vehicles that house their financial resources) have much greater decision-making authority and discretion than institutional fiduciaries in regard to how they invest their assets. Family offices, by managing their assets for total performance of financial return with social and environmental impacts, are in many ways best positioned to incubate the new and emerging impact investing approaches of coming years. Together with the variety of public-private partnerships discussed earlier, families may seed, innovate, anchor, subordinate, enhance, and leverage capital in creative ways that institutional investors can often only dream of. Their existence is nascent—as of this writing, the new 100% Impact Network has recently held only its fourth meeting—yet the appeal of managing all one's resources on an integrated, total portfolio basis is clear to a new generation of fiduciaries and an existing generation of asset owners seeking to attain the greatest possible level of integrated performance for their capital. Many will watch to see how these families execute their strategies, and many others will be the beneficiaries of their increasing impact investment acumen.

Leading Trend Indicators

- Family office networks and associations will begin offering sessions on "100 Percent Impact" and Total Portfolio Management strategies.
- As more principals seek to advance an impact investing vision, they will require new forms of investment research, will develop new wealth management practices, and engage new types of advisors—all in pursuit of an impact agenda.
- As family offices manage larger pools of capital in alignment with an impact agenda, watch for a growing number of foundations and other asset owners to replicate or be informed by their experiences.

■   ■   ■

These developments are really only the start; we would encourage you to identify your own list of Top Ten trends in impact investing. As impact investing continues to grow and expand into mainstream investment practice, we will see the creation of many of the elements that come with a new and vibrant market:

- There will be new innovations in capital structure and management.
- New opportunities will be created for those coming into the space with their own visions and insights in regard to how capital might best be used to create impact with sustainable financial performance.

- New job categories and career paths will be pioneered.
- Growing interest on the part of the general public will need to be fed with reliable, practice-based information and stories depicting the power of capital to create positive change in our world.
- New cycles of virtuous innovation, entrepreneurship, and institutional transformation will be unleashed.

Regardless of the particulars or whether we ultimately land five or ten degrees off True North, the changes are coming—and are indeed already under way.

Watch for them.

Track their development.

Structure your investments accordingly.

There is no guarantee of future success, but there is also no need to move blindly ahead. As our own research has shown, there is a rapidly growing body of knowledge regarding how to "do" impact investing, a rising pool of talent to guide the execution of impact investing strategies, and a studied track record of emerging success on which to build the successful investment strategies of the future.

8

Concluding Reflections

EVEN AS THE ULTIMATE SCALE OF THE TRANSFORMATION we're undergoing
is as yet unknown, we are clearly moving through a period of
profound change in how we understand the nature of capitalism
and the purpose of capital itself. The days of pursuing long-term
profit without consideration of social and environmental factors
are gone, just as the age of our truly understanding how capital
might be applied for impact is opening before us. The lessons we've
learned from the twelve funds profiled in this book and from the
leading practitioners who contributed to this work are clear:

- Mission First and Last has enabled funds to maintain fiscal
  discipline while embedding impact within investment strategies, moving beyond the artificial bifurcation of impact versus
  financial performance.
- Policy Symbiosis has played a central role in advancing impact
  investing.
- Catalytic Capital has been key to anchoring and expanding
  impact investing funds of every stripe.
- Multilingual Leadership has enabled the field to benefit from
  knowledge grounded in a host of silos, while leveraging
  that knowledge for new applications and success.

These lessons, together with the deeper insights presented both
in this book and in our original fund case studies, also indicate
something else:

*Impact investing is moving from its early period of many experiments
and voices toward an integrated period of linking its various communities of
practice into an arena of Collaborative Capitalism.*

Furthermore, impact investing's early period of engaging in public discourse based on anecdote and opinion is giving way to a single discourse based on knowledge, experience, and research.

We hope this first deep, long-term research initiative is not the last. The field as a whole must pay greater attention to defining terms, understanding true impacts, and moving from conjecture to intentional analysis. The work presented in this book, and in prior research, available at www.pacificcommunityventures.org/impinv2, offers a starting place for the field's next phase of development. We look forward to participating with our colleagues in continuing to raise the bar with regard to documenting the continuing evolution of impact investing.[1]

On the basis of our observations and analysis, and the experience of others at this point in the field's development, we know:

- Business and investors have the wherewithal and desire to manage financial capital for deep impact. We must now work to lock in the mission of impact investing funds by establishing clear purposes, strategies, and performance benchmarks for the most effective allocation of capital.
- Public officials see a clear opportunity to create an enabling environment of regulatory and policy supports to complement private capital and the innovation of social entrepreneurs the world over. We need to work to continue the field's record of nonpartisan promotion and create the policy bridges needed for impact investing to continue its development, regardless of elections and ideology.
- Investors are intrigued by the possibilities for leveraging private capital, philanthropic investments, and public capital in order to bring new investment strategies to market, unleashing new flows of capital into underserved communities and markets. We need to know more with regard to how best to structure impact capital and maintain its focus while allowing investors to earn a fair return on their investments.
- Community and cross-sector stakeholders are critical to the future success of impact investing. Their vision and voice is not a "nice to have" but central to attaining the ultimate goal of impact. We must ensure that we forge better avenues to engage

a diverse, challenging constituency and work to ensure impact investing advances not only private financial returns but also the community and environmental justice we seek.

In chapter 7, we explored the Top Ten global trends impact investors should be aware of as they develop and execute investment strategies. In addition to being aware of these trends, impact investors also need to be cognizant of the challenges and questions that remain. Our world is littered with well-intentioned initiatives and allocations of precious capital to underperforming strategies. We would be well served not to lead with our press releases and events, but rather let our actions and results tell the story of our work.

Ongoing Challenges for the Field's Development

We offer the following, limited list of ongoing challenges for the field of impact investing:

Early Development

Early-stage, impact-oriented enterprises are particularly starved of capital; they present a difficult opportunity for investors to get their heads around, as Monitor's excellent research report *From Blueprint to Scale* discusses at length.[2] Yet this segment of the impact investing market is especially critical. All businesses start out small and need capital. And through our research on the twelve funds in this book, we have seen that the approach to investing at the earliest stages of a company's or market's development tend to be highly innovative, providing a powerful testing ground for the realization of Collaborative Capitalism in practice. Ongoing work to understand where capital from individuals (family and friends) meets public and philanthropic resources, and ultimately institutional money, is essential, not to mention the numerous technical and capacity-building supports that are needed along the way.

Definitions and Terms

As hard to believe as it is for those who have been a part of this discussion over multiple years, many continue to debate and define the particulars of what constitutes impact investing. More important, specific and detailed terms and concepts continue to be refined and explored. The field would be well served by the adoption of a big-tent approach to this challenge, wherein we acknowledge that all capital may create impact and all forms of corporation may be managed for change. As we have previously stated, at its core the fundamental premises of impact investing are, quite frankly, not that hard to understand. Yet as with many things, the devil is in the details. We should get comfortable with that reality and seek to be crystal clear with regard to how we define the particulars of each strategy, fund, or investment opportunity, rather than spending exorbitant time making sure we are all on the same road before we start our individual journeys. That said, many will continue to explore how various concepts may best be applied in particular circumstances and what ideas might best be advanced from rhetoric to practice—and that is also fine!

Metrics, Measurement, and Evaluation

Although some impact investing strategies have been reviewed and assessed relative to their real impact and contribution to value creation, the reality is that the majority of impact investing strategies presently being executed presume impact on the basis of claims and intent—not of demonstrated, research-based analysis. Relative to the level of analysis applied to many philanthropic and business strategies, this should come as no surprise. But the fact is, all of us promoting the practice of impact investing as a tool for advancing community development and social justice need to raise the bar on how we define that impact and how we then track and assess performance. There are three parts to this discussion. First is simply the fact that most organizations receiving impact investing funds do not have adequate or sophisticated management and reporting systems in place. Second, many organizations (nonprofit and for-profit) view such metrics requirements as a cost of doing business in order to receive funding—not as a requirement for an organization managing for impact, much less an organization that should seek to be "data driven" in order to inform firm decision making and strategy development. Third, there are fundamental challenges regarding how best to link capital allocations with claims to the generation of impact. Each of these three issues raises significant challenges for impact investors and should be at the center of our discussions with regard to tracking, measuring, and, finally, assessing the impact aspect of impact investing.

Postmodern Portfolio Theory and Total Portfolio Management

Although there are certainly questions with regard to executing impact investing as a single, direct investment strategy, growing numbers of asset owners from across a wide spectrum are exploring how best to conceive of and then execute impact investing as part of a Total Portfolio Management strategy. As previously discussed, such an approach would seek to allocate capital and assess its performance across the spectrum of philanthropic, near-market-rate, and market-rate capital investment. The downturn of 2008 demonstrated significant shortcomings in the traditional assumptions of modern portfolio theory (that by managing investments across a range of strategies carrying various risk-and-return profiles, we can "diversify away" risk and balance a portfolio in pursuit of various levels of financial return).[3] As mainstream markets have come roaring back since 2013, the question remains: How do we best advance a new, postmodern portfolio theory that effectively integrates consideration of social and environmental risks and rewards as a part of an informed, strategic portfolio management process? In addition, although various actors (including one of this book's authors [Jed]) have promoted concepts of Total Portfolio Management and Activation, additional research is required if we are to formalize such practices and promote them to a wider audience of mainstream investors.

Defining Roles and Responsibilities

A big-tent approach to impact investing implies that all participants in the capital market have a role. For example, a sustainable approach to investing in public markets more broadly will ultimately advance the same conditions—an outcomes orientation, additional transparency, and attention to constituency—that drive impact investing and Collaborative Capitalism, bolstering the capacity for investors with a different focus (on private markets, for example) to also achieve their impact objectives. It is one thing to say as much, but another to understand the implications fully. Impact investing in private funds—representing all of our twelve research subjects—provides a very bounded and therefore convenient locus for research. Once we move beyond these confines, addressing the challenges of understanding how, precisely, to manage outcomes, no matter the investor type and market, will be an altogether more ambitious undertaking, even as the experience of private funds provides a jumping-off point. For example, we might ask which large public companies or industry sectors have the potential to deliver the types of outcomes that are consistent with impact investing, and how might it be possible to track these outcomes and create funds that seek intentionally to deliver them?

Stakeholder Voice

Constituents are highly diverse and can include investors, governments, employees, community members, nonprofits, customers, suppliers, and others. Many of these groups may not communicate their desires effectively or efficiently. Thus key questions become challenging, such as: In an impact investment with multiple stakeholders, are the interests of investors more important than the interests of other stakeholders, such as beneficiaries or customers? If not, how can these interests be effectively managed?

Once you posit the notion that an impact fund or business must be responsive to the needs of stakeholders, you set the expectation that these needs will be considered. A fundamental question for those engaged in Collaborative Capitalism raised in chapter 1 is how to create the relationships and feedback loops that make the constituency process feasible, actionable, and, of increasing importance, binding. The new emergence of corporate forms like benefit corporations are one potential answer to this; we expect others will emerge around the globe as well, as different countries have different laws and norms around organizational power dynamics. The best division between what is regulated in legal terms and what emerges as a behavioral norm is also unclear as of yet. Which of these solutions will be most effective and how will we know? It will take probably a decade or more to discover the answer.

Using the Right Tool for the Right Problem

As impact investing continues to evolve and we learn more about its relative effectiveness and performance, it is critical not to over-promote the practice or fall victim to the notion that it represents some sort of panacea for the problems confronting us around the world today. Although certain concepts of impact investing (such as Total Portfolio Management) are broad and strategic, other practices (such as direct investment) are applicable only in certain situations in pursuit of certain outcomes. Of course, most of those involved in impact investing would be the first to acknowledge the limits and constraints of some of its practices; however, in many of our public debates, impact investing is presented as the critical innovation that will advance our common agenda. Instead, in our public discussions and private strategy sessions, we need to seek greater clarity with regard to when a defined and specific impact investing strategy offers the greatest promise of optimizing impact and when other related tools (traditional grants and social service provision, venture philanthropy, shareholder advocacy, and so on) may be more effective. Many of us affirm and practice an approach to impact investing as a lens through which *all* investments are assessed relative to the nature of their potential impact, and so may draw on a variety of defined investing strategies in its execution. In contrast, those promoting one tool within the impact tool kit (social impact bonds, for example) should be cautious in promoting a single hammer for all the nails in the world.

The Road Ahead

Finding the answers to many of the challenges we've raised in this book as well as those being raised in discussions elsewhere—and engaging the larger community to share our insights—will require a determined ongoing effort and significant investment of time and resources. Yet a commitment to field building remains crucial. In the absence of deeper research and analysis, we will continue to be driven by anecdotes and limited circles of knowledge—all of which will stifle the ultimate development of this promising area of investment practice.

And, of course, investment is not the only critical factor in the future success of impact enterprises and efforts. All actors have a role to play in ensuring that the field develops in the most efficient and effective way possible, leveraging the insights of those who succeed and capturing the lessons that come from unanticipated outcomes and experiences. Entrepreneurs can work to "bake in" a commitment to learning and dissemination as a part of their business strategy and organizational culture. Institutional investors can work to capture their knowledge and convene colleagues to explore experiences. Policymakers can create larger, virtual platforms to disseminate the best policy frameworks and initiatives. And corporations can come down from Davos to more effectively and directly engage their constituencies.

The stakes are high.

If impact investing spurs the socialization and growth in Collaborative Capitalism that we believe it will, for the first time in history we will be responding to some of the world's most difficult challenges appropriately, proportionally, and sustainably—through massive deployment of the world's global capital markets.

We know there is the very real possibility it can be done.

All that remains is to continue our shared efforts to move from vision to practice and from innovation to impact.

Impact Investor Resource Guide

In this section, we offer a brief overview of each of the tool kits in chapters 3 through 6, providing an easy reference for readers eager to learn the practices of Mission First and Last, Policy Symbiosis, Catalytic Capital, and Multilingual Leadership. Each of the chapters in question includes additional detail if a recommendation strikes a chord. We also include a general listing of organizational websites, blogs, and conferences of interest, and a catalog of all the authors' reports, blog articles, and case studies linked to the research project.

Chapter 3: Impact DNA (Mission First and Last)

"And although these funds may have been created with a more inherently collaborative set of 'genes' than other funds, these genes only mutate into organizational DNA—and create the conditions for success—over time. The specific practices are discernible, in other words, and can be learned."

Table RG.1 The Mission First and Last Tool Kit

Step	Strategies
Gaining clarity: use the investment thesis of change as an anchor for understanding, internalizing, and communicating precisely the value you propose to add.	Think hard about how, precisely, your investment is making an impact, compared to others (through extensive research, reflection, and engagement with peers).

Table RG.1   (*Continued*)

Step	Strategies
	The investment thesis of change includes six elements: • The "change," or social outcome, that is being pursued • The source of capital for pursuing that change • The fund's investment approach • The fund's investment recipients • The activities (outputs) of investment recipients made possible by the provision of capital • The outcomes that these outputs will lead to, and how they will be measured.
Aligning internally: the way you structure, govern, and manage your fund speaks volumes to mission.	Think concretely about operational and ownership strategies that will ensure that a fund's entire staff, board, and any other affiliated parties are on the same page and working collaboratively toward shared goals, including using the following questions: • Does your governance structure include a mission perspective? • How strong and resilient are your internal feedback loops? Do they incorporate feedback from external stakeholders? • Are there concrete opportunities to embed mission in compensation strategies and through other operational policies and practices?

Table RG.1 (*Continued*)

Step	Strategies
	• What resources do you commit to tracking and reporting impact? Does the effort feel cursory or foundational? • What resources are available to staff and other direct stakeholders for learning, through opportunities including formal training, participation in field-building events, or peer groups?
Aligning externally with investors and other stakeholders: tune in to the motivations of investors, and the needs of a broader set of stakeholders, including their investees, the markets they operate in, and their users or customers.	Diagnose your performance in implementing formal paths to external alignment. Another set of questions should be useful: • Are you familiar with what others are doing? Which funds are at the top of their game on alignment, and what does best practice look like? • Is there external buy-in for your internal practices and policies? • Have investors rallied around a relatively targeted set of social performance indicators that are consistent with your investment thesis of change? • Do investees clearly understand your mission, and vice versa? Are you supporting the mission-oriented needs of investees, and do you report to your investors and other key constituencies not just on fund

Table RG.1 (*Continued*)

Step	Strategies
	performance—that is, social outcomes—but on the fund *process* of engaging externally? • Do you actively engage in field building and work with peers on issues related to alignment?
Tracking and reporting impact: tap a range of resources to develop robust accountabilities.	Commit to, and implement, high-quality impact evaluation, which includes • Clearly established and stated social and environmental objectives • Performance metrics and targets related to these objectives, using standardized metrics wherever possible • Monitoring and management of the performance of investees against these targets • Reporting on social and environmental performance to relevant stakeholders Identify resources for both understanding impact evaluation as a practice more broadly, and the specific metrics and methods available to apply or adapt.

Chapter 4: Symbiosis as Strategy (Policy Symbiosis)

"Urgently and respectfully cultivate a deep partnership with government, rather than being reactionary when it is too late. The market is only now taking shape. This is the moment for impact investors to embrace the role of public policy in their work."

Table RG.2   The Policy Symbiosis Tool Kit

Step	Strategies
Acquire knowledge: know your market and the applicable policies.	Review the literature (and scan the market) with the goal of understanding the full array of policies that might be harnessed to increase the probability of both social and financial success in your space—not just those that act directly on your own organization. Join sector and field-level trade groups. Broaden your reading list. Verify and contextualize what you discover in consultation with peers, independent experts (for example, legal advisors), and core constituents, including investors and investees, who are themselves subject to the influence of policy.
Build partnerships: share your experiences as a leading practitioner and strengthen relationships with public officials and other constituents that make impact investing possible.	Be open and proactive about engaging with the public sector, including by considering the following questions: • Are there industry convenings where policymakers are not present? If so, why not? • Is there more you could do to help policymakers? • Do your political leaders at the local, regional, or national level know what you do? • Have you identified areas of shared concern with public officials?

Table RG.2 (*Continued*)

Step	Strategies
	• Are there any initiatives you could be pursuing jointly with public officials?
	Share your insights as a practitioner with public officials:
	• Blog regularly. • Maintain an active presence on social media. • Partner with established thought leaders. • Publish white papers and other research reports. • Participate on conference panels. • Participate in "advocacy days" together with peers. • Provide formal feedback on particular policy initiatives.
Be visionary: embrace public purpose as a strategic objective.	Position your small but innovative impact within the bigger picture of social change that many policymakers have in mind. Have a robust investment thesis of change and articulate it boldly. Embrace the public purpose in your investment thesis of change, and ensure that this is confidently communicated to public officials.
Proceed with integrity: commit publicly to the highest ethical standards.	Sign on to public principles of ethical behavior. Demonstrate and communicate that operating with the highest standards of integrity is plain good business.

Chapter 5: The New Deal (Catalytic Capital)

"[Fund managers] who want to leverage Catalytic Capital will need to take the time to understand, in an engaged way that builds trust between parties, the real strategic interests of stakeholders and the alignment of these interests with your own."

Table RG.3   The Catalytic Capital Tool Kit

Step	Strategies
Know how: learn the tools of structured finance and multiparty transactions.	Study other transactions; talk to lawyers, accountants, and financiers; or start doing deals in the space and learn what some of the variations and norms are within your investment area of focus.
	Partner with third parties who have this knowledge.
Know who and why: understand the motivations of different types of investors and the way they use their capital to achieve various ends.	Read and do research outside your comfort zone and think about what other kinds of companies, funds, or partners may actually have an interest in the outcomes you care about.
	Cast a wide net and make lists of different kinds of partners based on geographic, impact, industry, and stage interests. (Imagine a sample investment in the portfolio and prepare an informal "ecosystem analysis" for that company.)
	Attend industry conferences, make new connections, ask a lot of questions, and try to figure out ways to build collaborative relationships with new parties.
	Find the right anchor or seed investor for your own fund,

Table RG.3 (*Continued*)

Step	Strategies
	recognizing that a large portion of your limited partners will have strategic, and not just financial, reasons for investing.
Think expansively: revisit strategic objectives and approaches and determine whether you could be playing a more catalytic role.	Put the spotlight back on yourself and consider the following sample questions: • What kind of catalytic role do you want to play, and which kinds are not acceptable to you? • Will you structure relationships for a set of diverse parties, or do you prefer to let someone else do that, and to step in when the opportunity seems to match your own interests? • What kind of leverage is most needed by your stakeholders? • What can you learn from your investees or other partners about what has been tried before? • How can you take advantage of other experts outside of your networks to help build a knowledge base of best practices that your fund can use going forward?
Invest strategically: focus your efforts on an approach aligned with the organization's mission.	Hone your ideas through interaction; don't assume that one size fits all or that your plan in the abstract will work when it's time to get detailed. • Examples of engagement include meetings and networking, research, and communications.

Table RG.3 (*Continued*)

Step	Strategies
Review collectively: track your catalytic impact individually, but also by examining the deal and the sector holistically, assessing the way your impact has influenced and coordinated with others.	Revisit best practices in tracking performance, with a focus on catalytic impact. For example: • If you were a seed investor in a deal, how much capital was leveraged afterwards? • If you were a sustaining investor, how well did that work for the fund or enterprise—has it met the recipient's own sustainability goal? Don't be afraid to work directly with constituents, including investees, coinvestors, and actors in other parts of the market. Seek advice and support from third-party experts around best practices in your field. Share results and findings publicly so that other managers can learn from your work.

Chapter 6: Multilingual Leadership

"Impact investors seeking to maximize the value of Multilingual Leadership to their firm must *recognize the type of multilingual expertise and relationships that will best enable them to reach their goals.*

As investors educate themselves and build their teams, they should do this in a way that *strategically incorporates the interdisciplinary background of founding team members and of new hires, and contributes to the continued learning processes of the company,* as well as those of potential partners."

Table RG.4   The Multilingual Leadership Tool Kit

Step	Strategies
Learn: frame your goals and work through the distinct lenses of the business/finance, nonprofit/philanthropic, and public sectors.	Study the priorities and key concepts of the three sectors: • The public sector seeks to improve the quality of life for all citizens, in part by focusing on the concepts of market systems, failures, and externalities; public goods; and efficacy and scale. • The financial sector seeks primarily to maximize risk-adjusted returns, focusing on the concepts of risk mitigation and return on equity, efficiency, supply and demand, and price and willingness to pay. • The nonprofit sector seeks to do good in the world, focusing on the concepts of theory of change and of catalytic investment and innovation, and the clear articulation of demonstrated outcomes. Look out for articles written by representatives from different silos—and those working hard to "bridge the divide," such as the Global Learning Exchange on Social Impact Investing, an initiative of the UK Cabinet Office, the Impact Investing Policy Collaborative, and the World Economic Forum. Create conditions in your workplace that accommodate both formal and informal training and mentorship.

Table RG.4   (*Continued*)

Step	Strategies
Adapt: clarify your role by identifying core strengths and opportunities to add value.	Test your investment thesis of change against the following core, cross-sector elements: • Does it address a market failure? • Is it consistent with other (noninvestment) approaches to addressing the social outcome at hand? • Is it catalytic, with the power to change market systems and bring new actors to the table? Identify the key government, philanthropic, and financial stakeholders that are active in your focus area. Draft communication materials to test knowledge and messaging. "Find your voice" by workshopping ideas and language internally and with key external, cross-sector stakeholders.
Act: operationalize cross-sector approaches and play a truly multilingual role in the market.	Recruit multilingual leaders to your team. Invite multilingual leaders you admire to join a board or advisory board. Provide your current employees with a continuing education allowance to pursue classes that relate to your impact area. Continue to raise the bar on performance measurement. Advocate for policy that enables progress in your area of impact investing.

Table RG.4 (*Continued*)

Step	Strategies
	Volunteer with or donate to organizations that address your area of impact. These groups may be future strategic partners.
	Do pro bono work that applies your core skills to the impact areas in question.

Resources

These are the organizational websites, blogs, publications and conferences we feel may be of interest to the reader. All can be found easily through www.google.com.

Websites

Acumen

B Lab

Blended Value

CASE at Duke University

CASE i3 Initiative on Impact Investing

Case Foundation

CASE Notes Fuqua blog

Echoing Green

Global Learning Exchange on Social Impact Investing

Huffington Post Impact

ImpactAlpha

ImpactAssets

Impact Investing Policy Collaborative

InSight at Pacific Community Ventures

MaxImpact

Next Billion

Pacific Community Ventures

SOCAP

Skoll Centre for Social Entrepreneurship

Stanford Social Innovation Review

US National Advisory Board on Impact Investing

World Economic Forum

Conferences

Confluence

Impact Capitalism Summit

Investors' Circle

Impact Investing Exchange, Singapore (IIX)

Milken Institute Capital Markets Conference

Sankelp Forum

Skoll World Forum

SRI Conference

Social Capital Markets Conference (SOCAP)

The SRI Conference (formerly, SRI in the Rockies)

TBLI Europe and US

US-SIF

Project Catalog

This book builds on the authors' research with Pacific Community
Ventures, CASE at Duke University, and ImpactAssets from
2012 to 2014, which included numerous published reports,
blog articles, and case studies, listed in the following sections.

Reports

"The Impact Investor: The Need for Evidence and Engagement,"
March 2012, available at http://www.pacificcommunityventures
.org/reports-and-publications/the-impact-investor-best-practices
-in-impact-investing/

"A Market Emerges: The Six Dynamics of Impact Investing," September 2012, available at http://www.pacificcommunityventures .org/reports-and-publications/the-impact-investor-a-market-em erges-the-six-dynamics-of-impact-investing/

"Impact Investing 2.0: The Way Forward—Insight from 12 Outstanding Funds," November 2013, available at http://www.pacificcom munityventures.org/impinv2/wp-content/uploads/2013/11/ 2013FullReport_sngpg.v8.pdf

"Impact Investing 2.0: The Way Forward, Executive Summary," November 2013, available at http://www.pacificcommunity ventures.org/impinv2/wp-content/uploads/2014/01/2013 ImpactInvestor_exec-summary.pdf

Blog Articles

"Six Dynamics Describe How Impact Investing Is Unique," September 2012, available at http://www.huffingtonpost.com/ben-thornley/six-dynamics-describe-how_b_1914353.html

"The Pioneering Impact Investor," October 2012, available at http:// www.huffingtonpost.com/ben-thornley/impact-investing_b_ 2003431.html

"Mission Meld: A Case Study on Alignment in Impact Investing," October 2012, available at http://blogs.fuqua.duke.edu/case notes/2012/10/18/mission-meld-a-case-study-on-alignment-in-impact-investing/

"Advancing Impact Investing Platforms—Promise and Peril!" October 2012, available at http://www.nextbillion.net/blogpost. aspx?blogid=2993"Closing in on the Crux of Impact Investing," June 2013, available at http://www.huffingtonpost.com/ben-thornley/closing-in-on-the-crux-of_b_3381169.html

"Impact Investing 2.0—What $3 Billion Tells Us about the Next $300 Billion," September 2013, available at http://www.huffingtonpost .com/cathy-clark/impact-investing_b_3850296.html

"Opening the Curtain on the New 2.0 Era of Impact Investing," November 2013, available at http://www.huffingtonpost.com/ ben-thornley/opening-the-curtain-on-th_b_4227984.html

"Success in Impact Investing Through Policy Symbiosis," February 2014, available at http://www.huffingtonpost.com/ben-thornley/success-in-impact-investi_b_4849740.html

"Impact Investing and Global Finance: The Big Picture," April 2014, available at http://www.huffingtonpost.com/ben-thorn ley/impact-investing-and-global-finance_b_5150545.html

"Mission-Driven Returns," June 2014, available at http://www .ssireview.org/blog/entry/mission_driven_returns

Case Studies

The following twelve detailed case studies are freely available online at http://www.pacificcommunityventures.org/impinv2/downloads-and-resources/:

Aavishkaar India Micro Venture Capital Fund

ACCIÓN Texas Inc.

Bridges Ventures Sustainable Growth Funds I and II

Business Partners Limited Southern African SME Risk Finance Fund

Calvert Foundation Community Investment Note

Deutsche Bank Global Commercial Microfinance Consortium I

Elevar Equity Unitus Equity Fund and Elevar Equity II

Huntington Capital Fund II, LP

The W.K. Kellogg Foundation Mission Driven Investments

MicroVest I, LP

RSF Social Finance Social Enterprise Lending Program

SEAF Sichuan SME Investment Fund, LLC

Notes

Preface

1. For a brief but concise overview of the trends in impact investing, see the Case Foundation's "Short Guide to Impact Investing," at http://casefoundation.org/impact-investing/short-guide.

Introduction

1. World Economic Forum. (2013, September). *From the Margins to the Mainstream—Assessment of the Impact Investment Sector and Opportunities to Engage Mainstream Investors.* http://www3.weforum.org/docs/WEF_II_FromMarginsMainstream_Report_2013.pdf.
2. Webster, B. (2013, December 24). "The Best of 2013: What's Next for Impact Investing? The Value of a Formal Fund Structure to Maximize Impact." Next Billion. http://www.nextbillion.net/blogpost.aspx?blogid=3159.

Chapter 1

1. The term *Collaborative Capitalism* is not new. The writings of Joe Echevarria, CEO of Deloitte LLP (see "Collaborative Capitalism: The Power of Business and Government Working Together," January 22, 2013, http://globalblogs.deloitte.com/deloitteperspectives/2013/01/collaborative-capitalism-the-power-of-business-and-government-working-together.html); Eric Lowitt's work on the collaborative economy (see "Nine Tips for Success in the Collaboration Economy," *Guardian,* August 7, 2013, http://www.theguardian.com/sustainable-business/tips-success-collaboration-economy); and work by others all have discussed the new precepts of leadership from a cross-sector and

enterprise point of view, including coauthor Jed Emerson, in 2003 in his seminal research work, *The Blended Value Map*, http://www .blendedvalue.org/wp-content/uploads/2004/02/pdf-bv-map.pdf.

2. Snowdon, G. (2011, November 18). "Richard Branson: 'Capitalism has lost its way.'" *Guardian*. http://www.theguardian.com/business/ 2011/nov/18/richard-branson-capitalism-lost-way.

3. Freeland, C. (2013, November 20). "Is Capitalism in Trouble?" *Atlantic*. http://www.theatlantic.com/magazine/archive/2013/12/ is-capitalism-in-trouble/354683/.

4. Rodin, J. (2013, November 14). "'Impact Investing.' *New York Times*. http://www.nytimes.com/2013/11/22/opinion/impact-investing .html?_r=0.

5. United Nations. (2011). *Financing for Development*. http://www.un .org/esa/ffd/.

6. Milway, K. S., and Goulay, C. D. (2013, February 28). "The Rise of Social Entrepreneurship in B-Schools in Three Charts." *Harvard Business Review*. http://blogs.hbr.org/2013/02/the-rise-of-social- entrepreneu/.

7. See also Hurst, A. (2014, April). *The Purpose Economy*. Elevate, Boise, ID. http://www.amazon.com/dp/1937498298/?tag=googhydr-20& hvadid=31592535157&hvpos=1t1&hvexid=&hvnetw=g&hvrand= 16684400209860371963&hvpone=18.74&hvptwo=&hvqmt=b& hvdev=c&rcf=pd_sl_kx7wd54fh_b.

8. Career Advisory Board, DeVry University. (2011, January 28). "Exec- utive Summary—The Future of Millennials' Careers." http://www .careeradvisoryboard.org/public/uploads/2011/10/Executive- Summary-The-Future-of-Millennial-Careers.pdf.

9. Deloitte. (2012, January). *The Millennial Survey*. http://www.deloitte .com/assets/Dcom-CostaRica/Local%20Assets/Documents/Estudios/ 2012/120124-cr_Millennial_Survey_2011.pdfwatch
   Liesel Pritzker Simmons and Ian Simmons, cofounders of Blue Haven Initiative, explain their view of this trend in the six-minute video "Millennials Take a Stand for Impact Investing." (2014) Vor Video. http://vorvideo.com/latest-videos/millennials-take-stand-impact- investing/.

10. Deloitte. (2014, January). *Big Demands and High Expectations: The Deloitte Millennial Survey, Executive Summary*. http://www2.deloitte .com/content/dam/Deloitte/global/Documents/About-Deloitte/ gx-dttl-2014-millennial-survey-report.pdf.

11. Emerson, J., and Little, T. (2005, September). *The Prudent Trustee: The Evolution of the Long-Term Investor*. Rose Foundation for Communities

and the Environment. http://www.rosefdn.org/downloads/prudent trustee.pdf.

12. CalPERS, *CalPERS Investment Beliefs,* Adopted September 16, 2013. http://www.calpers.ca.gov/eip-docs/about/pubs/board-offsite.pdf. For the original discussion of these ideas, see Thornley, B. (2013, September 20). "The Question of Mainstreaming Impact Investing." *Huffington Post.* http://www.huffingtonpost.com/ben-thornley/the-question-of-mainstrea_b_3949731.html.

13. Watch Janine Guillot explain this in the three-minute video "Impacting the World's Largest Pension Funds." (2014). Vor Video. http://vorvideo.com/latest-videos/impacting-worlds-largest-pension-fund/.

14. Mercer. (2012, January). *Through the Looking Glass: How Investors Are Applying the Results of the Climate Change Scenarios Study.* http://www.ifc.org/wps/wcm/connect/df5b210049f05559b354ff21a6199c1f/How_investors_are_applying_climate_change.pdf?MOD=AJPERES

15. Fulton, M., Kahn, B. M., and Sharples, C. (2012, June 12). *Sustainable Investing: Establishing Long-Term Value and Performance.* http://ssrn.com/abstract=2222740 or http://dx.doi.org/10.2139/ssrn.2222740.

16. O'Donnel, N., Poon, J., Carty, I., and Sokolovskaya, A. (2013, June). *ESG Reporting on the London Stock Exchange.* Advocates for International Development. http://a4id.org/sites/default/files/user/LSE%20ESG%20reporting.pdf.

17. http://www.opic.gov/opic-action/overview.

18. Volans. (2013). "Evolution." http://volans.com/about/evolution/.

19. Olsson Center for Applied Ethics. (2013, January 2). "The Future of Capitalism." http://blogs.darden.virginia.edu/ethicalworld/2013/01/02/the-future-of-capitalism/.

20. Deloitte. (2014). "Sustainable Supply Chain." http://www.deloitte.com/view/en_US/us/Services/additional-services/deloitte-sustainability/sustainable-operations-supply-chain/index.htm.

21. World Economic Forum, with InSight at Pacific Community Ventures and the Initiative for Responsible Investment. (2013, April). *Breaking the Binary: Policy Guide to Scaling Social Innovation.* World Economic Forum. http://www.weforum.org/pdf/schwabfound/PolicyGuide_to_ScalingSocial%20Innovation.pdf.

22. United States Conference of Mayors. (2013, June). "A New Era for Public Private Partnerships Transforming Smart City Technology and Sustainability Infrastructure." http://www.usmayors.org/resolutions/81st_Conference/tc16.asp.

23. Thornley, B., and Brett, D. (2013, November). *Impact Investing 2.0 Case Study: Deutsche Bank Global Commercial Microfinance Consortium 1.*

Pacific Community Ventures, CASE at Duke University and Impact Assets. http://www.pacificcommunityventures.org/impinv2/wp-content/uploads/2013/11/casestudy_deutsche_v7.pdf.

24. For more discussion of how these factors interrelate, see J.P.Morgan Global Social Finance Research. (2012, October 1). *A Portfolio Approach to Impact Investment.* http://www.jpmorganchase.com/corporate/socialfinance/document/121001_A_Portfolio_Approach_to_Impact_Investment.pdf.

25. See, for example, Clark, C., and Emerson, J. (2012, January). "A New World of Metrics: Trends in Monitoring Social Return." *Investing for Impact: How Social Entrepreneurship Is Redefining the Meaning of Return.* Credit Suisse Research Institute. http://sites.duke.edu/casei3/files/2013/03/CREDIT-SUISSE_investing_for_impact.pdf.

26. For an in-depth discussion of this topic, please see one of the first articles to address this theme: Emerson, J. (2003, Summer). "Where Money Meets Mission: Breaking Down the Firewall Between Foundation Investments and Programming." *Stanford Social Innovation Review.* http://www.blendedvalue.org/wp-content/uploads/2004/02/pdf-money-meets-mission.pdf.

27. See, for example: Emerson, J. (2002, May/June). "Horse Manure and Grantmaking." *Foundation News and Commentary.*

28. Ragin, L. M. (2004, January 1). *New Frontiers in Mission-Related Investing.* F.B. Heron Foundation. http://fbheron.issuelab.org/resource/new_frontiers_in_mission_related_investing.

29. Gonzalez, A., and Rosenberg, R. (n.d.). "The State of Microcredit—Outreach, Profitability, and Poverty." http://www.microfinancegateway.org/gm/document-1.9.26787/25.pdf.

30. Morgan Stanley. (2013, November). "Morgan Stanley Establishes Institute for Sustainable Investing." (Press release.) http://www.morganstanley.com/about/press/articles/a2ea84d4–931a-4ae3–8dbd-c42f3a50cce0.html

31. Dees, J. G. (2011). "Social Ventures as Learning Laboratories." *Tennessee's Business* 20(1), 3–5. http://caseatduke.org/documents/Articles-Research/Social_Ventures_as_Learning_Laboratories-May_2011.pdf.

32. Clark, C., and Nicola, D. (2013, November 26). "Bringing Social Impact Bonds to the Environment." *Stanford Social Innovation Review.* http://www.ssireview.org/blog/entry/bringing_social_impact_bonds_to_the_environment.

33. Goldman Sachs. (2014). "Urban Investments." http://www.goldmansachs.com/what-we-do/investing-and-lending/urban-investments/.

34. Instiglio. (n.d.). "Social Impact Bonds and Development Impact Bonds Worldwide." http://www.instiglio.org/en/sibs-worldwide/.

35. Bloom, J. (2014, January 7). "Thin Margins, Deep Trust." RSF Social Finance. http://rsfsocialfinance.org/2014/01/thin-margins-deep-trust/.

Chapter 2

1. E.T. Jackson and Associates, Ltd. (2012, July). *Accelerating Impact: Achievements, Challenges and What's Next in Building the Impact Investing Industry.* Rockefeller Foundation. http://www.rockefellerfoundation.org/uploads/images/fda23ba9-ab7e-4c83–9218–24fdd79289cc.pdf.

2. Monitor Institute. (2009, January). *Investing for Social and Environmental Impact: A Design for Catalyzing an Emerging Industry.* http://monitorinstitute.com/downloads/what-we-think/impact-investing/Impact_Investing.pdf.

3. Domini, A. (2011, March 14). "Want to Make a Difference? Invest Responsibly." *Huffington Post.* http://www.huffingtonpost.com/amy-domini/want-to-make-a-difference_b_834756.html.

4. Pinsky, M. (2011, December). "'Impact Investing': Theory, Meet Practice." *Community Development Investment Review,* 48–52. http://www.frbsf.org/community-development/files/Pinsky.pdf.

5. O'Donohoe, N., Leijonhufvud, C., Saltuk, Y., Bugg-Levine, A., and Brandenburg, M. (2010, November 29). *Impact Investments: An Emerging Asset Class.* J. P. Morgan. http://www.jpmorganchase.com/corporate/socialfinance/document/impact_investments_nov2010.pdf.

6. World Economic Forum. (2013, September). *From the Margins to the Mainstream—Assessment of the Impact Investment Sector and Opportunities to Engage Mainstream Investors.* http://www3.weforum.org/docs/WEF_II_FromMarginsMainstream_Report_2013.pdf.

7. Some have argued that the idea of "additionality" is essential—that is, that an investment must increase the quantity or quality of an enterprise's social outcomes beyond what would otherwise have occurred through mainstream sources of capital (see Brest, P., and Born, K., in *Stanford Social Innovation Review,* "Unpacking the Impact in Impact Investing," at http://www.ssireview.org/articles/entry/unpacking_the_impact_in_impact_investing). Others, the three of us included, have argued instead that different types of capital, ranging from the philanthropic to the commercial, should not all be held to that same standard. We believe that being "catalytic"

and leveraging mainstream capital into impactful markets is an equally important contribution.

8. HM Government. (2013). *Growing the Social Investment Market: HMG Social Investment Initiatives 2013*. https://www.gov.uk/government/uploads/system/uploads/attachment_data/file/204990/HMG_social_investment_initiatives_2013.pdf.

9. J.P.Morgan Global Social Finance and Global Impact Investing Network. (2014, May 2). *Spotlight on the Market: The Impact Investor Survey*. http://www.thegiin.org/binary-data/2014MarketSpotlight.PDF.

10. US SIF Foundation. (2012). *Report on Sustainable and Responsible Investing Trends in the United States 2012*. http://www.ussif.org/files/Publications/12_Trends_Exec_Summary.pdf.

11. MIX (Microfinance Information Exchange). (2012, June). *Fiscal Year 2012 Annual Report: Microfinance Information Exchange, Inc*. http://www.mixmarket.org/sites/default/files/fy2012_mix_annual_report.pdf.

12. Consulting Group to Assist the Poor. (2013, November 27). *Trends in International Funding for Financial Inclusion*. http://www.cgap.org/data/trends-international-funding-financial-inclusion.

13. Initiative for Responsible Investment, US SIF Foundation, and Milken Institute. (2013, July). *Expanding the Market for Community Investment in the United States*. http://www.ussif.org/files/Publications/USSIF_Expanding_Markets.pdf.

14. US SIF Foundation, *Report on Sustainable and Responsible Investing Trends*.

15. Towers Watson. (2013, September). *The World's 300 Largest Pension Funds—Year End 2012*. http://www.towerswatson.com/en-US/Insights/IC-Types/Survey-Research-Results/2013/09/The-worlds-300-largest-pension-funds-year-end-2012.

16. InSight at Pacific Community Ventures and the Initiative for Responsible Investment. (2012, February). *Impact at Scale: Policy Innovation for Institutional Investment with Social and Environmental Benefit*. Pacific Community Ventures. http://www.pacificcommunityventures.org/uploads/reports-and-publications/ImpactReport_FINAL2.10.12.pdf.

17. "Spring in the Air: Bonds Tied to Green Investments Are Booming." (2014, March 22). *Economist*. http://www.economist.com/news/finance-and-economics/21599400-bonds-tied-green-investments-are-booming-spring-air?frsc=dg|c.

18. World Bank. (2013, August). "Green Bond Fact Sheet." http://treasury.worldbank.org/cmd/pdf/WorldBankGreenBondFactSheet.pdf.

19. "Spring in the Air." http://www.economist.com/news/finance-and-economics/21599400-bonds-tied-green-investments-are-booming-spring-air

20. Littlefield, E., Strauss, M., and Kimball, A. (2013, December). "Evaluating Past Impactful Investments to Create a Future Impact Investing Strategy." *From Ideas to Practice, Pilots to Strategy: Practical Solutions and Actionable Insights on How to Do Impact Investing.* World Economic Forum. http://www3.weforum.org/docs/WEF_II_Solutions Insights_ImpactInvesting_Report_2013.pdf.

21. O'Donohoe et al., *Impact Investments.*

22. Rockefeller Foundation. (2013, April 5). "New Impact Fund Launched to Fuel Impact Investing in Africa." (News release.) http://www.rockefellerfoundation.org/newsroom/new-impact-fund-launched-fuel-impact.

23. World Economic Forum, with InSight at Pacific Community Ventures and the Initiative for Responsible Investment. (2013, April). *Breaking the Binary: Policy Guide to Scaling Social Innovation.* http://www.weforum.org/pdf/schwabfound/PolicyGuide_to_ScalingSocial%20Innovation.pdf, 29.

24. Morgan Stanley. (2013, November 1). "Morgan Stanley Establishes Institute for Sustainable Investing." (Press release). http://www.morganstanley.com/about/press/articles/a2ea84d4–931a-4ae3–8dbd-c42f3a50cce0.html.

25. Initiative for Responsible Investment et al., *Expanding the Market.*

26. InSight at Pacific Community Ventures and the Initiative for Responsible Investment, *Impact at Scale.*

27. Etsy. (2013). *Etsy Values & Progress Report 2013.* http://extfiles.etsy.com/progress-report/2013-Etsy-Progress-Report.pdf?ref=progress_report_download.

28. Zweynert, A. (2013, September 27). "What Happens When a Social Enterprise and an Oil Giant Join Forces?" *Christian Science Monitor.* http://www.csmonitor.com/World/Making-a-difference/Change-Agent/2013/0927/What-happens-when-a-social-enterprise-and-an-oil-giant-join-forces.

29. Evergreen Cooperatives. (2012). http://evergreencooperatives.com/.

30. Bannick, M., and Goldman, P. (2012, September). *Priming the Pump: The Case for a Sector Based Approach to Impact Investing.* Omidyar Network. http://www.omidyar.com/sites/default/files/file_archive/insights/Priming%20the%20Pump_Omidyar%20Network_Sept_2012.pdf.

31. Clark, C., Emerson, J., and Thornley, B. (2012, October). *A Market Emerges: The Six Dynamics of Impact Investing.* Pacific Community Ventures, CASE at Duke University and ImpactAssets. http://www

.pacificcommunityventures.org/uploads/reports-and-publications/ The_Six_Dynamics_of_Impact_Investing_October_2012_PCV_CASE_ at_Duke_ImpactAssets.pdf.

32. SOCAP. (n.d.). "About SOCAP." http://socialcapitalmarkets.net/ about-socap/.

33. ACCIÓN East. (2013). "Microloans in the United States." http:// www.accioneast.org/home/support-accion/learn/microlending-in-the-united-states.aspx.

34. Bridges Ventures. (2009). "Measuring Social Impact." http://www .bridgesventures.com/measuring-social-impact.

35. See the Impact Investing 2.0 project site: www.bit.ly/impinv.

36. Koh, H., Karamchandani, A., and Katz, R. (2012, April). *From Blueprint to Scale: The Case for Philanthropy in Impact Investing*. Monitor Inclusive Markets. http://www.mim.monitor.com/blueprinttoscale .html.

37. Gonzalez, A., and Rosenberg, R. (n.d.). *The State of Microcredit— Outreach, Profitability, and Poverty*. Microfinance Gateway. http:// www.microfinancegateway.org/gm/document-1.9.26787/25.pdf.

Chapter 3

1. Rodin, J. (2013, May 8). "The Transformative Power of Philanthropy." Rockefeller Foundation. http://www.rockefellerfounda tion.org/blog/transformative-power-philanthropy.

2. Acumen Fund Metrics Team. (2007, January). "The Best Available Charitable Option." Acumen Fund. http://acumen.org/wp-con tent/uploads/2013/03/BACO-Concept-Paper-final.pdf.

3. ACCIÓN Texas Inc. (2014). "Our Impact." http://www.acciontexas .org/about/our-impact/.

4. For more of an overview on evaluation in impact investing, please see Clark, C., and Emerson, J. (2012, January). "A New World of Metrics: Trends in Monitoring Social Return." In *Investing for Impact: How Social Entrepreneurship Is Redefining the Meaning of Return*. Credit Suisse Research Institute. http://sites.duke.edu/casei3/files/2013/03/ CREDIT-SUISSE_investing_for_impact.pdf.

5. Clark, C., Rosenzweig, W., Long, D., and Olsen, S. (2004). *Double Bottom Line Project Report: Assessing Social Impact in Double Bottom Line Ventures*. RISE: The Research Initiative on Social Entrepreneurship. http://www.riseproject.org/DBL_Methods_Catalog.pdf.

6. Institutional Limited Partners Association. (2011, January). *Private Equity Principles*. http://ilpa.org/index.php?file=/wp-content/uploads/

2011/01/ILPA-Private-Equity-Principles-version-2.pdf&ref=http://www.google.com/url&t=1394723729.

7. Bannick, M., and Goldman, P. (2012, September). *Priming the Pump: The Case for a Sector Based Approach to Impact Investing.* Omidyar Network. http://www.omidyar.com/sites/default/files/file_archive/insights/Priming%20the%20Pump_Omidyar%20Network_Sept_2012.pdf.

8. J.P.Morgan Global Social Finance and Global Impact Investing Network. (2014, May 2). *Spotlight on the Market: The Impact Investor Survey.* http://www.thegiin.org/binary-data/2014MarketSpotlight.PDF.

9. Gawande, A. (2013, July 29). "Slow Ideas: Some Innovations Spread Fast. How Do You Speed the Ones That Don't?" *New Yorker.* http://www.newyorker.com/reporting/2013/07/29/130729fa_fact_gawande?currentPage=all.

10. RSBY is a state insurance scheme, administered by private insurers, for patients living below the poverty line.

11. Case Foundation. (2014, April). "A Short Guide to Impact Investing." http://casefoundation.org/impact-investing/short-guide.

12. Monitor Institute. (2009, January). *Investing for Social and Environmental Impact: A Design for Catalyzing an Emerging Industry.* http://monitorinstitute.com/downloads/what-we-think/impact-investing/Impact_Investing.pdf.

13. SJF Ventures. (2013). *2013 Positive Impact Report.* http://www.sjfventures.com/wp-content/uploads/2013/08/SJF-Pos_Impact_2013.pdf.

14. Global Impact Investing Network. (2011, December). *Impact-Based Incentive Structures.* http://www.thegiin.org/binary-data/RESOURCE/download_file/000/000/332–1.pdf.

15. "About Impact Investing." http://www.thegiin.org/cgi-bin/iowa/resources/about/index.html.

16. Bridges Ventures. (2014, January). *Shifting the Lens: A De-Risking Toolkit for Impact Investment.* http://www.bridgesventures.com/news/shifting-lens-new-report-bridges-bank-america-merrill-lynch-de-risking-impact-investments.

17. Root Capital. (2014), *A Roadmap for Impact.* http://www.rootcapital.org/sites/default/files/downloads/rootcapital_impactroadmap.pdf.

18. Jackson, E. T. (2013). "Interrogating the Theory of Change: Evaluating Impact Investing Where It Matters Most." *Journal of Sustainable Finance and Investment, 3*(2). http://www.tandfonline.com/doi/ref/10.1080/20430795.2013.776257#tabModule.

19. Clark, C., and Kleissner, L. (2013). *Toniic eGuide to Early Stage Global Impact Investing;* Toniic. (2012). *eGuide to Impact Assessment.* http://www.toniic.com/toniic-institute/.

20. Edens, G., Lall, S., (2014, June). *The State of Measurement Practice in the SGB Sector.* Aspen Network of Development Entrepreneurs (ANDE). http://www.aspeninstitute.org/sites/default/files/content/docs/pubs/The%20State%20of%20Measurement%20Practice%20in%20the%20SGB%20Sector.pdf.

21. IRIS. (n.d.). "Getting Started with IRIS." http://iris.thegiin.org/guides/getting-started-guide/summary.

Chapter 4

1. Social Investment Task Force. (2010, April). *Social Investment Ten Years On: Final Report of the Social Investment Task Force.* http://www.socialinvestmenttaskforce.org/downloads/SITF_10_year_review.pdf.

2. World Economic Forum, with InSight at Pacific Community Ventures and the Initiative for Responsible Investment. (2013, April). *Breaking the Binary: Policy Guide to Scaling Social Innovation.* http://www.weforum.org/pdf/schwabfound/PolicyGuide_to_ScalingSocial%20Innovation.pdf, 25.

3. Thornley, B. (2010, December). *Community Equity Capital: The Opportunities and Challenges of Growth.* InSight at Pacific Community Ventures. http://www.pacificcommunityventures.org/uploads/reports-and-publications/Community_Equity_Capital_InSight_2010.pdf.

4. Bannick, M., and Goldman, P. (2012, September). *Priming the Pump: The Case for a Sector Based Approach to Impact Investing.* Omidyar Network. http://www.omidyar.com/sites/default/files/file_archive/insights/Priming%20the%20Pump_Omidyar%20Network_Sept_2012.pdf.

5. Federal Reserve Bank of San Francisco. (2009, June). *The Economic Crisis and Community Development Finance: An Industry Assessment.* http://www.frbsf.org/community-development/files/wp2009-05.pdf.

6. Ibid.

7. Yellen, J. L. (2014, March 31). "What the Federal Reserve Is Doing to Promote a Stronger Job Market." (Speech at the 2014 National Interagency Community Reinvestment Conference, Chicago, Illinois.) Board of Governors of the Federal Reserve System. http://www.federalreserve.gov/newsevents/speech/yellen20140331a.htm.

8. Federal Reserve Bank of San Francisco and Low Income Investment Fund. (2012). *Investing in What Works for America's Communities.* What Works for America's Communities. http://whatworksforamerica.org/pdf/whatworks_fullbook.pdf.

9. Working Cities Challenge. (2014). "Our Goal." http://www.bostonfed.org/workingcities/.

10. "CDFI Coalition." http://www.cdfi.org/policy-and-advocacy/.

11. Opportunity Finance Network. (n.d.). "CDFIs: Investing in Opportunity." http://ofn.org/sites/default/files/ABOUTCDFIs_Factsheet_051613.pdf.
12. Cameron, David, MP. (2013, June 6). "Social Investment Can Be a Great Force for Social Change." (Speech delivered at the Social Impact Investment Forum, London). GOV.UK. https://www.gov.uk/government/speeches/prime-ministers-speech-at-the-social-impact-investment-conference.
13. World Economic Forum et al. *Breaking the Binary*, 25–27.
14. Ibid., 31–33.
15. NeighborWorks America. (2014). "NeighborWorks Impact Data." http://www.nw.org/network/stateimpactasp/impact_landing.asp.
16. Living Cities. (2014). "History." http://www.livingcities.org/about/history/.
17. Living Cities. (2014). "Leadership and Influence." http://www.livingcities.org/how/leadership/.
18. Living Cities. (2014). "Frequently Asked Questions." http://www.livingcities.org/faq.
19. Brett, D. (2013, November). *Impact Investing 2.0 Case Study: Aavishkaar India Micro Venture Capital Fund*. Pacific Community Ventures, CASE at Duke University and ImpactAssets. http://www.pacificcommunityventures.org/impinv2/wp-content/uploads/2013/11/casestudy_aavishkaar_v6.pdf.
20. US Small Business Administration—Investment Division. (2012). *The Small Business Investment Company (SBIC) Program, Annual Report FY 2012*. US Small Business Administration. http://www.sba.gov/sites/default/files/files/SBIC%20Program%20FY%202012%20Annual%20Report.pdf.
21. Thornley, B. (2013, March 20). "Big Government. Big Impact. Big Data. Big Lessons." *Huffington Post*. http://www.huffingtonpost.com/ben-thornley/small-business-investment-company-program_b_2908696.html.
22. Australian Department of Education, Employment and Workplace Relations. (2013, June). *The Social Enterprise Development and Investment Funds: Progress Report*. http://docs.employment.gov.au/system/files/doc/other/sedifprogressreport2013_2.pdf.
23. World Economic Forum et al. *Breaking the Binary*, 28–30.
24. Ibid., 31–33.
25. USAID. (2014, April). "About DIV." http://www.usaid.gov/div/about.
26. USAID. (2013, November 6). "USAID's New Approach Unlocks $1 Billion in Private Financing for Development." (Press release).

http://www.usaid.gov/news-information/press-releases/nov-6–2013-usaids-new-approach-unlocks-1-billion-private-financing-development.

27. US Small Business Administration. (n.d.). "Certified Development Companies." http://www.sba.gov/tools/local-assistance/cdc.

28. World Economic Forum et al. *Breaking the Binary,* 22–24.

29. Ghosh, A. (2013, May 8). "Now, a Regulatory Body to Set Norms for Impact Investment." *Economic Times.* http://articles.economictimes .indiatimes.com/2013–05–08/news/39117121_1_vc-investments-vc-funds-vineet-rai.

30. Speirn, S., (2013, Fall), "Mission-Driven Investments Can Help Philanthropists Become More Effective Grantmakers." *Stanford Social Innovation Review.* http://www.ssireview.org/up_for_debate/impact_investing/sterling_speirn.

31. Pfund, N., (2013, Fall), "Impact Investors Can Help Shape the Culture of Young Companies." *Stanford Social Innovation Review.* http://www .ssireview.org/up_for_debate/impact_investing/nancy_pfund.

32. World Economic Forum et al. *Breaking the Binary.*

33. Mahmood, A. (2013, November 7). *The Ethical Dimension in Impact Investing.* Impact Investing 2.0. http://www.pacificcommunityven tures.org/impinv2/asad-mahmood-the-ethical-dimension-in-impact-investing/.

34. Global Impact Investing Network. (2013). "About Impact Investing." http://www.thegiin.org/cgi-bin/iowa/resources/about/index.html.

35. Smart Campaign. (2014). *The Client Protection Principles.* http://www .smartcampaign.org/about/smart-microfinance-and-the-client-pro tection-principles.

36. Principles for Responsible Investment. (n.d.). *The Six Principles.* http://www.unpri.org/about-pri/the-six-principles/.

Chapter 5

1. Bannick, M., and Goldman, P. (2012, September). *Priming the Pump: The Case for a Sector Based Approach to Impact Investing.* Omidyar Network. http://www.omidyar.com/sites/default/files/file_archive/insights/ Priming%20the%20Pump_Omidyar%20Network_Sept_2012.pdf.

2. Thornley, B. (2010, December). *Community Equity Capital: The Opportunities and Challenges of Growth.* InSight at Pacific Community Ventures. http://www.pacificcommunityventures.org/uploads/reports-and-publications/Community_Equity_Capital_InSight_2010.pdf.

3. Ibid.

4. Ibid.

5. Clark, C., Allen, M., Moellenbrock, B., and Onyeagoro, C. (2013, May). *Accelerating Impact Enterprises: How to Lock, Stock, and Anchor Impact Enterprises for Maximum Impact.* CASE at Duke University. https://dl.dropboxusercontent.com/u/7845889/AcceleratingImpact Enterprises.pdf.

6. Kolodko, G. W. (1991, January). "Polish Hyperinflation and Stabilization 1989–1990." *Economic Journal on Eastern Europe and the Soviet Union,* 9–36.

7. Global Impact Investing Network. (2013, October). *Issue Brief: Catalytic First-Loss Capital.* http://www.thegiin.org/binary-data/RESOURCE/ download_file/000/000/552–1.pdf.

8. Chung, A. and Emerson, J. (n.d.). *From Grants to Groundbreaking: Unlocking Impact Investments.* Impact Assets Issue Brief #10. http:// www.impactassets.org/files/Issue%20Brief%2010.pdf.

9. Read and watch a video with more of Laurie's comments here: Webster, G. (2014, March 5). "Capacity + Capital = Impact." *CASE Notes* (blog). http://blogs.fuqua.duke.edu/casenotes/2014/03/05/ capacity-capital-impact-2/.

10. Ibid.

11. See the UK Cabinet Office's Centre for Social Impact Bonds for more information on the Social Outcomes Fund: http://blogs.cabinet office.gov.uk/socialimpactbonds/outcomes-fund/ or "UK Cabinet Office: About the Social Outcomes Fund." http://iipcollaborative .org/wp-content/uploads/sites/3/2014/05/SOF_IIPC-v21.pdf.

12. Ibid.

13. For a discussion of an entrepreneurial ecosystem analysis, see Bloom, P. N., and Dees, J. G. (2008, Winter). "Cultivate Your Ecosystem." *Stanford Social Innovation Review.* http://www.ssireview.org/articles/ entry/cultivate_your_ecosystem.

14. Reisman, J. Gienapp, A., and Stachowiak, S. (2007, December 5). *A Guide to Measuring Advocacy and Policy.* Prepared by Organizational Research Services for Annie E. Casey Foundation. http://www.aecf .org/upload/PublicationFiles/DA3622H5000.pdf.

Chapter 6

1. Eggers, W. D., and Macmillan, P. (2013). "The Wavemakers." In *The Solution Revolution: How Business, Government and Social Enterprises Are Teaming Up to Solve Society's Toughest Problems.* Boston, MA: Harvard Business Review Press, 17–50.

2. Smith, G., and Kalil, T. (2014, April 4). "U.S. Global Development Lab Launches to Develop and Scale Solutions to Global Challenges."

USAID. http://blog.usaid.gov/2014/04/u-s-global-development-lab-launches-to-develop-and-scale-solutions-to-global-challenges/.

3. Archer, D., and Cameron, A. (2009). *Collaborative Leadership: How to Succeed in an Interconnected World.* Waltham, MA: Butterworth Heinemann, 115–123.

4. Bornstein, D. (2007). "Six Qualities of Successful Social Entrepreneurs." *How to Change the World: Social Entrepreneurs and the Power of New Ideas.* Oxford, UK: Oxford University Press, 241.

5. United Way. (2013, June 13). "United Way of Salt Lake Announces Results-Based Financing for Low-Income Preschool Students." (News release). http://www.uw.org/news-events/media-room-/news-releases/uw_resultsbasesfinancingnr.pdf.

6. Cranston, S. (2013, October 24). "Leapfrog Investments Raises Second Fund." *Financial Mail.* http://www.financialmail.co.za/features/2013/10/24/leapfrog-investments-raises-second-fund.

7. Office of Governor Deval Patrick. (2014, January 29). "Massachusetts Launches Landmark Initiative to Reduce Recidivism Among At-Risk Youth." (Press release). Mass.Gov. http://www.mass.gov/governor/pressoffice/pressreleases/2014/0129-at-risk-youth-initiative.html.

Chapter 7

1. J.P.Morgan Global Research, Rockefeller Foundation, and Global Impact Investing Network. (2010, November 29). *Impact Investments: An Emerging Asset Class.* http://www.rockefellerfoundation.org/uploads/files/2b053b2b-8feb-46ea-adbd-f89068d59785-impact.pdf.

2. World Economic Forum. (2013, September). *From the Margins to the Mainstream—Assessment of the Impact Investment Sector and Opportunities to Engage Mainstream Investors.* http://www3.weforum.org/docs/WEF_II_FromMarginsMainstream_Report_2013.pdf.

3. The three of us have each spent our careers advancing various aspects of this vision. Therefore, some of these ideas and insights have been explored in numerous papers related to the themes of this book and the field as a whole, and may not be presented here for the first time.

4. The notion of Total Portfolio Management has been described through Jed Emerson's "total foundation asset management and the unified investment strategy" and Carol Newell's more geographically targeted notion of "whole portfolio activation," as well as through Tides' paper on "total portfolio activation." The core notion across all is that investors have an opportunity and responsibility to leverage impact across all asset classes in alignment with their institutional focus or personal values. See Emerson, J., and Freundlich, T. *Invest with*

Meaning: An Introduction to a Unified Investment Strategy for Impact. ImpactAssets Issue Brief #1. http://www.impactassets.org/files/down loads/ImpactAssets_IssueBriefs_1.pdf; Humphreys, J., Solomon, A., and Electris, C. (2012, August). *Total Portfolio Activation: A Framework for Creating Social and Environmental Impact across Asset Classes.* Tellus Institute. http://www.tellus.org/publications/files/tpa.pdf

5. Ceres. (n.d.). "Investor Network on Climate Risk (INCR)." http://www.ceres.org/investor-network/incr.

6. Gilbert, D. (2014, March 20). "Exxon Agrees to Disclose Its 'Carbon Risk.'" *Wall Street Journal.* http://online.wsj.com/news/articles/SB10001424052702304026304579451642191953028.

7. Carbon Tracker. (2014). "Home." http://www.carbontracker.org/.

8. PricewaterhouseCoopers. (2013, March) *Responsible Investment: Creating Value from Environmental, Social and Governance Issues.* Apax Partners. http://www.apax.com/media/239914/pwc_ri%20in%20pe_survey_mar12.pdf.

9. KKR. (2012). *Creating Sustainable Value: Progress Through Partnership: 2012 ESG and Citizenship Report.* http://www.kkr.com/_files/pdf/KKR_ESG-Report_2012.pdf.

10. Instiglio. (n.d.). "Social Impact Bonds and Development Impact Bonds Worldwide." http://www.instiglio.org/en/sibs-worldwide/.

11. Bar-Yam, M., Rhoades, K., Sweeney, L., Kaput, J., and Bar-Yam, Y. (2002). *Changes in the Teaching and Learning Process in a Complex Education System.* New England Complex Systems Institute. http://www.necsi.edu/research/management/education/teachandlearn.html.

12. Wood, D. (2013, December). "The Current Limits and Potential Role of Institutional Investment Culture and Fiduciary Responsibility." World Economic Forum Investors Industries. *From Ideas to Practice, Pilots to Strategy: Practical Solutions and Actionable Insights on How to Do Impact Investing.* http://www3.weforum.org/docs/WEF_II_Solutions Insights_ImpactInvesting_Report_2013.pdf.

13. Emerson, J., and Little, T. (2005, September). *The Prudent Trustee: The Evolution of the Long-Term Investor.* Rose Foundation for Communities and the Environment. http://www.rosefdn.org/downloads/prudent trustee.pdf.

14. Hesse, A. (2008), *Long-term and Sustainable Pension Investments: A Study of Leading European Pension Funds.* Asset4 and German Federal Environment Ministry. http://www.sd-m.de/files/Long-term_sustainable_Pension_Investments_Hesse_SD-M_Asset4.pdf; Ness, A., (2010). "The Integration of ESG in Emerging Markets." Eurekaedge. http://www.eurekahedge.com/news/09_dec_ResponsibleInvestor_The_Integration_of_ESG_in_Emerging_Markets.asp.

15. EY. (2011). "Six Trends in Corporate Sustinability." http://www.ey .com/US/en/Services/Specialty-Services/Climate-Change-and-Sus tainability-Services/Six-growing-trends-in-corporate-sustainability_ overview.

16. Deloitte. (2013). "The Millennial Survey 2013: Future Leaders Say Business Must Encourage Innovation and Positively Impact Society." http://www2.deloitte.com/content/dam/Deloitte/global/Documents/ About-Deloitte/dttl-crs-millennial-innovation-survey-2013.pdf.

17. Schervish, P., and Havens, J. (2003). *Why the $41 Trillion Wealth Transfer Estimate is Still Valid: A Review of Challenges and Questions.* Chestnut Hill, MA: Boston College Center on Wealth and Philanthropy.

18. For examples of this, see Domini, A. (2011, March 14). "Want to Make a Difference? Invest Responsibly." *Huffington Post.* http://www.huffing tonpost.com/amy-domini/want-to-make-a-difference_b_834756.html and Pinsky, M. (2011, December). "'Impact Investing': Theory, Meet Practice." *Community Development Investment Review*, 48–52. http://www .frbsf.org/community-development/files/Pinsky.pdf.

Concluding Reflections

1. See the Impact Investing 2.0 project site: www.bit.ly/impinv.

2. Koh, H., Karamchandani, A., and Katz, R. (April 2012). *From Blueprint to Scale: The Case for Philanthropy in Impact Investing.* Monitor Inclusive Markets. http://www.mim.monitor.com/.

3. Anecdotally, there were impact investors who found that the only portion of their portfolio that did not decrease in value through the downturn were their investments in impact investing vehicles.

Acknowledgments

1. More of the participating organizations are listed on the Impact Investing 2.0 project's microsite: http://www.pacificcommunityven tures.org/impinv2/conclusion/appendix-a/.

Acknowledgments

The Impact Investor has been over three years in the making since we first committed to sharing the experiences and lessons of those funds that have delivered outstanding performance in impact investing. From the outset, this was not intended to be our story, but rather a conduit to the insights of others: leading investors and intermediaries in a field hungry for the knowledge they have to share. We are grateful, first and foremost, for the courage and collegiality of those who created and manage these funds, and greatly appreciate how freely they opened their doors to at least three sets of prying eyes—providing invaluable lessons, through their experiences, that are among the most enriching we have encountered.

Many investors, investees, and managers involved with these funds made themselves available to us. Our sincere thanks to all of those with whom we spoke or corresponded in recent years. And a special thanks to those who, through many months of intense conversations and collaboration, partnered directly with us to help navigate the unique terrain of each case study. This includes Vineet Rai and P. Pradeep at Aavishkaar; Janie Barrera and Celine Peña at ACCIÓN Texas Inc.; Michelle Giddens, Clara Barby, Brian Trelstad, and Maggie Loo at Bridges Ventures; Mark Paper and Nazeem Martin at Business Partners Limited; Jennifer Pryce, Andrew Parrucci, and Beth Bafford at Calvert Foundation; Asad Mahmood and Mark Narron at Deutsche Bank; Maya Chorengel, Johanna Posada, and Sandeep Farias at Elevar Equity; Tim Bubnack, Hope Mago, and Morgan Miller at Huntington Capital; Tony Berkley, John Duong, Neal Graziano, Dana Linnane, and Joel Wittenberg at W.K.

Kellogg Foundation; Gil Crawford and Dave Wedick at MicroVest; Don Shaffer, Ted Levinson, Taryn Goodman, and Melinda Cheel at RSF Social Finance; and Mildred Callear, Bert van der Vaart, and Bob Stillman at SEAF. These are just the funds' managers and staff. We also thank, collectively, all the limited partners and fund investors with whom we spoke, as well as the funded entrepreneurs. There were hundreds of people involved in our 360-degree interviews of the stakeholders in each fund, and every single conversation helped us.

The project itself has been something of an entrepreneurial effort. At each stage of its development, we have been fortunate to find enthusiastic backers and partners, without whom our research would not have been possible.

The earliest supporters of our work were the Annie E. Casey Foundation and RS Group, with whom we have enjoyed deep relationships over many years that, in their various ways, have led to this work. Through Christa Velasquez and then Tracy Kartye, Annie E. Casey has been a leading social investor and has quietly funded significant field-building initiatives connected to its relentless commitment to understanding the impacts of its efforts. That funding has supported Pacific Community Ventures thought leadership over many years, building the capacity of the organization for managing this particular project. Jed Emerson has been proud to be a team member of RS Group in Hong Kong for the past four years. RS Group's work in impact investing and social entrepreneurship has helped advance impact investing in Hong Kong and Asia. The team there also provided us with essential start-up capital needed to get this project off the ground. In particular, we extend our deep thanks to Annie Chen, RS Group's president, who is nothing short of visionary, providing an excellent example of how individual investors play a critical role in advancing impact investing practice.

Omidyar Network joined the effort soon thereafter as our lead supporter, bringing significant experience as one of the field's most important and innovative investors, and offering a powerful mix of institutional credibility and audacity. We are truly grateful for Omidyar's preparedness to help us scale a high-risk research project dependent on the willingness of private market actors to provide data, which was never a sure bet. Omidyar's enthusiasm for thought leadership is unabashed, as the publication *Priming the Pump* made clear in 2012, and it has provided a constant source of support, insight, and direction. Thanks particularly go to Paula Goldman and Rosita Najmi at Omidyar Network for their direct collaboration on the work and their detailed and thoughtful feedback throughout.

Joining our coalition of funders were the F.B. Heron Foundation, W.K. Kellogg Foundation, and Deutsche Bank. Thank you in particular to Kate Starr at Heron Foundation, and two others we have already thanked and will thank again: Tony Berkley at Kellogg Foundation and Asad Mahmood, then at Deutsche Bank. We discovered that each of these organizations believe in true partnerships with its grantees, an approach from which we benefited considerably.

To a growing community of research partners and funders we were eager to add a broader group of leading practitioners as an expert global brain trust, and set about creating a project advisory group. Many thanks to each of the individuals among this number for their invaluable feedback to our work along the way:

Rosemary Addis, Impact Investing Australia (formerly) Australian Department of Education, Employment and Workplace Relations
Wiebe Boer, Tony Elumelu Foundation
Francois Bonnici, University of Cape Town
Amit Bouri, GIIN
John M. Buley Jr., Duke University
Dirk Elsen, Triodos Bank
Brinda Ganguly, Rockefeller Foundation
Paula Goldman, Omidyar Network
Hilary Irby, Morgan Stanley
Jonathan Jenkins, the Social Investment Business
Oliver Karius, LGT Venture Philanthropy
Tracy Kartye, Annie E. Casey Foundation
Randall Kempner, ANDE
Robert Kraybill, Impact Investment Exchange Asia
Asad Mahmood, Deutsche Bank
Yasemin Saltuk, J.P. Morgan
Kate Starr, F.B. Heron Foundation

Our research effort had two homes (being a modern organization!): On the West Coast, we were housed at Pacific Community Ventures (PCV) in San Francisco, and on the East Coast we were housed at CASE at Duke University in Durham, North Carolina. PCV (www.pacificcommunityventures.org) is one of the most innovative community development financial institutions in the United States and has become known for the strength of its research and policy work, among other important programmatic initiatives. The research division of PCV, InSight, was built on a single contract with the California Public Employees Retirement System (CalPERS) ten years ago to track the social and economic impacts of CalPERS investments in California. InSight now stands as a leading provider of research and advice on impact investing. Beth Sirull, PCV's current president, arrived at PCV ten years ago to lead the CalPERS work and, as InSight's founding director, has been a tireless leader, advisor, and advocate for this research throughout. Others at PCV also played crucial roles, namely the contributing authors of our fund case studies and research, including Daniel Brett, Colby Dailey, and Brenna McCallick, all of whom provided nothing less than the rock-solid foundation for this effort. The project management and editorial leadership from this group have been simply outstanding. We also benefited early in the project's development from the relentless efforts of a then Georgetown MBA intern, Christopher Cox, and later from intern Katya Makovik and, critically in our final stages, a consultant and former PCV colleague, Sarah Ritter. Tom Woelfel also provided support for the earliest iterations of our research on best practices at PCV, supported by the Annie E. Casey Foundation. Thank you. And thanks also to those in the operational engine room at PCV who kept the project afloat, including Carolyn Clark, Allison Kelly, and Robyn Miller.

The Center for the Advancement of Social Entrepreneurship (CASE, www.caseatduke.org) was founded at the Fuqua School of Business at Duke University by J. Gregory Dees and Beth Battle Anderson in 2002. It is an award-winning research and education center that prepares leaders and organizations with the business tools needed to create lasting social change. CASE has educated more than a thousand MBA students working across the globe to drive social impact from within companies, nonprofits, and government. As a field builder, CASE has also worked with hundreds of organizations to help define, promote, and propel the field of social entrepreneurship, and has created distributed multi-sector partnerships focused on ways to help change the ecosystems social entrepreneurs need to succeed. In 2011, CASE launched the CASE i3 Initiative on Impact Investing to focus on the development of capital markets for social and impact enterprises. The launch of CASE i3 was rapidly followed by the formation of this research project, as a cornerstone effort to understand the factors that drive high performance, a kind of *Forces for Good* approach to impact investing. In 2012, CASE also partnered with USAID to create the Social Entrepreneurship Accelerator at Duke (SEAD) as part of USAID's Higher Education Solutions Network. Today, SEAD is a Duke-wide partnership of faculty, students, practitioners, and impact investors working to support the scaling of global health innovations around the world.

As an academic center, CASE has had the privilege of creating blended teams of faculty, students, and practitioners for its research. For this project, the most important contributions have been from the CASE i3 fellows and associates, a select group of MBA students who commit to working in teams on consulting and research projects across the globe, as well as to mastering targeted coursework on impact investing. The Impact Investor project stretched across two classes of fellows. In 2012–2013, the team was led by Greg Payne, and Brendan Mullen, Jack Buettell, Victoria Gandy, Ha Le, Jacqueline Westley, Jamie Attard, Jorge Mendes, and Mailande Moran contributed, with help from cochairs Scott Kleiman and David Nicola. In 2013–2014, a new team, led by Ha Le (who had spent the summer managing the project), came on board, and students Laura Mixter, Mary O'Donnell, Jorge Soriano, and Mitesh Tank participated, with help from cochairs Tony Wang and Grace Webster. Grace and Tony also worked hard to support our practitioner engagement efforts at SOCAP in 2013 and the Skoll World Forum in 2014. Fuqua alumni Abigail Lundy and Elana Boehm also became our copyeditors on all of the Impact Investing 2.0 case studies. The literally hundreds of interviews and documents we collected and analyzed during the course of this project would have been impossible to manage without the dedication of all of these students, and we are grateful for their help, questions, and insights along the way. We must also acknowledge the significant contributions of John M. Buley Jr., faculty member at CASE and advisor to the project; J. Gregory Dees, to whom this book is dedicated; Erin Worsham, CASE's executive director; and Matt Nash, CASE's former executive director, now serving as the managing director of SEAD. Each of these exemplary colleagues always lent an ear and a hand to whatever problem of the day we needed to solve—how to structure the research, negotiate a book contract, identify a colleague working in a certain area, finalize agreements among the partners, blog and tweet our findings, and more. This project has been a perfect example of the power of distributed teams working together for a common purpose, and we are quite proud that so many in our community were able to be part of the process of learning together about what has driven success in the field of impact investing.

Jed's work throughout has been a part of his engagement with ImpactAssets, which has also provided us with a significant platform of knowledge and relationships from which to draw. ImpactAssets is a leading nonprofit financial services group that combines promotion of various impact investing products and strategies with support for the field as a whole through its Issue Brief series and annual roster of leading impact investing funds, the I.A.-50. We extend our particular thanks to ImpactAsset's director of investment, Fran Seegull, whose suggestions and referrals were significant contributions to our work. Also, thanks go to Nathan Ranney for his research support as we drafted the text of the book.

Finally, from our figurative homes to our literal ones, we also dedicate this book to our families, the inspiration for our work. They are the constant sustenance on which we depend every day—and, in the last year in particular, every long night—as well as our best confidants, critics, and reality checks.

From Cathy

My deepest thanks go out to Greg Dees, for helping me personally and professionally in so many ways through our partnership over the last six years that they would be impossible to name. To Ben and Jed, for somehow always understanding what I want to say before I say it, and for supporting, challenging, and consoling me over the past two years, even if from the end of a conference line in Norway or Australia. (And Jed, for letting your dog, Ruby, slobber all over my foot back in 1998 while you explained SROI in the Presidio. It was the beginning of a long friendship!) To my husband, Mike, for being the anchor that allows me to float so freely, knowing you'll pull me back from my global explorations when you can see I need it. Thanks so much, honey. To my mother Lynne and late father, Richie, who taught me how both to take care of myself *and* make the world a better place, and helped me find delight in learning. To Jake, nine, for exploring Hogwarts, the Underland, and the Marram Marshes with me nearly every night over the past two years. We will always have friends in common, and I'm grateful. And last to Abby, six, my artist and my own little mermaid, for diving into life with the same joy you exhibit in any pool, and for fueling me up by telling me you love me more every night at bedtime.

From Jed

I express my sincere thanks to my coauthors, Cathy and Ben, who were gracious enough to invite me into this process and patient enough to wade through my cynical comments and jests to find the pearls I sought to offer. I thank the teams at RS Group (Hong Kong), Blue Haven Initiative (Boston), and the Gary Group (Denver), with whom I have the real pleasure of working and who give me real insight into how impact investing looks from the perspective of the asset owner and family member. And, of course, my thanks go out to my colleagues at ImpactAssets for their consideration and support. I also thank Adam Isbiroglu and Isabella Isbiroglu, who challenge me, make me laugh, and help keep my inbox remarkably free of e-mails! I offer particular thanks to my dad, Dr. Jim Emerson, for the great example he sets as an intellectual with both a sense of humor and humility. And, finally, to Mia, who puts up with my getting up at three in the morning to work and with my constant travel, which takes me away from our great home and walks in the Presidio or in the Rockies. Love to you, honey!

From Ben

The Impact Investor project has grown and developed, surged and struggled, cooperated and contradicted, alongside the journey from birth to toddlerhood of two irrepressible angels, Ellora and Asha, under the ever watchful and supportive eyes of my muse, Aviv. What an exhausting but fun time we have had together! To the loves of my life—thank you with all my heart. To my PCV family, amazing clients, and funders over many years (thank you Margot Brandenburg for bringing Cathy, Jed, and me together!), I am deeply indebted to you all. To my coauthors, Cathy and Jed, I have been inspired and forever changed by your experience, conviction, perspective, and support. Thank you for your partnership. To my parents, Carolyn and Andrew, thank you for the inspiration of your lifelong learning and pastoral commitments. I love you both. And finally, thanks to the greatest financial journalist of his generation, to whom I owe so much: my first boss and mentor always, Greg Bright.

■ ■ ■

There are so many others for whom we are grateful—our editors at Wiley, including senior editor, Alison Hankey; our ever-pleasant and insightful copyeditor, Michele D. Jones; and the designers of this book and our prior published research; and new funders like the Case Foundation, which led by Jean Case, Kate Ahern, Sonal Shah, and Sean Greene is providing action-oriented energy to impact investing. And of course, to our friends and compatriots in the field, including Rosemary Addis, Bob Annibale, Álvaro Rodríguez Arregui, Matt Bannick, Margot Brandenburg, Audrey Choi, Michael Chu, Katherine Fulton, John Goldstein, Katie Grace, Jonathan Greenblatt, Lisa Hall, Pamela Hartigan, Bart Houlahan, Carla Javits, Kevin Jones, Bonny Moellenbrock, Abigail Noble, Tracy Palladjian, Debra Schwartz, Abby Jo Sigal, Mitchell Strauss, David Wood, and so many more.[1]

To all of those we've listed here, and to other colleagues we have neglected to thank and will regret not having taken this opportunity to acknowledge, this book is for you. We've all been collectively building this field so long that we cannot name each of you, but you know who you are! The book is also dedicated to further partnerships and opportunities for learning. We cherish them, as we believe they exemplify the new Collaborative Capitalism for which the future holds such tremendous promise.

About the Authors

Cathy Clark is a professor at Duke University's Fuqua School of Business, where she directs the CASE i3 Initiative on Impact Investing as part of the award-winning Center for the Advancement of Social Entrepreneurship (CASE). Clark has been an active pioneer, educator, and consultant for twenty-five years in the fields of impact investing and for-profit and nonprofit social entrepreneurship. She helped develop the standards for B Corporations, taught at Columbia Business School for a decade, and managed impact investments at Flatiron Partners and the Markle Foundation. Currently, she helps manage the Social Entrepreneurship Accelerator at Duke (SEAD), a $10 million global health accelerator that is part of USAID's Higher Education Solutions Network, in collaboration with Duke Medicine and Investors' Circle. She also coordinates global research for the $4.5 billion of impact assets under management in funds rated by B Analytics with data from over eleven thousand impact entrepreneurs in twenty-nine countries. In 2013 she was selected as the academic member of the US National Advisory Board for the Social Impact Investment Taskforce established by the G8.

Jed Emerson is strategic advisor to three family offices (each of which is managing total net worth on an impact/sustainable basis) as well as chief impact strategist of ImpactAssets, a nonprofit financial services group. Emerson has played founding roles with some of the nation's leading venture philanthropy, community venture capital, and social enterprises. He is the author of numerous articles and papers, and is coauthor of *Impact Investing:*

Transforming How We Make Money While Making a Difference (Jossey-Bass, 2011). He coined the term *blended value,* has done extensive consulting for investors in Europe and Asia, and has worked with firms across the investment spectrum, from strategic philanthropy and mission-related investing to sustainable private equity and public equities.

Ben Thornley is the founder and managing director of ICAP Partners, a consultant and collaborator on the business of impact investing, and a strategic advisor to Pacific Community Ventures (PCV) and REDF, two prominent San Francisco–based nonprofit organizations deploying debt and philanthropic capital to social enterprises. Ben was a managing director at PCV prior to creating ICAP Partners, where he led PCV InSight, the global research and consulting practice in impact investing. Ben was responsible for cocreating a number of prominent research partnerships in that position, including on impact investing best practices with CASE at Duke University and ImpactAssets, and on the role of policy in impact investing, with the Initiative for Responsible Investment (IRI) at the Hauser Institute for Civil Society at Harvard University and the World Economic Forum. He built the Impact Investing Policy Collaborative (IIPC) with the IRI, a global network of researchers and public officials, the Accelerating Impact Investing Initiative with IRI and Enterprise Community Partners, which focuses on developing a US policy platform, and the Global Learning Exchange on Social Impact Investing, an output of the UK's 2013 presidency of the G8 coconvened by the IIPC, UK Cabinet Office, and World Economic Forum. Ben continues to advise institutions including CalPERS, Citi, the Annie E. Casey Foundation, and The California Endowment through PCV InSight's work as a prominent third-party evaluator of the social and economic impacts resulting from over $25 billion of investments, across asset classes.

Index

Page references followed by *fig* indicate an illustrated figure; followed by *t* indicate a table.

335